INTERCULTURAL COMMUNICATION

INTERCULTURAL COMMUNICATION

A Practical Guide

BY TRACY NOVINGER

 UNIVERSITY OF TEXAS PRESS, AUSTIN

LIBRARY OF CONGRESS CATALOGING-IN-PUBLICATION DATA

Novinger, Tracy, 1942–
    Intercultural communication : a practical guide / by Tracy Novinger. — 1st ed.
        p.   cm.
    Includes bibliographical references and index.
    ISBN 0-292-75570-8 (cloth : alk. paper) —
    ISBN 0-292-75571-6 (pbk. : alk. paper)
    1. Intercultural communication.   I. Title.
    HM1211 .N68   2001
        303.48'2—dc21   00-036408

TO THE MEMORY

OF THE FREE SPIRIT OF

PHYLLIS ALICE GRIFFITH ELLSPERMAN

AND TO GLEN,

MI QUERIDO Y MI AMIGO.

CONTENTS

Preface

In our world of expanding technology and shrinking geography, people of different cultures have increasing frequency of contact and need for effective communication on a daily basis. Speaking a different language is an obvious obstacle to intercultural communication, but a greater and more difficult hurdle is to "speak" a different culture. Even though we may learn the words, the grammar, and the recognizable pronunciation of a language, we may still not know how to navigate around the greater obstacles to communication that are presented by cultural difference.

Communication specialists estimate that from two-thirds to three-fourths of our communication takes place nonverbally through behavior. All behavior is communication, and since we cannot *not* behave, we cannot *not* communicate. During all of the waking hours that we spend with other human beings we "speak" volumes through the behavior our culture has drilled into us.

Each of us is conditioned by our culture from birth. We learn when to speak up and when to keep quiet. We learn that some facial expressions meet with approval and others provoke a reprimand. We are taught which gestures are acceptable and which are not, and whether we can publicly unwrap a gift; we learn where to put our hands at a meal, whether or not we can make noise with our mouths when we eat, which table utensils to use or not use, and in what fashion we may use them. We learn how to address people in a manner approved by our culture, what tone of voice to employ, what posture is censored and what is praised, when and how to make eye contact and for how long, and countless other things that would be impossible to remember consciously and use all at the same time when interacting socially. This communicative behavior is learned so well that it becomes internalized at a subconscious level. We are primarily aware of deviations from our prescribed cultural norms, and we tend to negatively evaluate any such deviations.

Since we learn our cultural behavior in units, it is a useful artifice to compare cultural differences in units. To learn to communicate across cultures more quickly and more effectively, we can apply a framework of categories of potential obstacles (cultural units) to our own and to a target culture.

Part I of this book addresses the need for successful communication across cultures and defines what constitutes a culture. Next, an original taxonomy of potential intercultural communication obstacles is constructed from the literature of communication, anthropology, psychology, sociology, business, and current events, as well as from interviews with persons of multicultural backgrounds. The categories are explained, and many are illustrated with anecdotes.

Part II applies the framework of obstacles outlined in Part I to the differences in cultural units of the United States and Mexico. This application demonstrates how these cultural differences create misunderstanding and ineffectual communication in commonly occurring business and social situations.

Part III prescribes an effective approach to intercultural communication between any two cultures, using the framework of potential obstacles to efficiently obtain results. We can act consciously to transcend the rules with which our own culture grips us.

Acknowledgments

Although I am indebted to persons too numerous to mention for insight into intercultural communication, I would like, nonetheless, to expressly thank a number of people who encouraged, informed, and assisted me. Any strengths of this work derive in great measure from their support. In expressing my appreciation, I do not imply that the following persons either agree or disagree with specific details or with the contents of this book. To Dr. Philip Gaunt, Director of the Elliott School of Communication at Wichita State University, Kansas, *un merci très particulier* for sharing his knowledge and for guidance. My thanks to Beatriz de la Garza, Ph.D., J.D., for her supportive friendship and interest, and to friends Nancy Hamilton and Arciela Izquierdo Jordan, J.D., for their feedback. Guillermina Flores de Padilla, Assistant Director of the Benjamin Franklin Library at the Instituto Mexicano Norteamericano de Relaciones Culturales de Nuevo León in Monterrey, graciously helped me when I showed up as an unannounced foreign visitor. I also thank Georgina Silva Ramírez de Domínguez for a warm welcome in Monterrey, Mexico.

For their input, I would also like to acknowledge Jane "Juanita" Smith Garcés, Maria Eugenia Dubois, Philip Russell of the Mexico Resource Center, Isabel Gereda Taylor, J.D., Robin Wasson, Allan Adams, Allert Brown-Gort, Evelyn Sierra Hammond, Ph.D., and Herb Brandt.

I have been blessed over the years with the enduring friendship of Marcia Barros Parisi of São Paulo, Brazil; Elvira Paiva Andrade of Santos, Brazil; Repeta Tetauru of Tahiti; and Geneviève Trouche, currently of Paris, formerly of Algeria and Tahiti. And special thanks to the Mexican people for the warmth and great courtesy they have unfailingly extended to me on many visits to Mexico.

I have a personal tie to the Latin Americas and especially appreciate the opportunity to have focused on Mexico in an attempt to illumine the difficulties of intercultural communication. On the Caribbean island of Aruba, where three generations of my family lived, I, too, called my cousins' grandfather, Luís Guillermo López of Mexico, "Grandpa." He was my godfather—my *padrino*—and I have many cousins (*primos hermanos*) with López and Cantú surnames.

The renowned Benson Latin American Collection at the University of Texas at Austin was a valuable library resource. And to Theresa May, my energetic editor at the University of Texas Press, *gracias, obregado, merci.*

INTERCULTURAL COMMUNICATION

PART ONE

THE GLOBAL PERSPECTIVE
OF INTERCULTURAL COMMUNICATION

ONE

Why Communicate across Cultures?

The most universal quality is diversity.
— MONTAIGNE, 1580

Isolated cultures stagnate; cultures that
communicate with others evolve.   —T. SOWELL,
RACE AND CULTURE 1994

INTERCULTURAL INTERFACE

A well-dressed Mexican pulled up in a taxi to the Palacio de Justicia in Lima, Peru. Armed guards were standing on the steps ascending to the building. The passenger paid and thanked the driver and opened the door of the cab, intent on the information he had come to get. As he leaned forward and put one foot onto the pavement, a cold rifle muzzle jabbed him in the temple and jerked his attention to matters at hand. The Peruvian guard holding the rifle shot two harsh words at him. The Mexican reddened, emerged from the taxi, and drew himself erect. With a sweep of his arm, he retorted three words: "¡Qué! ¿Nos conocemos?" (What! Do we know each other?) With a half bow the guard lowered the rifle and courteously gestured the man up the steps, speaking in deferential tones. What happened here? What did the guard with the gun say that triggered this reaction from the Mexican? And what in the Mexican visitor's behavior and those three Spanish words instantly changed the Peruvian guard's attitude and demeanor?

IN SPITE OF OURSELVES

We cannot not communicate. All behavior is communication, and we cannot not behave.[1]

Even a person who does not want to "communicate"—who sits huddled with arms folded and head down—communicates that he is trying to avoid communication. By nature, communication is a system of behavior.[2] And because different cultures often demand very different behaviors, intercultural communication is more complex than communication between persons of the same culture.[3] All communication takes place in the matrix of culture, therefore difference in culture is the primary obstacle to intercultural communication.

Communication specialists estimate that two-thirds to three-fourths of all communication is nonverbal. The average varies from culture to culture, but what this statistic essentially means is that a person communicates in great part by nonverbal behavior, behavior being gestures, facial expressions, tone of voice, dress, body language, the rituals (such as courtesies) one observes, etc. Our culture teaches us our behavior from birth, and most of our behavior is unconscious. Therefore—in addition to the words that we intentionally use—through our behavior we unconsciously communicate during all of the waking hours that we spend with other human beings. We "speak" volumes outside of our awareness and often in spite of our conscious choices.

Although our verbal language comes to us naturally, only the most ethnocentric can believe that their own is a "natural" language and that other societies speak some distortion of it. Yet, when it comes to the nonverbal language of behavior, most people believe that their own is a natural form of communication that foreign people have learned badly, not evolved to, or lost.[4] If we understand that we need to translate verbal language, we should be able to understand that we also need to translate nonverbal language.

THE CULTURE GRIP

Most of us probably think of ourselves as persons who operate through our own free will. Much of the time, however, this is not true.

The Mexican visitor and the Peruvian guard participated in a communication exchange that was deeply embedded in the hierarchy and formality inherent in Mediterranean-based cultures. With the interrogation, "¿Que quieres?" (What do you want?), the guard had addressed the visitor with the familiar verb form in Spanish. The familiar form of address in most Spanish-speaking countries is used only with family members, close friends, former classmates, or children. The reflexive reaction of the man arriving was indignation, even though the circumstances were dangerous. His retort "Do we know each other?" was a powerful cultural rebuke. The automatic response of the guard was to amend his discourtesy and reply in the formal style of address for the visitor to please go about his business. Fortunately for the Mexican visitor, this incident turned out well. He would not have responded in such a manner if he had stopped to think about the logic of challenging a gun with indignation and three Spanish words—but the point is that he did not think. Cultural conditioning controlled the behavior of both men, including he who held the gun and the apparent power. Neither man went through a conscious thought process.

Our behavior is taught to us from birth, and it is taught to us so that we will conform to the culture in which we live. We learn when to speak up and when to keep quiet. We learn that certain facial expressions meet with approval and others provoke a reprimand. We are taught which gestures are acceptable and which are not, and whether we can publicly unwrap a gift; we learn where to put our hands when at the table, whether or not we can make noise with our mouths when we eat, which utensils to use or not use, whether toothpicks are acceptable and, if so, in what fashion we may use them. We learn how to address people in a manner approved by our culture, what tone of voice to use, what posture is censored and what is praised, when and how to make eye contact and for how long, and countless other things that would be impossible to consciously remember and use all at the same time when interacting socially.

This behavior is learned so well—so that we can pass social scrutiny by the ever-alert antennae of our peers and be admitted to their group—that the behavior becomes internalized below the level of our conscious thought. We operate in great part on this elaborately written subconscious program, leaving only a small percentage of our actions to be governed by conscious choice and thought. We most often become aware of the subconscious behavior that we expect from ourselves and therefore from others when someone *violates* the pattern that we have come to expect. Such a violation raises our internalized rules to a conscious level of awareness.

CONSIDER THE CONTEXT

From culture to culture the proportion of nonverbal behavioral communication varies relative to the verbal communication that is used. Communication styles that focus relatively more on words to communicate and less on behavior—the context in which the words are used—are said to be "low-context." "High-context" cultures, in contrast, rely relatively more on nonverbal context or behaviors than they rely on abstract, verbal symbols of meaning. The difference in style is similar to that of time being conveyed to the second by the precise, numeric display of a digital watch, as compared to telling time by the halting movement of the hands of an analog grandfather clock. This dissimilarity in communication styles between low- and high-context cultures creates frequent, significant obstacles to intercultural communication.

A high-context message is one in which more of the information is contained in the physical context or internalized in the person receiving it, and less in the coded, explicit, transmitted verbal part of the message. A low-context communication is just the opposite. The focus is on vesting more of the information in the explicit verbal code.[5]

Low-context communication can be compared to interfacing with a computer. It is a system of explicit prompt and response exchanges. If the computer does not read an inaccurate response's programming, then it does not compute. North Americans have a low-context communication style and intend to transmit their messages primarily in words spoken, which are amplified or overridden relatively less than in many other cultures by nonverbal signals such as gestures, silence, eye contact,[6] or ritual.

Thus a low-context person consciously focuses on words to communicate, but a high-context person is acculturated from birth to send and receive a large proportion of messages through behavioral context, both consciously and unconsciously. When this high-context person receives a verbal message from a low-context person, misunderstanding is necessarily created when the high-context person erroneously attributes meaning to nonverbal context when such meaning is not intended. This same high-context person will then, in turn, communicate much by context along with a verbal message. The low-context person may not apprehend, much less understand, much of the contextual nonverbal message that is being expressed. The low-context person relies primarily on words themselves for meaning when, in fact, the context probably contains the real message.

The distinction between high- and low-context cultures does not mean that context is meaningless in low-context cultures. It means that culture dictates a large variation in degree of importance of the context to communicative meaning.[7]

READING THE SIGNS

In many societies with a high-context communication style, such as Japan or Mexico, it is considered impolite to respond with "no" to a request. The courteous response of "maybe" or "I will try" is clearly understood as "no" to a person familiar with that culture and contextual ritual. A person from a low-context culture will typically ignore the ritual (context) because he is accustomed to focusing on the words. He takes the words spoken literally and treats them as being information specific. This low-context person is then incensed or offended when he does not get what he expects. If he protests, the high-context person cannot understand why the low-context person wants to force a rude response, or why the low-context person is being rude by insisting.

When an Occidental moves to French Polynesia, she may be frustrated at receiving what appears to be no response at all when asking a question of a Polynesian. It may be days or months (or never), before she realizes that the person addressed has just responded "yes" by an almost imperceptible raising of the eyebrows. Though she would understand the nodding of the head that by convention signals assent in many Western cultures, she relies on words and does not even see the subtle, unfamiliar nonverbal reply. Moreover, before she becomes familiar with Polynesian culture, she would not know how to interpret the answer correctly if she did notice it. In Greece, for example, the same eyebrow "flash"[8] means no. Even so, some nonverbal messages are obvious. Clearly a different message is sent and received by the delivery of a bouquet of roses than by the delivery of a person's severed ear.

One cannot rely on the similarity of communication styles between two Western cultures, nor even on the similarity of styles between two Spanish-speaking countries. There are, for example, many differences between Colombian and Venezuelan cultures. Colombia is very formal; hierarchy (class) is paramount. In comparison, Venezuela is more informal. Venezuelans make a point of being equal to persons in high or important positions. They more commonly use the familiar *tu* form to address each other than do many other Spanish-speakers. This difference may have evolved because of Venezuela's oil production, which raised living standards and afforded more public education, making the general public here less class conscious than that in Colombia.[9]

North American writers, diplomats, soldiers, and tourists traveling in Europe after World War II found that many of the people they dealt with spoke English. It was easy to assume that everybody attached the same meanings to the same words in the same language and that Europeans and North Americans understood each other. But it quickly became apparent that, because of differences in culture and in daily activities and practices, a common language did not necessarily facilitate communication or comprehension.[10]

Today we come into contact with cultures that are foreign to us more than ever before. Technology has expanded contact between cultures in the postmodern world beyond traditional boundaries, thereby creating an urgent need to focus on intercultural communication.[11] We have become so mobile that distances no longer matter,[12] and we no longer have a national economy. The United States' economy now engages the economies of all other developed nations at a global level.[13]

Alvin Toffler wrote that "the transnational corporation . . . may do research in one country, manufacture components in another, assemble them in a third, sell the manufactured goods in a fourth, deposit its surplus funds in a fifth, and so on."[14]

THE OBSTACLE COURSE

Our global village is turning out to be an unstable and often unfriendly place, with ethnic nationalisms taking center stage.[15] Competent, effective intercultural communication has become critical for our well-being and survival. Individuals and organizations struggle to cope with problems in living and working with people of other cultures[16] on a daily basis. And in the accelerating pace of face-to-face and technologically facilitated interaction, it becomes ever more desirable to achieve intercultural communication competency as quickly as possible.

In order to increase our much-needed intercultural communication competency, it is helpful to know what kinds of obstacles commonly occur when we attempt to arrive at acceptable shared meaning across any cultural boundary. Recognizing potential obstacles will help avoid, overcome, or steer around potential pitfalls. To proceed on this course, we need to define some terms that will be used:

Intercultural: A macrodefinition of "intercultural" is used, indicating one or several differences between communicators relating to language, national origin, race, or ethnicity, rather than a microdefinition that, for example, might indicate the difference in "culture" between the Women's Bar Association and a local electricians' union in the United States, or between a group of engineers and a group of musicians. This book addresses the obstacles in communicating across cultures that are *inter*national, rather than targeting diverse, *intra*national subcultures (sometimes called co-cultures) that share the experience of living in the same polity, such as the United States of America. More precisely, the term "intercultural communication" shall mean an international "transactional, symbolic process involving the attribution of meaning between people from different cultures." [17]

Cross-cultural: This term will be synonymous with intercultural.

Etic: Etic is a communication term that means viewed from an external, *inter*cultural perspective, that is, culture-general. The word "etic" was coined by United States linguist Kenneth L. Pike by extraction from the word phonetic, and the word's pronunciation rhymes with "phonetic." Etic refers to cultural characteristics that pertain to, or are raw data of, a language or other area of behavior, without considering the data as significant units functioning within a system. "The etic view is an alien view—the structuring of an outsider." [18] The etic view can tell us that a certain tribe pierces nose, ears, and lips to wear bone and shell adornments—a list of alien behavioral characteristics.

Emic: Emic is a communication term that means viewed from an internal, *intra*cultural perspective, that is, culture-specific. The word "emic" also was coined by Pike and was extracted from the word phonemic. Its pronunciation rhymes with "anemic." Emic refers to cultural characteristics that pertain to or are a significant unit that functions in contrast with other units in a language or other system of behavior. "The emic view is monocultural, with its units derived from the internal functional relations of only one . . . culture at a time." [19] An emic view can show how the wearing of certain bone and shell adornments by members of a given tribe clearly labels members as to their rank, rights, wealth, and marriage eligibility, and is used by the culture to order daily interaction. The emic view *explains* alien behavioral characteristics.

North American: This term will refer to an English-speaking citizen of the United States of America (not a Canadian or Mexican) who is an anglophone. Often this will be a North American of northern European origin, but the term European American seems more awkward and would exclude true anglophones of other heritages. An anglophone of northern European origin is sometimes called an "anglo," but this term has a different connotation than anglophone. One should note that Mexico is in North America, and that residents of Mexico, Central America, and South America all live in the "Americas," and are therefore Americans. When interacting with countries of the Americas, rather than saying "I am an American," a citizen of the United States of America can more precisely refer to him- or herself in Spanish as a North American. It is better still in Spanish to use *estadounidense,* which is taken to mean a citizen of the United States of America even though the full names of a number of countries in the Americas begin with "United States."

In our quest for increased understanding, using a list of the types of obstacles that most commonly arise when attempting to communicate across cultures will give us a practical, etic template to apply to a specific foreign culture. Looking at the selected culture from the outside, we can go down the list of the categories in which breakdowns commonly occur. We can consider each category to see if it appears to be an area that impedes communication between our own and the target culture.

However, we also need to emically examine the internal cultural system of the "other" culture. Other societies frequently mandate verbal and non-verbal behavior for daily situations of personal interaction that are quite different from what is prescribed and considered appropriate in one's own. We will, of course, easily recognize prescribed verbal and nonverbal behavior that differs from the norms of our own culture. We can then increase our understanding of behavior that seems foreign or inappropriate by trying to comprehend the function within a given culture of the behavioral units that we question.

THE STAGNATION OF ISOLATION

Different cultures in the world have developed different skills according to the time, place, and circumstance in which they unfold, because cultural features evolve to serve a social purpose. The result today is that different people may confront in different ways, with varying degrees of effectiveness, the same challenges and opportunities, because cultures differ in their relative effectiveness for particular purposes.[20] Persons with diverse viewpoints must communicate in order to set conditions under which all can flourish[21] and to profit from the exchange of efficient ways of dealing with life circumstances. Sociologist Thomas Sowell points out that, historically, the Balkanization of peoples into small and isolated groups has resulted in cultural retardation.[22] Further, human tolerance suffers as communication declines.[23] It is imperative that cultures be able to communicate with each other for practical reasons.

We will all benefit from intercultural communication, for over the millennia of human history, cross-cultural experiences have been associated with a society's achievement.[24] Throughout history, cultures have beneficially crossed in the world's great trading centers. They also cross through migration. Today we can see this tendency toward achievement in "immigrant nations" such as the United States, Australia, and Brazil. These nations exhibit social and economic dynamism, optimism, and adaptability that are rare among societies that are more closed. Immigrants bringing a foreign culture affect the nation that receives them, even while the receiving nation in turn reshapes the immigrants.[25]

In setting out to cross cultural boundaries, and before examining potential pitfalls, we need first to begin with a map of cultural territory.

TWO   # What Constitutes a Culture?

Culture is communication and communication is culture.[1]

The plane finally landed in Tokyo, after the long flight from the West Coast of the United States. Annie Nimos had changed into fresh business clothes before arrival, because she would be met by the owner of the firm with whom she had corresponded for a year for her import business. She had placed several orders by correspondence, and business had gone smoothly, but this would be the first time she and the owner would meet. After finally getting through customs, she saw a gentleman with a sign in his hand that said "Mrs. Nimos" and made her way toward him. Tanaka-San, the owner of the firm, as well as another man and woman who were employees, had come to meet her. There were bows and *herros*, and the younger man stepped forward to offer to carry her laptop computer. She started slightly when he greeted her: "Hello. Welcome to Tokyo. How old are you?"

COMMUNICATING WITH THE OTHER

Some communication specialists propose that all communication is intercultural,[2] because there are microcultural differences between one family and another, or even idio-cultural differences between two persons. But this is not a useful stance in the attempt to communicate successfully across national cultures, as culture is commonly defined. The act of understanding and being understood is more complex in a broad intercultural range than in a narrow intracultural situation. The variables of mind, senses, and medium are, in part or great measure, the products of the communicator's particular culture.[3] Further, cultural differences present greater obstacles to communication than do linguistic differences.[4]

Although Mrs. Nimos had had contact with diverse cultures in South America and in Europe, this was her first trip to Japan. The personal question as to her age caught her off guard, because in the West such a question would be considered intrusive and offensive. After momentary hesitation she told the young man her age. He nodded and seemed satisfied, maybe because she was older than he had expected. Later in the visit, reflecting on her welcome at the airport, she was able to relate the question about her age to the importance of hierarchy in Japan. Age is an important factor in situating a person in the Japanese cultural hierarchy. For her Japanese business counterparts to feel comfortable that they knew the proper way to address and to relate to her, they needed to know her age.

In a later conversation, at a dinner with several Chinese students working on doctoral degrees in the United States, Mrs. Nimos recounted her experience in Japan, seeking another Asian perspective. On hearing the story, the men nodded instantly with understanding and said that age is important for the same reason in China. However, they elaborated, when communicating with family members generation becomes an important factor that overrides age. Xu Lia explained that he has an uncle who is almost the same age as he and a cousin who is twenty years older. Xu Lia must address the young uncle with the respect accorded to the older generation in the family, and he addresses the older cousin as a peer because the cousin is of the same generation as Xu Lia.[5]

We can best understand intercultural communication as cultural variance in the perception of social objects and events.[6] The differences commonly defined as cultural include language, nationality, ethnicity, values, and customs. And although communication between subcultures or microcultures within a given polity is not our focus, understanding how barriers to communication arise because of cultural differences certainly will increase one's communication skills with all people.

The elimination of geographic and social barriers by current communication technology constantly crosses cultural boundaries and confronts us with the Other, one who is other than us, in some way alien and diverse.[7]

Communicating with the Other may be the key to our survival,[8] and the identity and attributes of the Other are rooted in culture.[9] Central, then, to the issue of intercultural communication is the concept of what constitutes a culture.

CONCEPT OF CULTURE

There are many concepts of culture, ranging from the simple to the complex:

1. Culture is just "the way we do things around here." [10] Culture is the set of norms by which things are run — or simply "are." [11]
2. Culture is the logic by which we give order to the world.[12]
3. Culture refers to "knowledge, experience, meanings, beliefs, values, attitudes, religions, concepts of self, the universe and self-universe, relationships, hierarchies of status, role expectations, spatial relations, and time concepts" accumulated by a large group of people over generations through individual and group effort. "Culture manifests itself both in patterns of language and thought, and in forms of activity and behavior." [13] Culture filters communication.

Anthropologist Edward T. Hall, in his catalyzing work *The Silent Language,* states that culture is not one thing, but rather a complex series of interrelated activities with origins deeply buried in our past. He treats culture in its entirety as a form of communication. Culture is communication and communication is culture.[14] In a living, dynamic circle, culture governs communication and communication creates, reinforces, and re-creates culture.

Even though humans may be the only animals to have culture, they are not the first to be social. They did not, in their special wisdom, invent society. Even the earliest complex animals were born into a social system to which they had to adapt if they were to subsist. Society is an adaptive necessity for human existence, and communication is the system of co-adaptation that sustains society. However, we need to remember that even though communication is necessary to sustain life, other peoples who do not communicate precisely as we do, do not immediately die.[15]

Human communication contains two kinds of messages. The first is intermittent in occurrence and can be referred to as the new informational aspect. The other is the continuous, relational aspect of interpersonal communication. The conveyance of new information is no more important than the relational aspect of communication, because the latter keeps the communication system in operation and regulates the interaction process. Communication in the broadest sense is the active aspect of cultural structure.[16] The information content of communication often takes the form of a low-context verbal message, and the relational aspect is more often communicated nonverbally as a contextual metamessage.[17]

To understand how humans adapt to their society, we can conceptually break down the social system of a culture into units of prescribed behavior for given situations. Hall characterizes these units as situational frames in society. A situational frame is the smallest viable unit of a culture that can be "analyzed, taught, transmitted, and handed down" as a complete entity. Examples of such units might be "greeting," "gift-giving," "introductions," "eye contact," and "table manners." As children, we start learning in units the behavior for each situation that is considered appropriate for our culture. These situational units are culture's building blocks, and they contain social, temporal, proxemic, kinesic, linguistic, personality, and other components. Since we can more easily learn a new culture by using manageable analytic units,[18] looking at common cultural "situations"—the units that differ from culture to culture and constitute potential obstacles—can aid us in achieving effective intercultural communication.

Difference in the situational units of a culture creates communication obstacles in the *process* of verbal and nonverbal interaction between persons. But since culture as a whole gives rise to obstacles of *perception*, it is also imperative to broadly consider cultural information such as history, religion, form of government, preconceptions, and values.

Culture gives humans their identity. It is the total communication framework for words, actions, body language, emblems (gestures), intonation, facial expressions, for the way one handles time, space, and materials, and for the way one works, makes love, plays, and so on. All these things and more are complete communication systems. Meanings can only be read correctly if one is familiar with these units of behavior in their cultural context.[19]

Anything that can properly be called cultural is learned, not hereditary.[20] But these learned ways of interacting gradually sink below the surface of the mind and become hidden controls that are experienced as innate because they are ubiquitous and habitual. Culture organizes the psyche, how people look at things, behave, make decisions, order priorities, and even how they think.[21]

We are, all of us, already cultural experts, but we are experts in our own cultures and almost totally at a subconscious level. Our trained subconscious antennae can read insincerity when words and nonverbal communication are incongruent, and we can anticipate aggressive actions from subtle cues. But this same finely tuned sub-subconscious interpretative ability will misread cues that have a different meaning in another culture, and when this happens we have a reaction based on misinformation, often without our being aware of the mechanics leading to our response.

Our own cultural maps are so familiar, like a home neighborhood, that we do not need to make them explicit; it is only in foreign cultural territory that we need an externalized map.[22] When one can successfully describe an informal pattern in a culture, then others in the same culture can immediately recognize it because they already have acquired this pattern. By explicitly putting cultural patterns or rules into words, these informal and subconscious patterns can be more easily taught.[23] In fact, the only important process in the survival of cultures is transmission,[24] i.e., communication.

Although culture is learned, Hall points out that it is very difficult for culture X to teach culture Y to use nonverbal communication forms, because all groups tend to interpret their own nonverbal communication patterns as universal.[25] We constantly and silently communicate our real feelings in the language of nonverbal behavior, which is elaborately patterned by our culture.[26]

Consequently, to communicate across cultures, we need formal training not only in the language but also in the history, government, and customs of the target culture, with at least an introduction to its nonverbal language.[27] Humans are linked to each other through hierarchies of rhythms of language and body movement that are culture-specific. We cannot adequately describe a culture solely from the inside without reference to the outside, nor vice-versa,[28] which dictates an etic-emic approach.

CULTURE IS NORMATIVE

As children, we learn through subliminal, but clearly discrete, signals the directives, the prohibitions, the encouragements, and the warnings that govern our consistent association with other members of our society. Our systems of verbal and body-motion languages are flexible and malleable, but they are adaptive and functional only because they are systematically organized.[29]

Every society seems to have strict normative regulations of communication, a kind of communication traffic order.[30] In fact, all human behavior is subject to normative social control, and each bit of behavior (Hall's situational unit) becomes an element in a code. This normative structure is what gives human behavior its communicative power.[31] One communicates by how one adheres to or deviates from the norm. The particular set of rules that transforms a person into a human being derives from requirements established in the ritual organization of social encounters.[32] However, we should bear in mind that at some time in history some culture has justified or condemned every conceivable human action.

When a person is born into a society, a system already exists into which the person must be assimilated if the society is to sustain itself. If the person's behavior does not become predictable to the degree expected, then he or she must be accorded special treatment, which can range from deification to incarceration. In some societies the person who does not assimilate will be allowed to die. Ultimately the goal is to make the person's behavior predictable enough that society can go about the rest of its business. In every society, in order to attain membership, a person must gain control of the pattern of, and be incorporated into, the society's communication system.[33]

Human communities select their cultural institutions from a great range of possibilities; the resulting configuration of choices from this matrix makes up the pattern of a culture, and patterning is what gives culture its intelligibility.[34] These cultural patterns are unique, not universal, but human beings have difficulty getting outside their own cultural skins in order to see this. To communicate effectively across cultures, we need to increase our understanding of our own unconscious culture.[35]

DEVIATION FROM CULTURAL NORMS

There is a public order. All of our interactions with others are governed by a learned set of rules—our cultural pattern—most of which unconsciously guide our behavior and consequently affect our communication. We draw on our learned rules to understand others' behavior.[36] Interacting through verbal and nonverbal language usage (what is said when, how it is phrased, and how one coordinates language with nonverbal signs) is not simply a matter of free choice; such usage is affected by subconscious and internal constraints that lie out of our immediate awareness.[37] We are sharply conscious of another's deviation from these rules—and we interpret meaning from such deviation. When engaging in intercultural communication, we often cannot understand the meaning of another's comportment, and we know that we do not understand. A yet greater peril to misunderstanding occurs when we think we understand and do not. We misinterpret. We can misinterpret such things as the dynamics of turn-taking, the use of space, eye contact, and smiling, to name only a few possibilities from a potentially infinite list.

An act can be proper or improper only according to the judgment of a specific social group, and one type of socially approved act, called a negatively eventful act, is of central importance. If this type of act is not performed there will be negative sanctions, but the act goes unperceived if performed properly.[38] The part of the human nervous system that deals with social behavior works according to the principle of negative feedback. Therefore, we are consciously aware primarily of *violations* of our unconscious rules of behavior; acts in compliance with the rules go unnoticed, as do the unconscious rules themselves as long as persons comply with them. We most frequently become aware of this hidden control system when interacting with other cultures, because often such interactions do not follow our unconscious rules.[39] The great gift of intercultural interactions is the opportunity to achieve awareness of our own cultural system, which has value beyond simply having a good or bad experience with an "exotic" encounter.

Teresa, raised in South America, married a man with a French father and a Russian mother, Antonina. The newlyweds lived with the husband's parents early in the marriage. Every morning the young woman would greet her father- and mother-in-law and kiss them on the cheek, as she was accustomed to greeting her own family. On occasions when the mother-in-law was irritated with Teresa, she complained that Teresa obviously didn't like her—that she "disgusted" and "repulsed" Teresa. Teresa was surprised by the choice of words and could not identify the basis for Antonina's complaint.

Several years later Teresa realized that she was accustomed to giving a Latin-style "kiss" good-morning—a kiss on the cheek—or more accurately, a brushing of cheeks. But all of her life, in the various countries in which she lived, Antonina kissed family and friends, both men and women, in Russian fashion. This was a kiss full on the mouth, and most people with whom she interacted accommodated her style. Antonina interpreted Teresa's turning of her head and the "cheek-kiss" as avoidance because of dislike and a critical attitude. The only person Teresa kissed on the mouth was her husband. Before her realization, Teresa had not connected Antonina's accusation of "disgust" with her morning greeting and its style.

CULTURE CLASHES

Millions of North Americans traveled to Europe after World War II, and a large number of European writers, intellectuals, and students traveled to the United States. Occasionally, the opportunity to live in and learn about a different society helped shatter the preconceived stereotypes that each had about the other. But most of these transatlantic explorations and cultural exchanges led not to mutual understanding but mutual suspicion, and not to greater sophistication but greater provincialism. Most of the travelers were champions of their own culture with an inability to appreciate any country but their own or to accept another society on its own terms.[40] Simple exposure to another culture does not guarantee better intercultural communication. Such encounters may result only in culture clashes and the reinforcement of negative stereotypes.

Antonina and Teresa's greeting behavior lay below their conscious thought. Antonina reacted strongly to the negatively eventful act of avoidance of contact on the mouth because she interpreted it as judgmental. It brought Teresa's behavior to a conscious level, although Antonina seemed able to verbalize only her reaction and not its cause. For Teresa the morning greeting was not a negative event, and the ritual stayed below a conscious level. It would have been helpful if Teresa had become consciously aware of her own and Antonina's cultural conditioning earlier in the relationship, because the offense perceived by Antonina added fuel to a long-lasting fire of contention. This type of misunderstanding is typical of how cultural differences cause difficulties in intercultural communication.

Australian Jill Ker Conway, in her autobiography *True North*, recounts that she was irrationally irked by what she perceived as the inefficiency of English life, the slowness with which things got done, and the relaxed confidence of all concerned that they lived at the center of the greatest intellectual community in the world. John, her North American husband, gave her advice to help her objectively observe rather than react. He urged her "to view the British as though they were an African tribe, complete with nose rings and elaborate tattoos, delightful to observe, just as one would any other strange culture."[41] She states that, like "every émigré, I was always keeping score, somewhere in the back of my mind, weighing and assessing what was good and bad about my new situation, testing the new society against my native one."[42]

Conway writes that there are climates of the mind. "Some expatriates never arrive spiritually in the new land." The light remains foreign, and the climate is perpetually measured by the standard of another geographic zone. The senses of sight and smell continue to be governed by the person's inner sense, always searching for the familiar sensations of childhood, just as some émigrés can never master the pronunciation of a new tongue no matter how fluently they speak it.[43]

We automatically treat what is most characteristic of our own culture (that of our youth) as though it were innate. We are automatically ethnocentric—we are thoroughly trained to be so—and we therefore think and react to anyone whose behavior differs as if that person were impolite, irresponsible, inferior, etc. We experience the behavior of another that deviates from our own unconscious cultural norms as an uncontrollable and unpredictable part of ourselves; a cultural type of identification grips us in its iron fist,[44] demanding conformity. And, as the misunderstanding between Antonina and Teresa over greeting style illustrates, a negative or positive reaction can be primarily one-way.

All societies lament the differences they encounter in others. Europeans have complained that the United States' past has little relevance to the experience of societies elsewhere on earth. The French have long believed that their culture is infinitely exportable and their history of worldwide significance. While North Americans tout their democracy, the French proclaim their civilization. The global attitudes of both nations are similarly grandiose.[45]

In dealing with other countries, many North Americans assume that all foreigners secretly wish to emulate the United States and expect them to remodel their institutions using the North American pattern. Richard Pells writes that North Americans tend to evaluate other countries by how closely they resemble the United States, including not only those nations' social institutions but also their plumbing and their kitchens.[46]

Many nations characterize a cultural difference such as the killing of one's sister for adultery as an uncivilized deviation from cultural norms. Differences as extreme as this example signal very fundamental differences in cultural patterns. In non-Westernized Arab settings the sister is a sacred link between families, and culture justifies such an act as preserving the central family institution, without which the society would perish or be radically altered.[47] Without accepting, condoning, or participating in practices unacceptable to our own cultures, understanding a different practice nonetheless aids in intercultural communication. It is true, however, that significant and fundamental cultural differences make communication difficult at best and, on some points, impossible.

DIVERSITY AND IDENTITY

In some North American subcultures, it is the practice to avoid direct eye contact with strangers in public when closer than twelve to fourteen feet. Persons belonging to a group that is used to visual involvement inside that distance will misread the avoidance of eye contact: miscuing of this type on the unconscious behavioral level is touchy and complex and in some contexts is interpreted as deliberate racism.[48] Many people from Asian and Latin American cultures avoid eye contact as a sign of respect. This is also true of many African Americans, particularly in the southern United States. Many North American employers, teachers, and similar "authority" figures interpret avoidance of eye contact as a sign of disrespect or deviousness.[49] In fact, we can picture a North American adult scolding a child who looks down: "You *look* at me when I speak to you!"—but in many parts of the world one never challenges authority by looking it in the eye.

In United States' urban centers, direct eye contact has taken new meaning among the younger generation. It acts much like a challenge to a duel and may provoke a physical altercation. The Code of Conduct signs at Universal Studio's City Walk in Los Angeles warn against "annoying others through noisy or boisterous activities or by *unnecessary staring* [author's emphasis]." [50]

An anglophone North American teacher may assume that most children want to get ahead and may try to encourage students with contests. Hispanic New Mexican children may appear lazy because they seem not to want to make the effort. This stereotype takes on new meaning when we learn that to stand out from one's peers in the Hispanic group is to place oneself in great jeopardy and is to be avoided at all costs.[51] The teacher is steeped in the individualism of North American culture; the child has been conditioned by collective Hispanic culture. Members of each group will be motivated differently.

People as cultural beings are not masters of their fate—they are bound by hidden rules as long as they remain ignorant of the hidden norms of their culture.[52] What is closest to ourselves is what we consciously know least well.[53]

In *Not Like Us*, Richard Pells writes that North American expatriates living in Europe found the experience to be an occasion for introspection, and the opportunity not only to explore another culture but also to "rediscover" one's own. James Baldwin during his long residence in France concluded that his cultural ties were neither to Europe nor to Africa, but that his identity was inescapably North American. Other writers and intellectuals had similar epiphanies and spoke of a cultural reawakening and of their greater awareness of the strengths and deficiencies of their own North American culture.[54]

To understand and accept the ways in which the minds of those in another group work constitutes the essence of cultural understanding; a by-product of such acceptance affords a rare glimpse of the strengths and weaknesses of our own system. Transcending or freeing ourselves from the grip of unconscious culture cannot be accomplished without some such self-awareness. The real job may be to understand our own culture, and to take other cultures seriously forces us to pay attention to the details of our own.[55] We may, in fact, need each other for self-definition. How can we know what is distinctively British, French, or Mexican without describing what is peculiarly German, Italian, or Dutch? How can we know what is distinctively Latin American without defining what is North American?[56]

ETIC/EMIC APPROACHES

Since some universal skills for intercultural communication apply across all cultures,[57] we can effectively utilize an etic (culture general) approach. But we also need to employ an emic approach to produce paradigms about a specific culture,[58] and therefore we need to investigate the culture with which we plan to interact in order to pinpoint cultural differences. Increasing difference-awareness through an emic approach ideally should engender the concept that we are different from others and not always that others are different from us. Sensitizing people to the idea that differences exist is a first step in attaining intercultural communication proficiency.[59] Intercultural communication competence and culture-specific communication competence must be viewed as two separate concepts that operate simultaneously to contribute to the successful outcome of a given intercultural encounter.[60]

In examining a culture from the inside to gain as much understanding as possible, we should always be alert for any cultural differences that may potentially present communication problems but that may not seem to fit any external list of categories. It is important not to lose sight of the fact that culture is active, not static, and is continuously evolving and changing. And even though this book specifically addresses *inter*cultural communication, the concepts presented will also be useful in everyday *intra*cultural communication. Ideally, we will learn to suspend judgment about any unfamiliar or offensive communicative behavior, verbal or nonverbal, and ask ourselves "How is this behavior useful, or how does it originate in culture?" or—perhaps occasionally—"Is this individual really just an obnoxious representation of him- or herself?"

In our own cultures, we acquire a cultural template for communication behavior that not only allows us automatically to handle routine encounters, but also consciously to adapt to new situations that arise. In addressing a foreign culture, using an etic, general approach combined with an emic, culture-specific approach will give us insight into how to arrive at acceptable shared meaning both in anticipated and unforeseen circumstances.

INTERCULTURAL COMMUNICATION OBSTACLES

The successful intercultural communication process best begins with goodwill on both sides. However, an individual's negative reactions and evaluations of a foreign culture may create intercultural communication barriers. Negative evaluations cause dislike rather than like, and avoidance rather than approach. They occur because the foreign culture deviates from the norms to which we are acculturated. These barriers are bicultural and monodirectional, reflecting unwillingness or inability to understand the norms of a foreign culture. The barriers are not necessarily reciprocal. Further, a single cultural difference may, in fact, be an absolute barrier if it violates one of a communicator's core values.[61] The isolation of women in harems and the practice of infanticide violate Western core values. Female sexual freedom violates core values of most Arab and Asian nations.

Culture is the matrix in which perception and verbal and nonverbal communication processes develop.[62] Factors in these three general communication groupings in turn affect culture as well as each other. The interrelationships are complex but can be usefully diagrammed (see Table 1).

TABLE 1.   Cultural Matrix

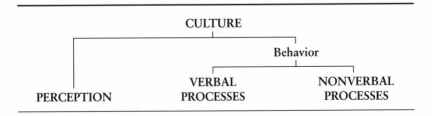

TABLE 2. Potential Obstacles to Intercultural Communication

Culture		
Perception	**Behavior**	
	Verbal Processes	*Nonverbal Processes*
CULTURE SPECIFIC	COMPETENCY	Chronemics (Time Sense)
Collectivism vs.	Accent	*Monochronic*
Individualism	Cadence	*Polychronic*
Face	Connotation	Context
Hierarchy	Context	Immediacy
History and	Idiom	Kinesics (Body Motion
Experience	Polite Usage	Communication)
Master Symbols	Silence	*Emblems (Gestures)*
Power	Style	*Eye Contact*
Preconceptions		*Facial Expressions*
Role	LITERACY /	*Haptics (Touch)*
Class	ORALITY	*Posture*
Gender		*Smell*
Rules		Proxemics (Space Sense)
Social Organization		*Fixed-Feature Space*
Family		*Semifixed-Feature Space*
Government		*Informal Space*
Thought Patterns		Physical Characteristics
Values		*Artifacts (Extensions of*
Worldview		*Self)*
		Physical Appearance
CULTURALLY		Vocalics (Speech
PERSONAL		Characteristics)
Adaptability		*Vocal Characterizers*
Attitude		*Vocal Qualifiers*
Ethnocentrism		*Vocal Rate*
Uncertainty		*Vocal Segregates*

As a navigation tool for foreign cultural territory, an original list of "obstacles" has been gleaned from intercultural communication research and literature. These obstacles have been sorted into the three general groupings and tabulated in taxonomic form. For an overview of a dynamic culture-as-communication whole, see Table 2 for this list of categories of common potential obstacles to intercultural communication.[63]

Table 2 will serve as a map to guide us in our attempt to communicate across cultural boundaries. The next three chapters will explicate the categories of potential obstacles to intercultural communication, so that we have a better chance of anticipating and recognizing—and therefore of avoiding or surmounting—these barriers.

THREE   # Obstacles of Perception

*Another culture can be different, without being
defective.*[1]

*Communication is like a kaleidoscope. Many units
of different sizes, shapes, and color make up the
whole picture. Any action, shift, or change adjusts
the pattern and the relationship of all of the units
to each other, thereby altering the picture.*

Monsieur and Madame Bertrand had invited a few good friends to dinner
at their Paris home. It was a crisply cold winter night. After dining sumptu-
ously and finishing late, Monsieur Bertrand was helping Madame Dubois
into her coat. The hosts and several guests were standing in the foyer.
Madame Dubois raised an arm to get it into the sleeve of her coat and
knocked a painting off the wall onto the tile floor. She and the hostess bent
down to examine the painting. Unfortunately, the fall onto the tile had damaged the frame. Madame Dubois fingered the damage. She said "It's damaged. I'm so sorry." Straightening up, she adjusted her coat and commented,
"What an awkward place to hang a painting. I couldn't avoid it." After good-
byes and effusive compliments about the wonderful delicacies of the dinner
and the selection of wines, Madame Dubois and her husband departed.

   Perception is the internal process by which we select, evaluate, and organize the stimuli of the outside world. From the time we are born, we learn

our perceptions and the resulting behaviors from our cultural experiences.[2] Behaviors "natural" to different cultures do not necessarily conflict,[3] but when they do, the conflict frequently causes communication problems.

Madame Dubois's apparent lack of concern for the painting that she damaged would probably cause ill will on the part of North American hosts. In North American culture, respect for a person's material possessions symbolizes respect for the person. More effusive apologies, and perhaps reparation, would have been both offered and expected in such a situation. But in France there is a different social network, and a possession does not symbolize the relationship. The friendship should be more important than a material possession, and the fact that Madame Dubois could rely on the relationship being more important than the damage to the painting was indicative of this cultural value and attitude, thereby reinforcing the friendship rather than causing a rift. This particular cultural difference between France and the United States is one that is especially difficult for both cultures to understand.[4] It is not that a material possession is more important than a friendship in the United States, it is that demonstrating respect for the possession of another *symbolizes* the importance one places on the relationship.

When we attempt to communicate with another culture, it is of great help to start out with an awareness of the principal types of cultural differences that can potentially impede communication—the arrival at acceptable shared meaning. We can classify these disparities as differences in perception and as differences in the verbal and nonverbal processes of communication. Drawing on studies by sociologists, psychologists, anthropologists, and communication specialists, on personal experiences of multicultural people, and on other sources, we can construct a number of common and significant categories of perception and process that cause difficulties when persons of different cultures attempt to communicate.

We will first consider the common communication obstacles engendered by culturally different perceptions, and next we will examine the obstacles that arise from verbal and nonverbal processes of communication. We will then see how this theoretical framework applies today to practical communication between two specific cultures: the United States and Mexico.

The categories of perception that commonly cause difficulties in intercultural communication are shown in Table 3.

Some explanation of each of the categories of potential obstacles outlined in Table 3 is necessary in order for us to understand how they apply to communication across cultural borders.

TABLE 3.   Obstacles of Perception

Culturally Shaped Perceptions	Personal Perceptions within a Cultural Framework
Preconceptions	Uncertainty
Collectivism vs. Individualism	Attitude
Face	Ethnocentrism
Hierarchy	Adaptability
History and Experience	
Master Symbols	
Power	
Role	
Gender	
Social Class	
Rules	
Social Organization	
Family	
Government	
Thought Patterns	
Values	
Worldview	

CULTURE SHAPES PERCEPTION

Preconceptions

Preconceptions so greatly affect intercultural communication that we will begin our discussion of obstacles caused by differences in perception with this category. Understanding that we all have preconceptions is a key to understanding how culture shapes perception. Culture engenders preconceptions in each and every one of us, in training us from birth in the behavior patterns to which we are expected to conform and which each of us in turn expects from others. We then carry these subliminal expectations or preconceptions into cross-cultural encounters, until we learn to suspend at least some of them because they may not be relevant to successful communication with a specific foreign culture. Prejudices and stereotypes are preconceptions.

If stereotypes are hardy, it is not because they necessarily contain some grain of truth. It is because they express the culture of the person who espouses the stereotype. A French person who says that North American children are rude refers to the French concept of child rearing, and the North American who maintains that the French are rude because they don't let you get a word in edgewise refers to the implicit rules of turn-taking in North American conversation.[5] Negative judgment or evaluation of a foreign culture fosters dislike and avoidance.[6]

People who use stereotypes make reality fit their preconceptions. A story that illustrates this is that of a patient who goes to a psychiatrist because he believes he is dead. The psychiatrist asks the patient if dead men bleed, and the patient answers that they do not. The psychiatrist then pricks the patient's finger and draws blood. The patient responds, "Well, imagine that, dead men do bleed."[7]

People tend to see what they expect to see and, furthermore, to *discount* that which conflicts with these preconceptions, stereotypes, or prejudices toward persons.[8] The different cultural identities of two persons attempting to communicate will encourage each to perceive the other as having group attributes, rather than as being a unique person.[9] Preconceptions can be positive or negative, but a significant problem they present in intercultural communication is that preconceptions often lie outside of awareness.[10]

Even though preconceptions are frequently misleading, there is nonetheless a wealth of evidence provided by anthropologists, sociologists, psychologists, and others that a culture does shape national character traits.[11] That the general public perceives "national" characteristics is summed up with good humor by a sign posted in an Italian restaurant. "Heaven is where the police are British, the chefs Italian, the mechanics German, the lovers French, and it is all organized by the Swiss. Hell is where the police are German, the chefs British, the mechanics French, the lovers Swiss, and it is all organized by the Italians."

There are reasons for these perceived identities:[12]

1. Members of a culture share common early experiences.
2. These experiences produce similar personality profiles.
3. Since the early experiences of individuals differ from culture to culture, personality characteristics and values differ from culture to culture.
4. This does not mean that all members of a culture behave the same, because there is a wide range of individual differences. Even so, most members of a given culture share many aspects of behavior to varying degrees.

Therefore, profiles of national character can be compiled without being stereotypes, and even though these profiles do not apply to every individual of a nation, they will apply to most. Stereotypes, on the other hand, apply to only a few people of a culture but are attributed to most.[13]

A stereotype can be called a cultural caricature.

Collectivism versus Individualism

One of the most fundamental ways in which cultures differ is in the dimensions of collectivism versus individualism. Individualists tend to be more distant in their personal interactions with others, and they must go through the process of acquiring affective relationships; collectivists, on the other hand, interact closely and are interdependent.[14] Individualists tend to be self-motivated and can be stimulated to achieve by individual competition. Collectivists, on the other hand, are better encouraged by appealing to their group spirit and by requesting cooperation.[15]

In studying cultural differences, French anthropologist Raymonde Carroll, who is married to a North American anthropologist, observes that a North American cultural premise is that "I" exist outside all networks. This does not mean that social networks do not exist or have no importance for the North American, but that I make or define myself—I myself create the fabric of my identity. This premise is evoked in a limited way by the expression a "self-made person." But in French collective culture, I am always a product of the networks that give me my identity, which can be questioned by anyone from the same French network. Hence Sartre's *l'enfer, c'est les autres*. But others are not always or only hell, because my network of relationships feeds, supports, defines and makes me significant, just as it can trap, stifle, and oppress me.[16]

Because in North America I am responsible for my identity, I have no reason to hide humble origins, for example. If I am successful, I can be proud. And if I come from high society, I am responsible for staying there and am myself responsible for any fall. This is why North Americans are not embarrassed by questions that French people find personally intrusive, such as "What do your parents do?" and why the biographies of North American public figures are not secret. If in the United States the brother of a national president is an alcoholic, this has no bearing on the president. The identity of the person in a collective culture, on the other hand, is defined much more by the person's social network than a social network defines a person in an individualistic culture. To ask a French person whom you meet "What do you do?" is "none of your business." [17]

Thomas Morning Owl, a member of the Confederated Umatilla Tribes in the state of Oregon, if asked "Shinnamwa?" (Who are you?) in the Sahaptin language, would not respond by giving his name. He would instead describe who his father is, his mother, and his tribe, and where they came from. Morning Owl comments that in North American society people have individual identities, but for the collective culture of Amerindians of the Columbia Plateau, a person is no one without reference to his or her lineage: "who preceded you, is who you are." [18]

Collective cultures place less value on relationships with out-groups (strangers, casual acquaintances) than do individualistic cultures. Therefore, persons of a collective culture, such as the Japanese, tend to focus most of their appropriately positive behavior on persons in their in-group, in order to maintain group cohesion, cooperation, and harmony.[19] Persons in out-groups are much less important. Individualistic cultures like the United States do not differentiate as much between out-groups and in-groups and therefore do not differentiate as much in their "friendly" behavior. This may partially explain the perception by other cultures that North Americans are overly or inappropriately familiar with strangers, or that their friendliness is shallow or insincere.

Further, collective cultures are less tolerant of variation in culturally prescribed behavior than are individualistic cultures.[20]

Face

Face is the value or standing a person has in the eyes of others. This standing can be a source of the person's sense of personal pride or self-respect. In many cultures maintaining face is of great importance, and one must take great care in disagreeing, criticizing, or competing.[21] Europeans are often amazed by the North American media's relentless exposure of U.S. problems and by the amount of self-criticism that takes place within the nation.[22]

Hierarchy

In a culture, differences can be accorded to the order of birth, order of arrival, and order of status. Hall states that societies will order people, situation, or station—but not all three simultaneously.[23] As a consequence, depending on the culture, people requiring a service might be attended to according to their age, in the order of their arrival, or in keeping with their perceived social rank.

Hierarchical organization of a culture affects people on a daily basis. "Flat" hierarchical organization affords an open and mobile society, whereas a steep hierarchy constricts social advancement.[24] The acceptance of hierarchy in a society is, by definition, an acceptance of inequality.[25]

In 1998 a twenty-four-year-old French citizen was appointed director of U.S. operations for a computer network-systems firm in San Francisco. Even though he is a graduate of one of France's most prestigious business schools, he maintains he would never have this kind of responsibility working for a French company. He explains that in the United States people will listen to you because of what you can do, not because of your age or where you learned to do it. But in France, age combined with knowledge are still not enough. Even when you are fifty years old and experienced, the status conferred by your school is the overriding factor in job opportunity. Your school ultimately determines your professional station in life, good or bad. Christian Saint-Étienne, a consultant and economics professor at the University of Paris–Dauphine, says that the rigid hierarchical system pushes bright and ambitious young people to leave[26] for environments where their opinions will carry more weight.

Different factors determine a person's rank in the hierarchy of different cultures. When Annie Nimos arrived for the first time in Japan, she was greeted with an opening query about her age. Her Japanese counterparts sought hierarchical information they considered essential in order to know the proper way to address and relate to her.

The difference in the hierarchical organization of cultures is a significant factor in intercultural communication. All living things have a pecking order.[27] The concept of hierarchical distance, which can also be conceived of as interpersonal power distance, affects the degree of formality that is used in communication style. A decentralized and democratic society encourages participatory communication,[28] while a centralized, authoritarian society discourages it. Japanese tradition, for example, is based on classification, rank, order, and harmony, in contrast to North American tradition, which is based on declassification, equality, exploration, and adventure (although there is, of course, some overlap).[29] Gender and minority statuses can affect one's position in the hierarchy of a culture.[30]

North American writers visiting Europe during the last half of the twentieth century remarked on the contrasts between the two civilizations. Europe is aristocratic in its culture and politics, with the upper classes demanding deference from those considered social inferiors.[31] In Mexico, also a hierarchical culture, people similarly prefer to maintain an authoritative distance and use very formal, although personal, courtesy. North Americans, in contrast, strive for impeccable democracy and egalitarianism in relating to others and as a result employ a far more informal style of communication.

Communication style in a steep hierarchical society serves to reinforce or create hierarchical difference between persons. Individuals will use forms of address that maintain social distance. In recognition of the hierarchy, they will tend to display positive emotions or behavior to persons who have higher status and negative emotions or behavior to persons who rank lower in status.[32]

An individual's communication style in a flatter hierarchical society decreases hierarchical differences. In a "flat" hierarchy, a speaker will use forms of address that demote the rank of persons at higher echelons and promote persons at lower ones, in an attempt to democratically minimize status differences and create equality. In the flatter hierarchy, there will be a tendency to display negative behavior toward higher-status persons to lower them to one's own status, and to display positive behavior toward lower-status persons to elevate them, because all persons should be equal.[33] Learned behavior is the opposite of that for cultures with a steep hierarchy.

A number of communication specialists studying gender differences in communication in the United States agree that women are more skilled than men at nonverbal communication. One of a number of plausible explanations is that women more often have passive or submissive roles and learn to read nonverbal communication cues to appease those in positions of power. If this is true, one can expect that in cultures with the steep hierarchical organization that equates to high interpersonal power distances, persons will be highly skilled in interpreting nonverbal communication cues.[34]

European intellectuals observe that the authority of persons in government and large corporations in the United States stems from the weight of public opinion in a democratic environment, rather than from hierarchical organization. North Americans in authority therefore strive to appear benevolent and democratic. Many European writers agree that the United States affords a fluid society where anyone can climb to the apex of the social pyramid, in contrast to the class divisions of Europe.[35]

The United States is organized with smaller distances in its social hierarchy than exist in the steeper social organization of many world cultures. The apparent lack of respect that North Americans express toward persons in authority, and the familiarity with which they interact with persons of lower status than themselves, can confuse or offend persons from cultures with steep hierarchical organization. For the purposes of successful—and enjoyable—communication, it is useful for people from other cultures to understand consciously that North Americans are conditioned by their culture to communicate in a manner that will decrease the hierarchical distance between themselves and people situated both at higher and lower levels in the social ranking system.

Hierarchy affects communication within a society. In a steep hierarchy, information slows down as it moves up the levels of authority, ending up in a bottleneck as it reaches the decision-maker who is overloaded with information.[36] On the way down, information moves quickly but is manipulated as a resource that enhances status and authority. Steep hierarchies breed concealment and misrepresentation of information.[37] In a flatter hierarchy, information flows more quickly and freely, with less distortion.

History and Experience

A person's life experience and a culture's history mold an individual's perceptions. In some cultures history is a part of the living present, and it colors people's perceptions of their lives on a daily basis. This would certainly be true in Israel and Palestine today, in a way that is not the case in the United States.

Some European writers claim that North Americans have no respect for the past, but others declare them emancipated from the "shackles" of history. Still others say that North Americans rarely look back because they are certain that the best lies in the future.[38]

Master Symbols

A culture may have strong political, religious, or other belief systems. As a result, there often will emerge a highly abstract master symbol that is agreed upon and respected by groups. If the social structure of a culture is tightly organized around such master symbols, such as the greeting "Allah is great" or the belief that "Christ is my savior," it will be difficult, and sometimes impossible, to share perceptions cross-culturally.[39] Master symbols represent core cultural values, a violation of which may be an absolute barrier to communication.

Power

When there is a significant discrepancy in power or status between groups, intergroup posturing tendencies are particularly acute and can present obstacles to intercultural communication.[40]

Cross-perceptions between the strong and successful and the weak and the poor differ. The strong attribute success or failure to individual traits and underestimate external factors. They tend to exaggerate their generosity and criticize lack of gratitude by recipients. The weak and poor attribute lack of success to the "system" rather than themselves. They see the successful as demanding and selfish. The disadvantaged seek recognition and respect, which the strong seldom give because they rarely understand the need.[41] One can see this phenomenon at work in interpersonal communication within cultures, as well as in communication between cultures.

Europeans tend to be ambivalent about the United States. On one hand they respect U.S. wealth and military strength, and on the other they fear U.S. motives and interference in domestic affairs. They have envied U.S. preeminence, which has caused them to exaggerate the nation's deficiencies. The United States is seen occasionally as a savior but more often as a necessary evil.[42] After World War II, Europeans, like the ancient Greeks, believed they could compensate for loss of political clout with their history of artistic and literary supremacy, in the role of guardians of "High Culture."[43]

Role

The role that society prescribes for persons can vary greatly by culture.[44] Cultures that have a high-context communication style will read a great deal of meaning into how a person adheres to, or deviates from, their culturally imposed role, and a culture often imposes severe sanctions for any deviation from a person's prescribed role. Cultures commonly impose roles by gender or social class.

GENDER.   Cultures regard some behaviors as masculine or feminine, and behavior associated with one sex is usually considered inappropriate for the other.[45] Society allocates patterning of gendered temperaments. Anglo-Saxon social convention, for example, discourages men from bringing aesthetic or nurturing feelings to consciousness, just as it took away men's tears in the nineteenth century. Social systems even control what should be thought and felt. This structures the psyches of both sexes to reproduce the society's desired ideal types.[46]

In fact, the rules for acceptable emotional display for the Arab male and female are the reverse of the rules for the North American male and female. The North American male is culturally trained to be stoic and undemonstrative. The culturally inculcated "stiff upper lip" of the male of Anglo-Saxon heritage appears cold and unfeeling in the Middle East, where the open weeping and uninhibited display of emotion of an adult male confirms a culturally approved sensitivity. A male exhibiting such open emotional display loses face in a North American environment. In the United States, emotional displays are considered more acceptable for females, whereas the Middle Eastern female is trained to be more undemonstrative than males of the same culture.[47] But cultures are relative. The span of accepted emotional display is toward the more controlled end of the spectrum in Asian societies. North American males and females both seem uncontrolled and embarrassingly demonstrative to many Asians.

Cultural differences in prescribed gender behavior can cause contempt or confusion in interacting. When an Arab holds the hand of another man to walk down the street, or when Latin men walk arm in arm, this behavior can be confusing to North Americans and Northern Europeans, to whom these signs of friendship carry homosexual overtones. Further, cultures also dictate how males and females interact with each other.

A domestic employee told a Dutch woman living in Pakistan that, because she was a woman, she had no authority either to direct her employee's housework or to fire him, and that only her husband had authority. A 1997 article in a travel magazine for Mexicans regarding their Huasteca region states that Mexican society does not view the independence of women kindly: they have always played a role that is economically dependent on men, although this is "changing."[48]

Annie Nimos moved from Brazil to the United States. She felt that something was not quite right when she walked in public places. After a month or two, she realized that she felt invisible. No one looked at her. Then she realized that she felt that no men looked at her. In Brazil, a man would stop on the street and watch a woman walk by, visually following her for a full 180 degrees. His eyes would take her in from head to toe. The woman would not acknowledge the presence of the man, although she was quite aware of it. In the United States, such an overt demonstration of interest would be considered threatening or inappropriate. The cues for expression of appreciation between the sexes were different in the two countries, and after Annie became accustomed to the different roles and cues she no longer felt like she had "disappeared."

SOCIAL CLASS. We all identify with a social class, consciously or unconsciously, and we sort others and ourselves into social classes when we interact. We use criteria such as income, occupation, education, beliefs, and attitudes. We also sort people into classes by grammar, accent, houses, cars, dress, and other factors. Our perception of another's social class affects how we communicate with them. Whatever system we use to sort people by class in our own culture, it can be more difficult to sort people from other cultures. The attributes present or lacking that we consciously or unconsciously use to assign people to a social "class" in our own culture may not apply to another culture. This may cause us to misinterpret a foreign person's station in life.[49] We consequently may not appreciate "who" they are in their own society or communicate with them in a manner that they find acceptable.

Social class can assign roles in a culture. Some societies have a very visible servant class, while others have none. Perhaps the best-known system is the Hindu caste system in India, with priestly Brahmins as leaders and the untouchables placed at the bottom of the hierarchy and consequently assigned the most distasteful tasks in society. Class may be determined by genealogical descent, as among European royalty. A British lord, even though not necessarily wealthy, plays a different community role than a gardener. In many cultures that were colonized by Europeans, lighter skin is associated with a higher social class, and darker skin with a lower class. The higher classes enjoy more privileged roles, and the lower classes are assigned manual labor. One Mexican family that could afford to educate only one son (the daughters were not considered because of their gender role) chose the son who was lightest in complexion, on the premise that he would more easily move into a privileged role in society than his darker-skinned siblings.

Rules

Customs, manners, courtesy, etiquette, and rituals are all rules of culture. Cultural rules are based on ideas and can govern bribery, nepotism, gifts, buying and selling, eating and drinking, the usage of time, the seating of guests, and social relationships.[50] Rules govern formality and ritual, and what types of interaction take place when and where.[51] There is not much leeway to custom (i.e., rules), such as "white tie with tails,"[52] or who should go through a door first.

In France, "door" protocol is prescribed and is a test of one's *savoir faire.* The French themselves describe this ritual as "la bataille de la porte" (the battle of the door). A door approached in tandem or in group requires evaluation of others' rank, your rank, and sex, to know in what order persons should go through and how much resistance to put up before preceding another person.[53]

North American guest professors in Europe have to learn a new etiquette. One does not simply drop into a colleague's office to chat. Rather one makes an appointment, sometimes weeks in advance, to meet and to talk—a formality that the spontaneous and gregarious North American finds difficult to understand. The French intellectual Jean Baudrillard noted that Europeans who live in crowded cities and cramped flats must pay more attention to manners and social niceties than do North Americans,[54] who have in their society's recent historical experience enjoyed much greater amounts of space than Europeans.

It is essential to know the manners (rules) of a target culture for successful intercultural communication.[55]

Social Organization: Government and Family

The institutions of a culture can be formal or informal and affect how the culture organizes itself.[56] The organization of the government and the family in any given culture is an important factor that affects intercultural communication. People may rely and therefore focus on a formalized government system to fill many of their material needs, as in Denmark, where abstract government laws and edicts carry great weight. In contrast, people may be able to rely only on an informal extended-family system of support, as in Mexico, where family relationships are of paramount importance and government rulings take second place.

Thought Patterns

Different cultures arrive at their concepts of reality in different ways. Their perception of reality may come through faith or belief, independent of fact. It may come from fact based on evidence, which is the most predictable concept of reality. Or a culture may perceive reality primarily through feelings or instinct, which is the most common basis for reality perception in the world.[57]

North Americans usually reason inductively, going from facts to theory, whereas Japanese and French logic is primarily deductive, from theory to facts.[58] From a given theory the French will proceed to its illustration in the "real world" with facts. In contrast, "facts" make up the real world for the British and North Americans: get the facts and then we'll talk. The French work from the abstract to the concrete, and North Americans and the British from the concrete to the abstract, which makes for different persuasive and presentation styles.[59] The result is that European writers state that North Americans distrust ideas as opposed to facts, and one proclaimed that North Americans "never" speak in abstract terms.[60]

Persons in different cultures also learn to learn differently: they may learn by rote, by demonstration, by guiding, by doing, and so on.[61] To process new information, people seek analogues for it within their own experience, and if they do not have any they are liable to distort or reject the new information. But an analogue may also cause misunderstanding: "Ruling circles" does not mean the same thing to a person of mainland China experience as it does to an Australian or North American.[62]

Different cognitive styles result in different perceptions of reality:

- Open-Minded versus Closed-Minded Approaches: Open- versus closed-minded approaches govern whether one seeks additional information.[63]
- Associative versus Abstract Thinkers: Associative thinkers filter data through a screen of experience; abstractive thinkers can more easily imagine something new. Rote education tends to produce associative thinkers; problem-solving education produces abstract, "scientific" thinkers.[64]
- Particularistic versus Universalistic Thinkers: Particularistic thinkers value personal relationships more than rules; universalistic thinkers value abstract rules and laws.[65]

Values

Values are the learned (through acculturation) organization of rules for making choices and resolving conflicts,[66] and differences in values can be an obstacle to intercultural communication.[67] To respect another culture's values can deny our own values as a basis for judgment. There is much debate over relative and absolute values.[68] Values regarding money, work, and success are often based in religion.[69] Religious values are manifested not only in dogma, but also in living patterns and outlook. Material welfare also affects intercultural communication.[70]

Different cultures' perceptions of well-being may be as opposite as contentment in being alive with minimal necessities and wanting to "die with the most toys."[71] Some cultures stress economic success, and others place more emphasis on intellectual pursuits, while still others focus on the spiritual dimension of living. Richard Pells writes that both European and North American exchange professors agree that greater value is placed on strong basic knowledge of science, literature, and philosophy in European universities than in their U.S. counterparts. It often seems to be in vogue to criticize the United States as being overly materialistic. Even so, many European writers concede that in spite of the faults they find with the United States, it is indisputably a place where ordinary people live well.[72]

In France, who you are is more important than what you have achieved, and what a person does is therefore none of your business. In contrast, in the United States and Australia, for example, what you have achieved—that is, demonstrated—is important.[73]

The most difficult thing for North Americans to understand in French culture may be the different ways in which the French affirm personal bonds or adherence to a group. Social debts situate a person in a network in France; financial debts do not—money is not part of the relational system. It is said that the French will discuss everything about sex and nothing about money. A North American who borrows a car will usually return it with more gas than when he borrowed it and will feel responsible for repairing any damage, because in North American culture consideration for a person's car symbolizes consideration for the person. But in France, if a car is very important, then it is the owner's responsibility not to lend it. "Things happen" and it is incumbent on the owner to safeguard and not to lend something valuable.[74]

A North American woman who lived for years in Iran recounted that on hot summer nights people put out chairs and mats on the rooftops of their homes to sit and to sleep. Every morning people would take everything back inside, because otherwise neighbors would fish for items with poles and take them. It was accepted that people should not "abandon" property in plain sight, thereby tempting their neighbors. It was the owner's responsibility to protect a valued possession by properly putting it away.

Worldview

This may well be the most important cultural perception and the most difficult to describe. It is a culture's orientation toward God, nature, life, death, the universe—the meaning of life and "being." [75] A person's view of the world synthesizes many of the categories of perception discussed. It has to do with such concepts as whether one sees oneself as master of one's fate or views the human condition as a product of destiny, whether a person should act individually or collectively as part of a group, whether people are basically equal or have a predestined rank in life, and what daily activities are most valued and praised by people in a culture.

PERSONAL PERCEPTION FILTERS WITHIN CULTURE

Uncertainty

A primary factor affecting intercultural communication is uncertainty.

We all have a strong need to understand both the self and the Other in interpersonal interactions—most people prefer to interact in predictable social environments. Interacting with a person from a foreign culture in the process of intercultural communication is often an unfamiliar experience. From the time we are born, there is pressure in our own culture for us to behave in a predictable manner to facilitate the functions of society, and there are penalties for noncompliance. [76] Because we are conditioned to conform, and because we expect others to conform to the norms of our own culture, a person's deviation from the rules with which we have been trained to comply makes us uncomfortable and uncertain. We cannot effectively use our subconscious programming in an unfamiliar behavioral environment, and therefore cross-cultural communication is more tiring and stressful than communication in our own culture. A high degree of unfamiliarity and uncertainty produces high anxiety or stress on the part of the communicators, and anxiety exacerbates the problems [77] presented by other intercultural communication obstacles.

The unfamiliar almost universally causes discomfort in people. As a result, most communicators involved in initial encounters first try to process information to assess the similarity between them. [78] In this uncertainty-reduction process, there are two important goals: prediction of the other's actions and causal explanations of observed behavior. [79] Reaching these goals is often difficult with people of "Other" cultures.

To be viable members of their social groupings, fish, birds, mammals, and humans must engage in significant symbolization; that is, all must learn to recognize, receive, and send ordered messages. In other words, the individual must learn to behave in prescribed ways that permit the other group members to recognize and *anticipate* the individual's behavior[80] in order to permit uncertainty reduction. Persons in high-context cultures may tend to reduce uncertainty about a target person more through in-group relationships than through frequency of communication.[81]

The need for uncertainty reduction is a significant element in intercultural communication.

Attitude

Attitudes are psychological states that influence overt behavior and distort perception; they cause interpretation of events in predisposed ways (as discussed in Preconceptions, above).[82]

A young man from France, when working in a small Kansas town, ordered lunch from a menu of few choices. His English was good, but he had a French accent. When the waitress heard the unfamiliar accent, she assumed that she would not understand him, and she stopped listening to what he was saying. A co-worker had to repeat in unaccented English the man's intelligible order of "a hamburger and fries."

Many people around the world react in this same manner to a foreign accent. The effort required to reduce uncertainty in intercultural interaction may be so great that it contributes to lack of motivation.[83] A necessary ingredient to overcoming intercultural communication barriers is honest desire.[84]

When a person exposed to a new culture is open-minded (see Adaptability, below) and disposed to be friendly and curious, remarkable changes in thinking can occur.[85] Attitude is an important factor in intercultural communication, because one person's perception of attitudinal similarity in another is a stronger correlate of attraction than that of cultural similarity.[86] How often have you heard the approving comment, "we speak the same language?" This statement by a North American usually does not refer to communication with a "foreigner," nor does it refer to verbal language. It rather indicates the attractiveness and ease of communication with a person when there is attitudinal similarity.

Ethnocentrism

When perceptions learned through acculturation are narrow and cause rigid behavior, they are ethnocentric.[87] Hall well describes this obstacle to intercultural communication. He gives the example that North Americans view the differences in other cultures as a result of their being "underdeveloped" North Americans.[88]

We are all inclined to evaluate a foreign culture on the basis of what we are used to at home and to conclude that our own country is infinitely better. Pells reports that a British Commonwealth Fund Fellow readily admitted that on making his first trip to the United States he did not question the validity of his subconscious acceptance of Britain as his model for comparison. In consequence, the visitor recognized that he "found much to criticize." In turn, numerous North Americans who traveled to Europe after World War II found it hard to adapt because their only frame of reference was life in the United States. They were not prepared to measure a civilization by the paintings on the walls or by the selection of custom-bound books on the shelves. They frequently judged European homes by the kitchens and bathrooms, which they considered outdated.[89]

Pells also writes that U.S. foreign policy sometimes seems hazardous to other people's health. The United States with hubris presents itself to the world as an omniscient practitioner of democracy, with the attitude that all nations should emulate its ideals. The real challenge for all of us in intercultural communication is to accept the idea that another culture can be *different without being defective*. To communicate well, we need to understand a culture's unique values, customs, and characteristics, rather than treat them as aberrant behavior.[90]

The quality of nonethnocentrism probably relates to the complex psychosocial development of a tolerant and strong personality. Such persons can think multidimensionally, are comfortable with uncertainty, and have high self-esteem. Ethnocentrism and empathy are opposites.[91]

Similarity assumptions also result from ethnocentrism. Unless there is overt reporting of assumptions, there is no chance of correcting misinterpretations.[92] North Americans may expect France to be peopled very much by persons like themselves (more difference might be expected in Tibet, for example) and underestimate the effect of an unfamiliar cultural environment. For example, one does not go around automatically smiling at people and returning smiles in France to foster goodwill. To smile at someone you do not know when introduced can be seen as a type of hypocrisy. In France, one reserves smiles for certain situations and reasons, and there are different kinds of smiles: a smile can be flattering, convivial, possessive, cynical, courteous, condescending—and much more.[93]

If cultural misunderstanding arises from the fact that surface resemblances in behavior can conceal profound differences in meaning, the inverse is also true. Surface differences may in fact represent similar meaning. If a French person breaks something in the home of friends, he may appear to brush it off, knowing he can rely on the bonds of friendship. In contrast, to North Americans respecting a friend's possessions symbolizes the esteem in which one holds the friend. Quite different surface behavior may confirm a friendship.[94]

You can never assume that addressing a multicultural or foreign audience is the same as speaking to a group of your own culture. North American speakers typically open with a joke, but this is not customary in Mexico or Canada, for example. And some anecdotes—for example, those that involve drinking—may offend persons of other cultures.[95]

Adaptability

Adaptability is our capability to alter the structure and attributes of our psychic system to meet the demands of the environment, and to suspend or modify our cultural ways to creatively manage the dynamics of cultural difference. This ability can reorganize the self from closed to open, from rigid to flexible, from intolerant to resilient, and from habitual to creative. A lack of adaptability impedes successful intercultural communication.

> Self-altering, creative adaptation capacity is the metacompetence for intercultural communication.[96]

Perception filters behavior and interaction—which are essential components of communication. As a useful artifice, perception has been broken down into the framework of units described above. But language is also an important ingredient in communication and is certainly responsible for many obstacles in communication between people of different cultures. Therefore, even though the vast subject of the verbal process of language in communication is not our main focus, the next chapter will present a few observations on the subject.

FOUR

Obstacles in Verbal Processes

Language perfectly represents cultural convention.

For simplicity, discussions of verbal processes in intercultural communication in this chapter will refer to verbal language as just "language."

Studying a language is an ideal example of the emic, internal approach to intercultural communication. Language perfectly represents cultural idiosyncrasies. There is no reason why, other than cultural convention, in English we should say "dog" to represent the mammal we know that this word represents, and that in Portuguese we should be required to articulate the sounds for the word *cão* to mean the same animal. And there is nothing in the sounds or in the appearance of the letters that we write to form each of these two words that somehow sounds or looks like a dog. The linguistic convention for how to verbally symbolize a dog is purely arbitrary and culture specific. The Portuguese word *ano* (year) and the Spanish word *ano* (anus) sound quite similar. To mistakenly substitute the Portuguese homonym for the word year in Spanish would be infelicitous. In many ways, culture itself is similarly arbitrary.

Language should be considered a mirror of its culture. It reflects the culture's content and nature.[1] Not only, however, is language a product of culture, but culture is a product of language, as well.[2] In fact, the Sapir-Whorf hypothesis essentially states that language is a guide to social reality and builds up the real world by the language habits of a group. No two languages are sufficiently alike to permit consideration that they represent the same social reality.[3] Consequently, one must learn the culture to learn its verbal language well.[4]

LINGUISTIC REALITY

Languages differ in what they allow one to say and in what they require one to say.[5] In the Navajo language, grammar requires that one define whether something is animate or inanimate, presumably according to what one has been taught to believe—or which one believes because one is so taught by language convention. According animate status to objects when using words to designate them forces the speaker into a certain perception of reality.[6] A similar, but more familiar, grammar requirement for an English speaker learning a foreign language would be the need to identify the gender of nouns as masculine or feminine, which is required in many languages, such as Spanish, French, or Italian.

Irish Gaelic does not possess equivalents of "yes" or "no," which seems unhandy to persons accustomed to this conciseness. Consequently, when speaking Irish Gaelic, people must construct circumlocutions such as "I think not" and "this is so" in place of these two words.[7]

Thomas Morning Owl, who teaches Amerindian languages of the North American Columbia Plateau to young people, explains that the identity of Sahaptin speakers is collective and comes from their lineage, rather than a person having an individual identity. If asked who they are, rather than give their name to identify themselves, Sahaptin speakers recite their ancestral lineage. "You are nobody without your lineage." To greet a relative in the Sahaptin language one says "papanaymusha" which acknowledges the family link. A person would be thought coldhearted without this acknowledgment. Morning Owl fears that young Amerindians are losing the key concepts of their culture with the loss of their languages. "When the language dies, we as Indian people die."[8]

Every culture has areas in which it needs to be particularly expressive. Trobriand Islanders in New Guinea have a hundred words for yams, which are an important food source, and the Maoris of New Zealand have thirty-five words for dung—although it is not clear what need this fills. Meanwhile, Arabs are a little unbelievably said to have six thousand words for camels and camel accoutrements, and Tasmanian aborigines have a word for every specific type of tree but no word that means just tree. Poignantly, the Araucanian Indians of Chile have a variety of words for describing different degrees of hunger.[9]

Tahitians have many names for one species of fish that they catch in the lagoons. Each noun denotes the size and the stage of maturity of the species—thereby causing and requiring a close and discerning focus both in speaking and in observation. Tahitians also use a whole glossary of words for the coconut, giving it a series of noun designators related to the size, maturity, and use of each coconut. Further, there is a whole lexicon of terms that apply to the coconut tree. The fish, the coconut, and the coconut tree play significant roles in the everyday life of the people. The litany of nouns that has evolved for the coconut, for example, seems to give "each" coconut an identity at a particular stage that is discrete, as opposed to the less precise use of an adjectival modifier such as a "small" or "young" generic coconut. How small? How young? Each developmental stage of the fish species and of the coconut acquires its own identity and reality through the use of a separate and distinct noun to designate it.

Mimosa was a Chinese woman born of immigrant parents in Tahiti and acculturated to the island. She made the decision to leave her French husband to marry another man. She tried to explain to her father that she did not love her husband but said that it was not possible for her to communicate with her father in his Chinese dialect on this subject. She volunteered that the problem stemmed from the fact that there was no word that she could use for "love" that was an equivalent to "love" in her Western language, which was French. She reported that the only words in the Chinese dialect that might apply to her circumstances were words that translate as esteem, honor, respect, duty, and similar concepts. If she told her father that she did not have any of these feelings or attitudes toward her husband, her argument only condemned her actions and reinforced her father's negative opinion. Any question of morality aside, the daughter and father could not discuss the subject. Because of language peculiarities, any explanation the daughter could give equated to her saying "I am a bad person," which precisely reflected her father's attitude.

The Sioux of North America have no words for "late" or "waiting," which reflects and affects the treatment of time in a culture. Truk Islanders have no past tense in their language and treat the past as if it were the present[10]—events thereby become indefinite in duration, and old conflicts remain immediate, as if they had just happened.[11]

Language affects our thought processes and how we perceive reality.

VERBAL COMMUNICATION

Speech behavior is one aspect of interactional communicative social behavior.[12] Language is not only a technical communication code, but nonverbal codes and other features of thought and behavior patterns stem from the structure and modes of a particular language.[13] In fact, some communication specialists classify both verbal language and patterns of thought as "verbal processes."[14] One of the most important design features of verbal language is its capacity to say or convey things that have never been said or conveyed before but will still be understood by another speaker of the same language.[15]

Language communicates in a context. Low-context cultures focus on explicit verbal codes. High-context cultures do not rely in the same way on verbal communication. They communicate relatively more by the context of nonverbal behavior, and the verbal content of their communication often is not meant to contain specific information but rather to be ritual behavior.[16] In many languages people will say, "How are you?" in greeting someone. For the person responding to describe exactly how they are doing or feeling is a surprising reply and not often welcome. The ritual response for North Americans, as for most Western cultures, is some form of "Fine, thank you," except in special circumstances.

The subject of language itself is vast and complex, so in our focus on the role that culture plays in communication, we shall address language only briefly. Viewed as an obstacle in intercultural communication, the problem of not knowing the language (the code) is self-evident. Regarding language, the principal areas in which obstacles arise in the verbal process of communication are as follows:

Verbal Processes of Communication
Competency
    Accent
    Cadence
    Connotation
    Context
    Idiom
    Polite Usage
    Silence
    Style
Literacy/Orality

Competency

A person may have different competencies in writing and in speaking a language.

Language competency is positively correlated to "attractiveness" in intercultural communication.[17] People tend to avoid communicating with persons whom they know or anticipate will not have adequate command of a language common to both parties to permit ease of communication. It is uncomfortable and embarrassing not to understand what a person is saying or not to have them understand you. The majority of people in a host country, for example, prefer to communicate with a foreign person who speaks the host country's language well.

A language barrier makes intercultural interaction more difficult than the intracultural interaction that takes place between persons who speak the same language.[18] In many countries it is essential to form close relationships in order to do business. It is difficult to do so without some knowledge of the country's language.

Many elements affect language competency.

ACCENT. The more closely a non-native speaker emulates the native accent and pronunciation of the target language, the better the non-native speaker will be able to communicate in that language. "Accent" can range from perfectly native pronunciation (no discernable foreign accent) to pronunciation of the foreign language using the same sounds that the non-native speaker learned in order to speak his or her own mother tongue (a very heavy foreign accent). The foreign speaker will be more or less intelligible to native speakers of the target language depending on where on the spectrum of native to foreign his or her pronunciation falls. In addition, native speakers will vary in their ability to interpret foreign sounds the non-native speaker uses to represent words in the target language.

CADENCE. Every language has its own cadence or rhythm, the emulation of which is necessary to achieve a native "accent" and which contributes to the understanding of the non-native speaker by the native speaker. Tonic accent affects cadence. English has a heavy tonic accent, such as the stress placed on the antepenultimate syllable of the word *CAN-a-da*. French does not have a tonic accent, and each syllable of a word is stressed equally. The pronunciation of *Ca-na-da* in French, with each syllable given equal stress, sounds to the ear of an English speaker as if the last syllable is being stressed (*ca-na-DA*) when, in fact, it is not. Cadence can also be considered to be a part of the vocalics, or nonverbal attributes, of a language.

CONNOTATION.   Connotative meaning of a symbol arises out of one's experience in the context of culture. Connotative and multiple meanings of a word are difficult to learn.[19] A French person who does not speak English well may not realize that using the word "dame" to refer to a woman has a negative connotation in North American English, whereas the cognate *dame* in French is very respectful. The words "lie," "fib," "equivocate," and "prevaricate" may be used synonymously, but each word carries a different shade of meaning. To say in English that a person lied is certainly more pejorative than to say that a person fibbed.

CONTEXT.   Nonverbal behavioral context affects, amplifies, explains, and supplements verbal language behavior, in addition to communicating on its own. Much has been said about communication by context in preceding chapters, and context will be further addressed in the following chapter on nonverbal communication processes.

IDIOM.   Idioms, jargon, figurative expressions, exaggeration/understatement cause misunderstanding.[20] Consider the North American expression "a can of worms," which is used to mean undesirable complexity or confusion. What mental picture must a foreign speaker of English attribute to this phrase? When communicating in any language with a non-native speaker, the avoidance of idioms, slang, and a large number of metaphors will greatly increase comprehension.

POLITE USAGE.   The actual language forms required in a target language may have no analogues in one's own and may therefore be difficult to learn or to use correctly.[21] In French and in Spanish, there are many circumstances when the use of the familiar *tu* form of address can be an insult or sexual invitation.

Not only can pronouns be formal and informal, there is also the matter of inflection. Mercifully, English pronouns are largely uninflected. For an English speaker to say "you" in German, she or he must choose between seven words: *du, dich, dir, Sie, Ihnen, ihr,* and *euch.* Such an unaccustomed panoply of choice may be good cause for communication anxiety.[22]

Polite usage closely relates to two perceptual categories of communication behavior: Hierarchy and Rules.

SILENCE. Silence is viewed by Asians as an important form of speech and rhetoric, and is used differently by different cultures.[23] The Japanese use an element of "speech" called *ma*, which is actually a silence gap and is an essential part of the Japanese language. North Americans are typically uncomfortable with such silences in conversation and often hasten to fill the gap. Silence can also be classified as nonverbal behavior.

STYLE. Different styles of expression are cultivated and appreciated in different languages—and therefore in different cultures. Ornate style, using an abundance of words chosen for their pleasant sound, connotation, and meaning, is prized in some languages. In other languages, economy of expression is sought. In U.S. universities, for example, professors in most disciplines encourage parsimony in verbal expression. They stress that one should use the fewest words possible to state an idea clearly, in accordance with the principle of Ockham's razor.

Literacy/Orality

Writing a language stabilizes it and develops a special kind of dialect. Most languages have never been committed to writing, but some languages (more correctly called dialects) have invested centuries in writing. In England or Germany or Italy where there are clusters of dialects, for example, one dialect has been developed in writing above all others and has become the national language. Such an established written language can be called a grapholect. The English grapholect has been refined for centuries by writers, theorists, grammarians, and lexicographers. In Germany, the text-based grapholect, or national language, is referred to as "high" German. Grapholects have massive vocabularies. The editors of *Webster's Third New International Dictionary* (1971) of the English language chose to include 450,000 words from some million and a half words of record. Oral languages can function with approximately five thousand words or less.[24]

Walter Ong states that writing develops codes in a language that are different from oral codes in the same language.[25] There are oral-based language codes and elaborated text-based language codes.[26] The oral-based code operates contextually in the daily lives of human beings, whereas writing concentrates meaning in language itself.[27] The oral-based code can be as expressive and precise as the elaborated text-based code in contexts that are familiar and shared by the speaker and hearer. But to deal with the unfamiliar expressively and precisely, an elaborated text-based code is imperative.[28]

Communication between a culture that primarily uses text-based language and a culture where language is oral-based has to successfully span a wider culture gap than would exist between two cultures that both tend to rely primarily either on text-based or oral-based language.

Many think that "good" grammar is used only by the literate and educated. However, all language has rules of grammar rules, which are indispensable to meaning; the rules may just be different from those of the standard, written, national "grapholect." However, it is imperative to note that, although oral or nonstandard dialects may be rule-based, in a profound sense no dialect in English, German, or Italian, for example, has the resources for communication of the standard grapholect. The grapholect has resources of a totally different order of magnitude.[29]

Ong also argues that only literate cultures have the key to symbolic, abstract thinking. Written language fixes thought and uses subordination and analysis. This kind of logic may escape a person from an oral language tradition. Sound is evanescent, and oral language strings thoughts together like beads on a string.[30]

Cultures can also promote or inhibit oral expression, and oral communication practices differ.[31] In some cultures, even an oral explanation is inadequate without visual or hands-on experience.[32]

In addition to the process of verbal communication through language, communication also takes place through the process of nonverbal social behavior. Behavior is dictated by culture, and differences in culture can therefore create significant barriers. We need to take a close look at the potential obstacles to intercultural communication created by nonverbal communication processes.

FIVE

Obstacles in Nonverbal Processes

We must learn to speak a foreign culture in the same way that we must learn to speak a foreign language.[1]

A woman in Brazil planned a long-awaited visit to her sister who lived in Colombia. In preparation for the trip, she purchased gifts for everyone in her sister's family. She could not decide what to take to her brother-in-law, David, but chanced to find the perfect gift. It was a life-size Brazilian *figa*, elegantly carved in lustrous mahogany, and it would look very nice on a coffee table or a desk. The *figa* is a hand gesture signifying "good luck" in Brazil. One makes a vertical fist, placing the thumb up between the index and middle fingers. It is like crossing one's fingers for luck in the United States. To display such a carving can make two statements. One is a statement of a person's appreciation of finely crafted objects, and the other is the symbolization of luck. On opening his gift, David broke out laughing. He rubbed his hands over the finely grained wood. Grinning, he pronounced, "This is most unusual. I will take it to my office and keep it on my desk. Thank you very much."

THE LANGUAGE OF BEHAVIOR

Literate persons who were concerned with the production of words and their proper usage proposed the early concepts of communication. They saw good communication as an unadulterated message entering the ear of the receiver and going through a clean pipe into an uncontaminated brain. Since these persons were devoted to the perfection of literacy, they unconsciously perceived spoken language to be an imperfect derivation of its written form. Written language is, however, a special shorthand derived from and representing the action of spoken language, and investigation further shows that communication is a system that makes use of all the channels of sensory modalities, not just vocalized words. We can no more understand communication by the exhaustive study of verbal language than we can understand physiology by an exhaustive study of just the circulatory system of the body.[2] We must therefore look beyond the verbal process to the nonverbal process that takes place between communicators, and we must be aware that a person's perceptions as well as nonverbal behavior color the message.

Many different messages are communicated nonverbally, in many different ways, and to accurately communicate nonverbally across cultures is complex. As he had promised, David took his gift to his office the next day and displayed it on his desk. The word quickly passed that *Sr. Ingeniero* had a distinctive wood carving from Brazil. The Colombian engineers all made the rounds to visit, chuckle, and examine the *figa*. David was the only engineer in the building to personalize his office with a well-executed, life-size representation of Colombia's equivalent of the North American obscene "finger" gesture.

Nonverbal communication behaviors do more than supplement or assist verbal communication. Not only do nonverbal behaviors act equally with verbal behavior to accomplish numerous communication functions, they also operate independently to achieve key communication goals. Further, nonverbal behaviors rarely occur in isolation. They usually form part of a larger system of behavior, and often increases in one nonverbal behavior causes decreases in other behaviors in order to maintain a stable level of sensory involvement.[3] Words can be replaced by touch or by eye contact. If we then wish to increase sensory involvement, we may choose to combine close proximity to a person with touch and with eye contact. We might do this to signal intimacy or extreme sympathy, and we may use this communicative behavior in place of words.

There is some debate as to whether communication takes place when nonverbal behavior does not *intentionally* encode and send a message. The unintentional transmission and reception of information is sometimes called indicative behavior rather than communication.[4] However, it seems clear that we do communicate both intentionally and unintentionally. We can try to dissimulate dislike for a person and yet still communicate our negative attitude. At times, we unintentionally communicate our impatience or irritation or condescension or disinterest. And sometimes a person's nonverbal behavior unintentionally communicates that the person's verbal message is a lie. Successful communication takes place when the communicators arrive at acceptable shared meaning of an intended message, or when an unintended message has been correctly interpreted. Miscommunication occurs when a receiver attributes erroneous meaning to a verbal or nonverbal message, whether the message was intended or unintended and whether or not the message was adequately or properly encoded and transmitted. Miscommunication has occurred when a person attributes a meaning of condescension, for example, to verbal or nonverbal communication and this attribution is erroneous.

Communication carries messages at least at two important levels. One level carries the content of the message, and another carries a metamessage about the relational aspect of the communicators.[5] Nonverbal communication often carries the information about the relation between the parties that are communicating, and verbal communication more often contains the content. More simply put, the content of the verbal question "What do you want?" is easy to understand. But this simple question can be asked in a variety of ways that contain more complex metamessages about how the parties do or will relate. Behavior such as tone and loudness of voice, facial expression, posture, and gestures can formulate the nonverbal part of the message. This same question can carry a nonverbal "relational" aspect that communicates concern, hostility, or impatience toward the receiver of the message. Culture will dictate the formality of wording of the question and the nonverbal behaviors that will accompany it. Therefore, in intercultural communication, understanding the meaning carried by even this simple question can be more complex than in intracultural communication.

Evidence suggests that there are some nonverbal signals that all members of the human species use and understand. But cultures formulate display rules that dictate when, how, and with what consequences these nonverbal expressions will be exhibited, and thus our ability to make pancultural generalizations as to their meaning is reduced. Even though people the world over may use the same expression for grief in private, their public display of grief by facial expression, tears, or crying may vary greatly because of cultural canons.[6]

Edward T. Hall states that "We communicate our real feelings in our silent language—the language of behavior."[7] Furthermore, he maintains that we are not fully aware of all that we communicate. The attributions that we make about nonverbal communication in other cultures are often wrong, and there is no available dictionary or code of intercultural nonverbal behavior.[8] In any case, if we are unaware of what attributions we have made, we do not question them. In addition, we should understand that people can intentionally manipulate nonverbal behavior,[9] just as they can manipulate verbal messages.

TO SPEAK OR NOT TO SPEAK

It is interesting to compare "conversation" patterns of people in France and the United States. Waiting in a long supermarket line to pay, the French will quickly show signs of impatience by rolling their eyes toward the ceiling, looking exhausted, stiffening, or by exchanging glances of complicity, but they usually do not speak to strangers in the line—all is expressed through nonverbal body communication. In the United States, custom is quite different. People often strike up general conversation to help each other pass the time, and they may casually show photos or exchange recipes. In contrast, a French woman introduced herself to a French couple in a North American supermarket when she heard them conversing in French and afterward apologized for coming up and actually speaking to the couple like that. She explained that she had become "very American."[10] The two cultures prescribe different modes of communication, encouraging and discouraging verbal exchanges in different circumstances.

SPEAKING CULTURE

Isaura is an international attorney who practices in the United States and has a Guatemalan father, a Mexican mother, and a North American husband. On a trip to Guatemala to visit family, she was at a party and rose to dance with her brother to some traditional music that always set her feet to moving before she even stood up. Antonio and Isaura made a handsome pair. Isaura executed the intricate footwork to the lively tune, head up, shoulders back, widely flipping her skirt with her hands, turning her body and flashing her eyes to accentuate the measures. Antonio quietly told her, "Isaura, estás bailando muy a la mexicana. Aquí no se baila el son así." (Isaura, you are dancing too much in the Mexican style. Here people don't dance the *son* like that.) Isaura then instinctively adjusted. For some reason, she had not made her usual culture switch. She bowed her head slightly and cast her eyes down, put her shoulders forward, held her skirt with her hands close to her hips, and closely reined in the range of her movements. Her whole demeanor changed as she projected the humility customary in traditional Guatemalan folk dances.

Much of human beings' communicative behavior evolved independently of their physiology, through adaptation to their culture. We must learn to speak a foreign culture in the same way we must learn to speak a foreign language.[11] Although the nonverbal communication of another culture is far more difficult to learn than verbal communication,[12] training in nonverbal communication for a target culture is nonetheless very helpful.[13]

When attempting to communicate with a target culture, the following basic categories of nonverbal communication can be used to anticipate or explain commonly occurring areas of difficulty:[14]

Nonverbal Processes of Communication
- Context
- Chronemics (Time Sense)
    Monochronic
    Polychronic
- Kinesics (Body Motion Communication)
    Emblems (Gestures)
    Eye Contact
    Facial Expressions
    Haptics (Touch)
    Posture
    Smell
- Proxemics (Space Sense)
    Fixed-Feature Space
    Semifixed-Feature Space
    Informal Space
- Immediacy
- Physical Characteristics
    Artifacts (Extensions of Physical Self)
    Physical Appearance
- Vocalics (Speech Characteristics)
    Vocal Characterizers
    Vocal Qualifiers
    Vocal Rate
    Vocal Segregates

We need to consider some of the implications of each of these categories with regard to intercultural communication.

Context

Because of its importance to intercultural communication, we will begin our discussion of the nonverbal processes of communication with the category of Context. It is difficult to overemphasize the importance of how different cultures use context differently to communicate.

Many obstacles to communication arise between high- and low-context cultures. High-context cultures emphasize formalized and stylized interaction rituals, which are a type of nonverbal behavior. The context communicates in place of "unnecessary" verbal expressiveness[15] or in addition to verbal language. Asians' awareness of the limitation of language places great importance on rigid and elaborate etiquette and customs (i.e., context), while a Westerner is usually only unconsciously aware of such limitation.[16] In both high- and low-context cultures, nonverbal cues are used to interpret verbal expression; nonverbal expression seldom occurs in isolation from verbal and other nonverbal cues.[17]

In cultures that are high-context in communication style, personal relations are very important, and face-to-face communication is the preferred mode. Written and telephone communication, as compared to personal interaction, do not provide a context as rich in the contextual cues that are carriers of meaning for the high-context communicator.

Verbal communication in high-context cultures often is information non-specific in content, the words used representing cultural rituals[18] rather than information per se. In contrast, the verbal content of communication in low-context cultures carries very specific, literal information.

Contextual communication takes place not only through nonverbal behavior, it also relies on knowledge that has been internalized by the communicators. A North American, Robert, who was living and doing business in Costa Rica had to pay a visit to a government office. Because of past experience, this time he was forewarned of the difficulty of locating an "address" in the Costa Rican capital of San Juan, where only some sixteen streets in the center of the city had names. No other streets in the country had names, and, furthermore, there were no street numbers assigned anywhere. Forearming himself, he listened carefully to high-context directions to the Ministerio de Hacienda. The ministry was located "two hundred meters west of the Coca Cola." He already understood that every one hundred meters really meant a block, no matter what the length of the block, so he knew he should go two blocks west of the Coca Cola plant. Confidently, he drove to the location indicated. There was no ministry. He drove around all the blocks in the area and still found none. Frustrated, he got out of the car and asked a pedestrian how to find the office he was looking for. The man nodded and told him that the office was two hundred meters west of the Coca Cola. Robert responded that he had looked everywhere around the Coca Cola plant in the next block and the ministry simply was not to be found in the neighborhood.

"Oh," replied the Costa Rican. "Not the new Coca Cola. The old Coca Cola. The one that was torn down. Where the market was built. The *Ministerio* is west of the 'Coca Cola' market."

In fact, Robert found the office two blocks west of the "Coca Cola" Market, a location that was now a market and not a Coca Cola plant. Not only did one have to understand directions given by physical context to navigate in San Juan, one also needed to be able to rely on one's own internalization of historical context in order to interpret directions. In asking for the location of something in San Juan, one might well be told that it was three hundred meters (which could be three very long blocks) east of the *higuerón*, but the big tree commonly used as a locator to give directions in that neighborhood had been cut down seven years before. Long-time residents knew, of course, where the tree commonly used to give directions stood before it was cut down. Certainly directions in Costa Rica are very high-context and do not rely on such low-context symbols as street names and numbers.

It is, nonetheless, important to bear in mind that since some two-thirds to three-fourths of communication is nonverbal, nonverbal communication still plays an important role in the communication style of low-context cultures. What is significant in an intercultural communication situation is the comparatively different proportion of communication that takes place via context when a high-context culture interacts with a low-context culture. Misunderstanding can arise both through misinterpretation and through lack of awareness of the messages being sent through context.

In a sense, all of the categories that follow can be said to operate as context in the nonverbal processes of communication. Furthermore, many processes usually take place simultaneously and are affected by or rely on the perceptions the communicators have internalized from their culture.

Chronemics [19]

Time can be measured formally by seconds, hours, days, months, years, by different calendars—or informally by moons and weather seasons, or other systems. People seem to easily understand the differences in formal time between cultures. But time can also be structured informally by a culture, and informal time elements are loosely defined, not explicitly taught, and typically operate outside consciousness. People therefore comprehend this informal structuring of time across cultures with less accuracy than their understanding of a formal time system. In addition, chronemic cues can be intentional or unintentional, and are often ambiguous. To further complicate matters, time cues have an ability to evoke strong emotional reactions.

Punctuality and waiting time are important elements of informal time, but what constitutes acceptable punctuality or waiting time can vary by culture and by situation. Arriving five minutes late for a business appointment in the United States usually elicits a brief apology, whereas arriving thirty minutes late in another culture would not merit mention.

Different perceptions of acceptable punctuality and waiting time can cause people to take offense where none was intended. However, these elements can also be used to send intentional messages, even in a culture such as the United States that is considered to be very low-context in communication style. The story is told that shortly after Harry Truman became president, a newspaper editor called on him. After waiting forty-five minutes, the editor asked an aide to convey to the president his annoyance about the long wait. Truman is said to have replied that the same editor had kept him cooling his heels for an hour and a half when Truman was a junior senator, and that as far as he was concerned, the editor still had "forty-five minutes to go." [20] In this situation, chronemic cues evoked strong emotions in both parties. Since different cultures conceive of or perceive time quite differently, this difference in perception greatly affects cross-cultural communication.

As mentioned, the North American Sioux have no words for "late" or "waiting," and Truk Islanders have no past tense in their language, treating the past as if it were the present. [21] These cultures would certainly "use" time differently than, for example, the punctual Swiss, who sometimes complain about the lax manner in which West Germans and North Americans treat time. Annie Nimos once boarded a train in Switzerland three minutes early, only to discover that she had taken the wrong train as she headed north. The train she had intended to board to travel south left *exactly* at the time scheduled, three minutes later.

The difference in perception of time greatly affects cross-cultural communication and frequently generates misunderstanding, misinterpretation, and ill will.

MONOCHRONIC CONCEPT. The monochronic concept indicates a linear and sequential approach toward time that is rational, suppresses spontaneity, and tends to focus on one activity at a time. People are punctual, efficient, and "get to the point" quickly. It is more typical of the Western than the Eastern world, and in the West predominates in North America and Northern Europe.

In the United States, particularly when communicating in a business environment, one may actually be asked to "get to the point," whereas in many countries to start out with "the point" too quickly is consummately rude.

POLYCHRONIC CONCEPT. Cultures that have a polychronic, or multiple-activity, "matrix" concept of time only loosely measure time with the symbols of a formalized system. Business relationships are personalized, based on trust, and take "time" to establish. It is "time" to move on to the next activity when the current set of activities is over. This approach toward time considers activity more important than the abstract measure of time by a clock. A polychronic concept of time is typical of Latin and Mediterranean cultures and, to some degree, Eastern cultures. Persons in polychronic cultures typically carry on many activities at the same time.

When trying to communicate, northern Europeans and North Americans tend to find multiple, simultaneous activities and conversations chaotic and difficult to follow. They may be overwhelmed when trying to meet with someone in a Latin American office while people come in and out, the secretary asks a question, the errand runner brings back a part for the car, the phone rings, and several conversations are carried on at once, and they may find social situations with multiple cross conversations and people talking all at the same time uncomfortable and confusing. They commonly state that such situations "drive them crazy." Certainly, for communication purposes, individuals from predominantly monochronic cultures have different personal capacities to adapt to polychronicity. North American accountants and North American musicians probably conceive of time quite differently. Even so, either a monochronic or polychronic treatment of time usually dominates in a given culture.

Polychronic cultures have different patterns of turn-taking when speaking than do monochronic cultures. Interrupting another speaker is not uncommon in a polychronic culture, and in fact may be taken as indicative of one's interest or enthusiasm, but interruption causes offense in some cultures. While some interruptions are acceptable in southern Europe and Latin America, conversational overlap is considered ill-mannered in northern Europe, and in the United States. Interruptions frequently frustrate Scandinavian and German negotiators when they conduct meetings in Italy, Spain, or Greece. Swedish researchers, in recording Spanish-Swedish negotiations, found that the Spaniards interrupted the Swedes five times more often than the reverse.[22]

Trying to carry on a conversation with someone from a culture with a turn-taking rhythm that we have not learned is as awkward as trying to dance with someone when you just cannot get in step. Annie Nimos grew up in South America and is married to a North American of Germanic heritage. Carl often states that he hates to be interrupted when he is speaking, and Annie knows she tends to jump spontaneously into conversations and interrupt. The two have discussed the different "cultures" that rule their respective family gatherings and, consequently, the different pattern of conversational turn-taking. Fortunately, this is an acknowledged difference between them and has become a subject of mutual analysis rather than dissension.

For people in polychronic countries, it is important to take time to get to know someone before deciding to do business with them. Business and social calls both take time and often require multiple visits, where one visit would suffice to accomplish the same purpose in a monochronic culture. In the view of a number of French writers, the legendary instant friendliness of North Americans is superficial, because it is so unlike the time taken in more polychronic France to painstakingly explore another's personality to achieve intimacy.[23]

Kinesics: Body Motion Communication

Edward Sapir wrote that we respond to gestures in accordance with an elaborate and secret code that is written nowhere, known by none, and understood by all.[24] Even though people can often identify a certain type of communication behavior when they see it, they may not be able to describe the behavior when asked.[25]

Body motion language, like vocalic language, culture by culture is composed of distinctive elements that can be, by rules for coding, combined in a virtually infinite number of ordered combinations that rule the communicative aspects of human behavior. We can term verbal language digital and body motion language analogic.[26]

According to Hall, we have specialized the language of the body to be congruent with everything we do, therefore it must be understood in its cultural context.[27] Just as there are no universal words or sound complexes that carry the same meaning universally (the symbols of verbal language are totally arbitrary), so there are no body motions, facial expressions, or gestures that have identical meaning across cultures. With regard to body motion language, Ray L. Birdwhistell wrote, "Not only is kinesic activity systematically patterned, but this pattern varies significantly from culture to culture and even from subgroup to subgroup."[28] Even so, there is a prevalent belief by persons of any specific culture that they themselves practice a natural pattern of movement—communication through kinesics—that people of other cultures must have learned badly, not evolved to, or lost.[29]

Research by Birdwhistell indicates that the body motion languages of French, Germans, and North Americans vary to a degree comparable to the range of differences heard when these languages are spoken. There is, at least for Western European languages, a set of necessary and formal body motion behaviors that are directly tied to linguistic structure. Studies show that the Kutenai of British Columbia move differently when speaking Kutenai than when speaking English. Fiorello La Guardia of New York spoke Italian, Yiddish, and American English. In studying film clips, kinesicists or any observer familiar with the three cultures could immediately determine which language he was speaking—even with the sound of the film clips removed. An equally manifest shift in behavior was evident in a U.S. Amerindian who spoke Taos and English, and also in a Lebanese who was similarly transformed when switching from English to Arabic to Parisian French. There is a systematic relationship between audible and visible communicative behavior. They are coercive and interdependent language systems.[30]

Cultures tend to concentrate activity in certain body areas and permit the activity of others only under certain limited circumstances, which is interesting in the study of national character.[31] Even on fairly casual observation, distinctions in body motion communication are so evident that the children of one family that frequently traveled internationally invented a body language game when waiting for inevitably delayed flights in airports. The children would try to guess from a distance the nationality of people (all in Western dress) from their gestures and body language. Then one of the children would sidle over near the speakers to hear what language they were speaking or otherwise identify nationality to see if their guesses were correct.

Birdwhistell also refers to people's movement as having "tertiary" sexual characteristics. Working with seven different cultures (Chinese, middle- and upper-class London British, Kutenai, Shushwap, Hopi, Parisian French, and North American), he found that persons in each culture could distinguish typically male communication behavior from typically female communication behavior. Two types of movement that can easily be identified are posture (including the angle at which legs and arms are held), and facial expression. Tertiary sexual behavior can be described as a learned and patterned communicative motion system that acts in some cultures to identify both the gender of a person and the social expectancies of that gender. It is not necessarily sexually provocative or responsive.[32]

North Americans have characteristics that are distinctly different from Europeans in how they occupy space with their bodies. A characteristic North American position is to sit with arms spread out, and a male will place his feet and legs apart. The position includes a slump and leaning back and is a type of sprawl that occupies a lot of space. This is rarely seen in a European, who will sit erect with legs and feet close together and arms placed close to the body, in a tight position occupying much less space.

Kinesics can be classified as follows:

EMBLEMS (GESTURES).   A gesture assigned a specific meaning in a culture is called an emblem. Gestures that are foreign to us create non-understanding, and we know we do not understand. More problematic are homomorphic (same or similar in form, but different in meaning) gestures that not only generate misunderstanding but can be insulting and inflammatory.[33] We think we understood, but we misinterpreted.

The North American thumbs-up gesture of approbation has obscene "middle-finger" meaning in many Middle Eastern nations, in Australia, and in Nigeria. Imagine the amazement of many global TV watchers when the U.S. presidential nominee signified his pleasure by the thumbs-up sign at the 1992 Democratic Convention.[34] The Brazilian gesture for good-luck made by forming the fistlike *figa* is an obscene gesture in Colombia. These homomorphic gestures may appear the same in form, but they carry different meaning in different cultures.

Body motion language is nuanced and complex. Any "dictionary" of gestures can be deceptive if too literal, as though a gesture carries precise, denotative meaning. A hand salute in the U.S. Army can satisfy, please, or enrage. By a shift in stance, facial expression, the speed or duration of the salutation, and in selection of inappropriate contexts for the act, the salute can honor, ridicule, demean, or insult the recipient. Awareness of this variability on an established pattern stimulated one of the primary breakthroughs in the development of kinesics as a communication discipline.[35]

In general, some ·search indicates that men use gestures more frequently than women, and the uneducated use gestures more frequently than the educated.[36]

EYE CONTACT. Cultures have explicit rules regarding eye behavior such as staring, frequency of contact, and lowering the eyes (lowering the eyes possibly being a universal sign of submission). The same behavior can have different meaning in different cultures, giving rise to misinterpretation. For example, in some cultures direct eye contact signifies honesty and attentiveness, while in others it shows disrespect and boldness—it can even signal aggression.[37] In North American culture, one can almost hear a scolding adult admonish a child, "You look at me when I speak to you!" In the same circumstances in most Latin American cultures, for the child not to lower the gaze and eyes is to disrespectfully challenge authority.

In public places, the French and North Americans may not attribute the same meaning to a nonverbal exchange, yet they believe the meaning to be identical. This reinforces negative opinions of each other. In a safe neighborhood, if there is eye contact of one North American passing another on the street, he or she will often nod, smile, and say hello. Having gone out walking, a respectable gray-haired man from France confided that if he were younger, he would think that pretty young North American women were encouraging contact. "They seem like such flirts" when they look and smile at you like that.[38]

FACIAL EXPRESSIONS. Communication research supports the view that there are some universal patterns of facial expression.[39] There appears to be the most agreement that happiness is recognizable. However, cultural rules may dictate the use of a facial expression for other purposes. In China and Japan "happiness" may express anger or mask sadness, both of which culture dictates one may not overtly show.[40] A Westerner may be confused by the smiling explanation of an employee in Japan that she was absent because her mother died. The employee is smiling because one should not inflict the unpleasantness of grief on others. A smile portrays friendliness in one society, embarrassment in another, and in yet another may contain the warning that unless tension is reduced, attack will follow.[41]

Physiologists have estimated that the musculature of the face can produce over twenty thousand different facial expressions.[42]

HAPTICS (TOUCH). Although human beings are born with a need for touch, as evidenced by studies showing that infants will not survive without adequate touching, cultures train humans as to what and how much touch is acceptable as they mature. People in collective cultures touch each other more than those in cultures that stress the individual.[43] The former are called high-contact.

Touch can cause misunderstanding in intercultural communication.[44] In South Africa, a vigorous handshake is desirable, but in Latin America this is considered hostile; some cultures will not shake hands when they want to show respect.[45] In Thailand, one does not touch another in public, and one never touches on the head.[46] Gender roles also influence touching rituals. Culture carefully dictates the variations of acceptable touch. An orthodox Jew or a fundamentalist Muslim will not shake hands with (touch) a woman as a greeting or when being introduced, because such touch of a nonfamily female is not culturally permitted. North Americans in many social or business settings usually consider a light touch on the forearm between a man and a woman nonintrusive. However, even a small variation in the length or pressure of such a touch might well carry sexual overtones.

Mr. Jalil, who came from the Middle East, called on an office in the United States to rent warehouse space. Mrs. Jones greeted him and stepped forward to shake his hand. Mr. Jalil backed up one step, placed his feet side by side, and put both hands in his pockets. He apologized, saying that his religious beliefs did not permit him to shake hands. They formalized the rental contract, and at that point Mr. Jones arrived at the office. Mrs. Jones introduced him to Mr. Jalil, and Mr. Jones reached forward to shake hands. Mrs. Jones was about to discreetly put her hand on her husband's forearm to discourage the action, when Mr. Jalil stepped forward and shook hands. Mrs. Jones realized that Mr. Jalil's beliefs did not forbid shaking hands; they forbade shaking hands with her because of her gender.

POSTURE. The meaning and use of body posture or stance can vary culturally. In the United States, a culture that values a casual and friendly attitude, people often sprawl when they sit or slouch when they stand. In many more formal European countries, such as Germany, a slouching posture is considered rude. Standing with hands on hips can be relaxed, bad manners, or a challenge depending on the culture. Sitting with legs crossed may be unacceptable depending on one's gender as well as on the culture with which one is interacting. Cultures also orient themselves differently to communicate. People may orient themselves very directly—face to face—to communicate, as in Arab countries, or they may assume a stance that is less direct, as in many Asian countries.[47]

SMELL.   Smell is one of our most basic modes of communication and can sustain a message when the person is gone. Arabs perceive smell as an extension of the person and actively smell others; North Americans are the least comfortable with smell.[48] It is said that an Arab should not deny his brother his breath.

Proxemics

A German fable tells this story. On a winter night, the porcupines gathered together to socialize. Because of the cold, they moved closer together for warmth, but this caused them to prick each other with their quills. So they moved farther apart, but then they became cold again. They continued to adjust themselves, until they found the optimum distance to be both warm and comfortable. That distance became known as "good manners."[49]

People communicate with space far more than is consciously apparent, and space affects behavior differently in different cultures.[50] Attitudes in the United States toward space that are dissimilar to those in Europe are illustrated by the concept of a frontier. In Europe, a frontier signifies a boundary or a barrier. In the United States a frontier symbolizes constant expansion and unobstructed movement.[51]

The wife of a North American Fulbright professor in Germany during the 1980s, like many compatriots, was struck by the confinement of cherished spatial boundaries: the fences between houses, the closed doors to rooms, lines drawn, and distinctions made. And a Frenchman's comparison of the behavior of children on a beach remarked that North American children roam far and wide because they are accustomed to lots of space. French children tend to stay by their parents on their "little sandy domain."[52]

The use of space to communicate can be usefully broken down into three categories.

FIXED-FEATURE SPACE. Fixed-feature space tells us what we do where and how. We know what behavior is appropriate in a dining room, in a bedroom, in a ballroom, or in a church.[53] People wrest and defend space (territoriality) and use space to indicate status or rank by the amount or location of their territory.[54] The use of space reflects the centralization of modern French culture. Streets of cities radiate out like wheel spokes from the center—just look at a map of Paris. The French use public space, like sidewalk cafes, to socialize.[55]

SEMIFIXED-FEATURE SPACE. Semifixed-feature space extends this function to movable objects. Some cultures easily move furniture, and others do not.[56] One German executive working in the United States actually had the visitor's chair in his office bolted to the floor because it so greatly disturbed him to have a visitor reposition the chair when sitting down in front of his desk. In France, subordinates' desks cluster around their manager's central desk. Germans keep the doors in their offices and homes closed. Privacy and property are sacred.[57] Rank or status can be communicated by placement of tables, seating, and so on.[58]

The quickest way not to be invited back into a French home is to go wandering around through the rooms. The doors to the bedrooms—and especially the bathroom—are kept closed and mean keep out. However, in an office in France, a closed door does not mean a "closed door policy." It only means that you have to open it to go in. North Americans working in France are astonished when they close an office door for privacy to reprimand or fire a person, only to have Monsieur Dumont or Madame Bertrand walk right in.[59]

INFORMAL SPACE. Informal space includes the distance maintained in interpersonal encounters, which varies culturally.[60] In some cultures people stand and sit very close when interacting, and they make negative judgments—such as coldness, condescension, or disinterest—about those who interact at a greater distance. One can, on the other hand, intrude into another's zone of personal space and be perceived as pushy, disrespectful, or sexually aggressive.[61] Culture usually determines orientation (whether persons interact face-to-face or side-by-side), as well as whether people wait in line or jockey for the best position to be served.[62]

Waiting in line for service of some sort is an experience common to most people. *Resquillage,* or line-jumping, in France pushes a sensitive button for most British and North Americans. While it is inconvenient to those who are waiting, the French may secretly admire the daring of the loner who cuts in at the front of the line. Think of all the world-class French explorers, aviators, mountain climbers, solo seafarers, and deep sea divers.[63]

The English are strict about lines and will wait a long time. It is said that a study was done to see just how far one could push the English and still have them respect their rules for waiting in line. In a public place two phone booths were labeled, one for men and one for women. By circumstance, a line formed at the women's booth, where people were waiting some twenty minutes to use the phone. One woman joined the line briefly, and then walked over to the men's booth, used the phone, and came out. Observers for the study approached her and asked what made her decide to leave the line for the women's booth and use the men's booth. She replied, "I'm French. I don't wait in line. These English are crazy."

At a motor vehicle licensing office in the United States, there was the usual long line of people waiting for their picture to be taken for their drivers' licenses. An Armenian woman standing in line stepped forward for her turn and signaled four other people to join her. She was told that she could not hold extra places. Disappointed, the rest of her family went to the end of the line to again wait, but this time standing in line. In the former Soviet Armenia, holding places in line was acceptable. In the United States, a social service agency had difficulty with Soviet immigrant applicants who would push and fight to win the attention of staff, which was a tactic that worked in their former countries. But North Americans are strict about their rules for lines. Democracy and efficiency rule that "first come, first served." Some agencies found it necessary to go to an appointment-only system to manage these cultural queuing differences.[64]

A North American who lived in Colombia for thirty years commented that on repatriating to the United States after so long, she found that she was no longer accustomed to the use of space in local supermarkets. In Colombia one has to be very aggressive in such activities as getting merchandise and maintaining a place in line. She found that she kept running into people in the aisles and in lines with her cart until she readjusted to the different use of space and timing.

Immediacy

Actions that simultaneously communicate warmth, closeness, and availability for communication are immediacy behaviors that signal approach rather than avoidance and are typical of cultures that have high physical contact (high-contact), as contrasted to low-contact cultures.[65] It is assumed that persons approach things they like and avoid things they dislike, so people interpret immediacy behaviors as communicating positive or negative evaluations of the interaction partner. The nonverbal cues most often associated with immediacy have to do with a person's sense of space, such as interpersonal distance, and with body motion communication, such as touch, gaze, body lean, and head and body orientation (facing).[66] These nonverbal cues have different meaning in different cultures. Further, expression of emotion is more permissible in some cultures than in others, and in some cultures for a man to publicly even speak to a woman may be unacceptable.[67]

Nonverbal immediacy behaviors are interrelated and compensate for one another, as well as compensating for the verbal level of immediacy. One cannot discuss what meanings are being expressed by touch or distance without taking into account other components, such as eye contact. Even if touch is inhibited by culture, one can signal a close relationship by adopting a close conversational distance and increasing gaze. Adding several cues together can intensify immediacy signals.[68]

A Frenchwoman walked up to a bank teller at the Banque de l'Indochine in the capital city of Papeete, Tahiti, and stopped at the counter. She stood so straight she almost leaned back, chin tucked in, feet together, elbows close to her sides. With precise diction and a carefully modulated voice, she said "Bonjour, Madame" to the teller. She stated her business, using the formal *vous* pronoun and "pointed" (*pointu*) Parisian French. The Polynesian teller's face closed in, as if she had been greeted with a slap rather than "good day." The Frenchwoman seemed unaware of the teller's negative reaction and continued assertively with impeccable French courtesy. The Polynesian teller responded to the customer's questions with curt replies, volunteering no information. The teller was minimally cooperative and could not be called "friendly." The Frenchwoman was able, nonetheless, to complete her transaction.

The next customer to approach the teller was a Polynesian. She walked up to the counter and put an elbow on it. She leaned slightly forward and to one side, with relaxed body posture. In a soft, singsong voice, she smiled and said in French, "Hi, there. You doing all right?" The teller responded. The customer continued, "I need to send some money to Raiatea. Can you help me?" ending her question with an informal vocal segregate. The teller assisted the customer with the transaction in a pleasant manner and was quite helpful.

There can often be hostility in communication between the Polynesians and the French in Tahiti. Although there are historical and power issues that affect communication between the two cultures, aside from these factors the different use of immediacy displays is an important element. Continental French are culturally trained to be formally courteous and to maintain distance in addressing people whom they do not know well. They also tend to have a confrontational style of communicating. Polynesians are informal and gregarious. Their communication style is open and warm, inviting communication. They acknowledge the party they are addressing in a personal manner. They are nonconfrontational and indirect in style. To a Polynesian, the formal and distant manner of the French is offensive. Sitting in the bank lobby in Tahiti, or in the Post Office on the *quai*, one can observe a parade of verbal and nonverbal communication styles of cultures as diverse as Polynesian, French, Chinese, and an occasional Australian or North American. One can clearly distinguish the different use of immediacy displays.

Some of the French who have lived in French Polynesia for a length of time have adapted, and they consciously or unconsciously adopt island immediacy displays to communicate with Polynesians. They modify the formality of their posture and body language and use pleasant facial expressions with less intense gaze. They soften their tone of voice and may switch to the familiar form of address, depending on the person to whom they are speaking. They use a more personal ritual of greeting to acknowledge the person they are addressing. Polynesians then perceive them as less demanding and condescending. The French who are able to employ island immediacy displays communicate with far greater success and less friction in everyday encounters than do the French who communicate in a Continental style. Polynesians respond with greater warmth and cooperation to island "immediacy." But we should not forget that to abandon one's reserve and formality of style would not meet with much success in a Paris bank or shop. Polynesian-style immediacy displays would be received as intrusively personal and inappropriately familiar. Each culture generally perceives the other's use of immediacy displays as lacking in respect. Quite simply, the rules are different.

Physical Characteristics

ARTIFACTS (EXTENSIONS OF PHYSICAL SELF). People communicate, consciously or unconsciously, by extensions of themselves,[69] such as their dress, gifts, property, jewelry, even briefcases or cars. These extensions are interpreted differently in different cultures. Informal dress that is acceptable in one culture may be considered in poor taste or even insulting in another. Physically observable "markers" of cultural difference such as Arab, African, or Amerindian dress in a setting where European-style clothing predominates, or vice-versa, may heighten persons' perceptions of dissimilarity and consequently impact negatively their desire to communicate.

It is often a shock to Mexicans at their consulates in the United States to see how some people will dress to come to the consulate for business or to obtain information—attributions about their status, education, and other characteristics are made to a greater extent than would be made by North Americans.

In Tahiti, a young Chinese man showed up to look at a Porsche convertible for sale by the regional manager of LAN Chile Airlines. The manager was biculturally French and Chilean, both of which are formal, hierarchical societies. The prospective car purchaser was dressed in shorts, an undershirt, and rubber thongs, and was smudged with flour. The manager did not want to show or let him drive the expensive car. Local staff took the manager aside and persuaded him to treat the prospective buyer's interest seriously, and the manager acquiesced. Several hours after seeing the car the baker returned with a paper bag full of cash—an enormous sum for the time and place—and happily left as the new owner of the prestigious vehicle. In Tahiti it is more difficult than in most places to judge a person's education, status, or wealth by artifacts.

PHYSICAL APPEARANCE.   Physically observable "markers" of potential cultural difference such as hair, facial features, body conformation, or skin color accentuate persons' perceptions of difference.[70] This is significant because the higher the perceived similarity between two individuals, the greater their attraction to each other[71] to communicate.

Vocalics

The voice is a rich channel in the system of nonverbal communication. Vocalic cues are among the most powerful cues in the nonverbal repertoire and, next to kinesics, are the largest in number. The term vocalics encompasses any vocal-auditory behavior except the spoken word.[72] Some vocalic cues are so brief as to be missed in intercultural communication.[73] Cultures have dominant vocalic patterns, and there are numerous subcultural variations.[74] The use of vocalics has different meaning in different cultures. Vocalics indicate how something is said, rather than the actual meaning of the words, and can be divided into four categories.[75]

VOCAL CHARACTERIZERS.   Characterizers are vocalizations such as laughing, crying, yelling, moaning, whining, belching, yawning. A belch can signify having eaten well, or that one has bad manners.[76]

VOCAL QUALIFIERS.   Volume, pitch, rhythm, tempo, resonance, and tone are vocal qualifiers. Loudness of voice connotes sincerity and strength to Arabs but seems aggressive to North Americans; an Arab may view a North American's lower volume as a sign of weakness.[77] North Americans often think Latin Americans are arguing when they are just having a conversation. Qualifiers such as voice volume, pitch, and tone give this false impression. This is also true of French speaking style. In the United States, North Americans often thought that a French father and his adult son were arguing when they were having an ordinary conversation.

VOCAL RATE.   Vocal rate is the speed at which people speak. A fast talker may be viewed as glib and untrustworthy in one culture but as intelligent and involved in another.[78]

VOCAL SEGREGATES.   Sounds such as "un-huh," "shhh," "ooh," "uh," and "mmh" are vocal segregates. The Japanese use an essential gap or silence interval that is called *ma*; this silence makes North Americans uncomfortable.[79] In Brazil a sibilant "ssss . . . " typically voices male approval of a passing female, although to the North American it may sound like a disapproving hiss.

Having constructed a framework composed of categories of perception, verbal processes, and nonverbal processes that frequently cause obstacles in intercultural communication, we will now apply this framework to two specific cultures to see how differences can cause communication obstacles. To apply our framework of categories, we will focus on Mexico and the United States. In addition to providing information that is specific to the cultures of these two countries, this application will demonstrate how the foregoing framework of categories can be used to identify potential problem areas for communication between any two cultures.

PART TWO

TWO WORLDS
The United States and Mexico

The Mexico–United States Cultural Environment

Communication between the United States and Mexico will always be difficult but never impossible.[1]

The successful U.S. corporation Corning and the giant Mexican glass manufacturer Vitro, in Monterrey, formed a cross-border alliance in 1991 that seemed blessed. They both had histories of successful joint ventures and a global orientation, and both were still headed by founding families. In February of 1994, however, Corning handed back Vitro's $130 million dowry and called the match off. Francisco Chavez, an analyst with Smith Barney Shearson in New York, said, "The cultures didn't match. . . . It was a marriage made in hell."[2]

On a day-to-day basis, no single country affects the national interest of the United States in more ways than Mexico. On an economic level, in 1993 Mexico had become the United States' second largest trading partner, after Canada. Mexico was buying 70 percent of its foreign purchases from the United States, which in turn absorbed 67 percent of Mexico's exports.[3] One year after the 1993 signing of the North American Free Trade Agreement (NAFTA), statistics from the U.S. Commerce Department measured Mexico's imports from the United States as equal to the combined U.S. imports of Germany, France, Italy, China, and Russia.[4] Jesus Reyes-Heroles, Mexican ambassador to the United States in 1998, pointed out that by 1997,

trade between Mexico and the United States had reached $170 billion—
double the amount in 1993. Reyes-Heroles called the success of NAFTA a
well-kept secret.[5]

But even greater success is available to those who will take the time to
understand cultural differences, whether they be Mexicans or North Americans. The twenty-five-month business union between Corning and Vitro
that held such great potential was damaged by constant cultural clashes that
proved fatal. Corning managers did not expect to have to wait for important decisions. The manner of decision-making in U.S. and Mexican cultures is different. One needs to know that only high-level executives in Mexico can make decisions, and Vitro's decision-makers were often busy with
other matters. Vitro—as is typical of Mexican businesses—was more hierarchical in structure than is the norm in the United States. In Mexico, a loyalty to fathers and *patrones* somehow carries over to modern corporations.
As a matter of loyalty or tradition, decisions are often left to a member of
the controlling family or to top executives, and the opinions of mid-level
managers are usually not requested. The cultural gap separating the two
businesses amounted to a different approach to work, which was reflected
in scheduling, decision-making, and etiquette. Cultural disparities hurt the
two companies' ability to react together to a fast-changing market with a
stronger peso, increased overseas competition, and a rethinking of market
strategies by both Vitro and Corning. The cultural hurdles to successful business seemed insurmountable, so the two companies called off the promising
joint venture.[6]

The failure of the Corning-Vitro alliance was unfortunate. Many think
that Mexico offers the greatest business opportunities that North Americans
will see in their lifetimes. In the 1950s and 1960s "Made in Japan" signaled
an inferior product to much of the world, but the Japanese made a remarkable change in the quality of their production in just a few decades. Mexico
today may be on the same track to significant change—and some say that
now is the time to establish a market presence.[7] Henry Kissinger wrote that
Mexico's propensity to import from the United States is the highest in the
world with or without NAFTA. In the next century Mexico will have a popu-
lation of more than one hundred million, our de facto open borders make
friendly relations a vital national interest, and twenty million Mexican residents in the United States link the interests of the two nations on the human
level.[8] Cuauhtémoc Cárdenas, who was elected mayor of Mexico City in
1996, campaigned in Chicago for Mexican votes.

LOOKING NORTH AND SOUTH

If sovereignty divides nations, then migration connects them. From 1981 to 1986, U.S. officials counted 1.1 billion persons entering the country from Mexico. There is a certain amount of xenophobia in the United States, and many North Americans wonder, as James Fallows put it, if Mexican immigrants will assimilate, further stretching the country's cultural fabric, or whether the volume of the influx will finally tear it.[9] It has been found that immigrant children will have cultural premises profoundly different from those of their parents. They are influenced by their own as well as the new culture, and a hybrid culture results. Although immigrants are usually completely acculturated in two generations,[10] they also influence the culture into which they assimilate.

Mexico and the United States are destined to come closer despite the worst of their governments' intentions. Mexican culture and the Spanish language will migrate north, and North American political attitudes and consumer tastes will travel south. Growing bonds will connect people and families in both countries, and over time the United States may deal more with Mexico as a relative than a neighbor. Economic and social integration is reshaping both countries.[11]

Given the importance of trade and, in addition, concerns about drug trafficking and the fluid flow of migration back and forth across a 2,000-mile border, it would be of great value to achieve effective, efficient intercultural communication between the United States and Mexico. The geographical fact of such an extensive common border is in itself good reason for the two cultures to address the issue of communication, with a view toward solving common problems.[12] Such an achievement will take focused effort. Andres Oppenheimer, foreign correspondent for the *Miami Herald* with twenty years of experience in Latin America, found Mexico to be by far the most difficult country he had to cover.[13]

In considering the Mexico–United States cultural environment, we will not try to compare the totality of North American and Mexican cultures, an immense if not impossible task, but rather will attempt to identify the areas of contact that most commonly cause misunderstanding in communication between these two cultures. We need to begin by looking at the principal characteristics of the two countries that impact their communication with each other.

It is clear that cultural differences between the United States and Mexico give rise to obstacles in communication attempts between the two peoples. In order to logically manage and gain some understanding of these obstacles, we can generally group and discuss them by the common, global categories of potential obstacles to intercultural communication set forth in Table I. Not all of the categories constructed are equally applicable to these two cultures, nor are there clear boundaries because of overlap and the kaleidoscopic interaction operating between and among categories within the matrix of each culture. In attempting intercultural communication between Mexico and the United States, some categories emerge from the data as particularly significant because of their potential to cause frequent misunderstandings between the two cultures.

This approach "by category" will assist us in analyzing the differences in Mexican and North American perceptions that are instilled by distinct acculturation, and the differences in what is prescribed by these two different cultures as correct verbal and nonverbal behavior for given situations. Conscious knowledge of specific cultural differences will give us some understanding of the dynamics that create communication difficulties between the two countries. For clarity, we need to bear in mind that:

- *North American* means a citizen of the United States of America (not Canadians or Mexicans) who is an anglophone.
- *Mexican* means a citizen of the United States of Mexico (not a Mexican American) who is Spanish-speaking. Due to different history and life experience, it is to be noted that there is a Mexican-American culture that is distinct both from Mexican culture and from the dominant anglophone culture in the United States.

In order to gather genuinely emic (internal) data about North American and Mexican cultures, information about attitudes and prescribed behavioral units was extracted from opinions and viewpoints published in diverse books, periodicals, and etiquette books intended for local consumption in the United States and in Mexico. It was important to find the viewpoint of Mexicans addressing Mexicans and of North Americans addressing North Americans. Personal interviews also were used as a source of material, and both business and social practices were considered. In addition, opinions of well-informed third parties who are not natives of either country were valuable in trying to understand how each culture's subconscious is conditioned to behave and communicate. A British communications expert who lived and worked in Paris for many years commented that the obstacles that exist in communication between the British and the French, a similar pair of "Nordic" and "Mediterranean" cultures, closely parallel the difficulties that exist between North Americans and Mexicans.

The collection of data deliberately does not attempt to be exhaustive, but rather focuses on communication obstacles that are significant, common, and repetitive in occurrence among and between educated people who live at a comfortable socioeconomic level—thus comparing mangos to mangos. The aggregate of these data will help bring the disparate cultures of Mexico and the United States into focus for the person who wishes to communicate across their cultural border. The following discussion of the obstacles that arise in communication draws on the views of both Mexicans and North Americans, each perceiving the other culture as through a two-way looking glass.

CULTURE SHOCK

Alan Riding writes that stepping across the Mexico–United States border plunges one into a different world. Probably nowhere in the world are two countries so different juxtaposed—and probably nowhere in the world do two neighbors understand each other so little. Language, religion, race, philosophy, and history separate the two countries even more than economic development. The United States is two hundred years old and looks forward. Mexican culture is several thousand years old and gripped by centuries of past history and traditions.[14]

It was primarily Spanish soldiers that colonized Mexico, not the families of men, women, and children that colonized the United States. Consider also that many Jews immigrated to Mexico as far back as the Inquisition, and that the arm of the Inquisition reached into Mexico. Mexico is closer to Europe and Spain in culture than it is to the United States, and, through Spain, Mexico was influenced by Arab culture. The Moors, who brought Arab influences to Spain, were on the Iberian peninsula for some eight hundred years.

Although Mexicans intellectualize contempt for what some consider the materialistic culture of the United States, and though they believe that "clever" Mexicans can outwit "naive Yankees," ordinary Mexicans also admire North Americans for their organization, honesty, and affluence. Many average North Americans, if they think about Mexicans, envision serapes, sombreros, and siestas. They probably do not picture chic urbanites dressed in the latest European fashions, nor do they envision the fine manners and warm courtesy of the common person.

There are many aspects of behavior that most members of a given culture share to varying degrees[15] but, even so, few individuals are a perfect representation of their culture. Consequently, despite any general national traits or attitudes of a nation, we must remember:

- In intercultural communication, one deals with individuals, and there are exceptions to every cultural norm.
- Certainly many Mexicans and North Americans do not fit a national mold.[16]

Mexican culture and U.S. culture often engender distinct perceptions of, and prescribe different behaviors for, the same situation. A number of factors significant to communication shape the cultural environments of these two countries.

HISTORICAL AND POLITICAL FACTORS

Amerindians and Mestizos

Mexico's indigenous peoples enormously impact the culture of Mexico today, and Mexican writer Dr. Agustín Basave Fernández del Valle points out that there is a chasm of difference between the native peoples of Mexico and those of the United States. Mexico had a civilization built on Maya-Quiche, Olmec, Toltec, Aztec, Mixtec, Zapotec, Totonac, Tarasca, and other Indian cultures that included such traits as complex sociopolitical institutions, cosmogony, and fine arts.[17] The Olmecs, for example, had an elaborate dating system that included the concept of zero, unknown to their Roman contemporaries. The United States was populated by indigenous tribes that, for the most part, were nowhere near as advanced.[18]

Many words from Náhuatl—the language of the Aztecs—have been assimilated into Mexican Spanish,[19] and the world today gets words such as chocolate and tomato from Mexico's Aztecs.[20] The visitor to Mexico may need to contend not only with Spanish as the national language, but with references to people, things, and places that have commonly occurring names such as Cuauhtémoc, Quetzalcoatl, and Tenochtitlán.

To Mexicans, a number of Amerindian figures are historically very important. The woman known as La Malinche was given as a concubine to

Hernan Cortés, the conquistador of New Spain—as Mexico was known. La Malinche served as an interpreter and, loyal to Cortés, revealed an Aztec plot to kill the Spaniards. La Malinche also bore Cortés a son, and the role she symbolizes is significant to Mexican culture.

The United States claims to be the biggest ethnic melting pot of modern history, but Mexican author Basave points out that racial mixing with Amerindians was eschewed and that there still remains discrimination against Caucasian miscegenation with African Americans. The majority biological mixture in the United States is fundamentally European. While North Americans are proud of economic success and opportunity, in contrast, intellectual Octavio Paz stated that Mexicans take great pride in being a fundamentally mestizo country.[21] Basave sees the United States as a country of white families that imported black Africans and let in Mexicans.[22]

Poet and writer Octavio Paz states that although the language, religion, government, and culture of Mexico are occidental, "we are a people between two civilizations and two histories."[23] Basave writes that the United States was started up like a new business, without two millennia of rich Indian culture, while Mexico's version of a human being is essentially Hispanic-Indian.[24]

African Americans in the United States historically served only as cheap labor. While the Amerindians in Mexico filled a similar role, the Spanish nonetheless converted them to Christianity and educated them, and the native Amerindians became an essential part of the Mexican nation through biological and cultural intermingling with the colonizers. Amerindians are the backbone of Mexico. Basave's viewpoint is that Amerindians do not count in the United States. The colonists used the "sanitary rifle," and "the only good Indian was a dead Indian." It has been said with good reason that "México es . . . uno de los países mas equilibradamente mestizos en el continente." (Mexico is . . . one of the most evenly mestizo countries of the continent).[25]

The legacy of Mexico's mestizo culture is that there is very little racial prejudice in Mexico. A person who facilitates business liaisons between the United States and Mexico aptly points out that any discrimination in Mexico is more social than racial. From her perspective, it would appear that the United States sins twice in the area of discrimination. Not only is there racial prejudice, but there is clearly an element of social prejudice as well.[26] In Mexico today, there are fewer barriers to social mobility for mestizos even than in other Latin American nations. In the 1990s, mestizos visibly occupied seats of power in government and in business.[27]

Despite Mexico's general mestizo pride, like other New World countries with great racial mixing, the elite economic classes in Mexico tend by circumstance to be lighter skinned—and therefore lighter skin and hair can be prestigious. A few upper-class Mexicans are quick to state that they have "no Indian blood," and ads selling products from beer to cars often feature blondes.

Master Symbols

Mexicans are "Guadalupeans," venerating the dark Virgin Mary of Guadalupe. This patron saint of Mexico first appeared to an Amerindian, and she represents the blending of the Spanish and Amerindian races and cultures that is the essence of Mexico. The Virgin of Guadalupe also represents the homogeneity of religion in Mexico, and the veneration of the mother in the family.

Another master symbol is the Amerindian woman La Malinche, who has several faces. To some Mexicans, she popularly represents woman as a potential prostitute and traitor. To others, she symbolizes the mother of a mestizo culture (she bore Cortés's mestizo son). *Malinchismo* also symbolizes the veneration of foreign culture as superior to that of the Mexicans. La Malinche was loyal to Cortés, a foreigner, and the Spaniards' arrival in Mexico seemed godlike in fulfillment of Amerindian legend.

The Virgin of Guadalupe represents core beliefs of Mexico regarding spirituality, the family, and the mestizo nature of the Mexican people. That abstract measure of time, the clock, could be said to appropriately symbolize the technological society of the United States, a "chronocracy," with its reverence for efficiency and the success of economic endeavors (time equals money). Each culture is organized around its respective master symbol, and the resulting different focus of daily life impedes the sharing of perceptions.

History and Life Experience

It has been said of North Americans that they always look to the future, so that the future is always present in the past, whereas in Mexico the past is always present in contemplating the future.[28] Mexican writer Basave feels that in the United States there is sometimes a rough disdain for the past. He points out that Henry Ford did not hesitate to state that history is made up of lies.[29]

The Spanish conquered Mexico a century before the English colonized the United States. They founded a university as early as 1551 and introduced printing to the American continent. The U.S. universities of Harvard (1636) and William and Mary (1693) were founded a century later. The first book was printed in Mexico in 1539, while the first book in the United States was printed in 1640. New Spain had rich and varied literary and artistic production compared with the paucity of cultural production in New England.[30]

For some feeling for the different historical context in which people of the two countries live today, consider the cities of Monterrey in Mexico, and Denver in the United States. Both began as frontier towns, removed from their national capitals both then and now, and both have been industrial and trade centers for their areas. Both Monterrey and Denver have had significant mining industries, and currently both have large breweries. Both are currently financial centers for their regions. Both have beautiful vistas, with mountains rising up from each city's edge. Denver celebrated its first centennial as a city in 1961; Monterrey celebrated its fourth centennial in 1996. For two urban centers that have so many similarities, just by virtue of their age, there is a vast difference in the sense of history in the two cities.

Mexico lives its history. It still resents the loss of almost half of its territory to the United States in the nineteenth century, a loss that is referred to frequently by Mexican writers as a "mutilation." Also resented is U.S. military intervention as recently as 1916. Historian Stanley R. Ross writes that Mexicans perceive their relationship with the United States as shaped by "armed conflict, military invasions, and economic and cultural penetration." Military invasion began with a war that Mexicans call the "War of the North American Invasion." While most future-oriented North Americans are not aware that the event ever occurred, Mexicans with their focus on history cannot forget it. North Americans communicating with Mexicans should be sensitive to the importance of this historical event, and it will help communication if Mexicans do not blame current generations of Americans for the past invasion.[31] Mexico and the United States will have a difficult time overcoming the scars of their mutual past.

The Mexican Revolution, which began in 1910, was not just a changing of the palace guard. It overturned social order. Combat lasted nearly a decade, and the destruction of lives and property was far greater than that of the North American Civil War. Since this significant event ended so recently, it is not surprising that the revolution is so meaningful in Mexico today.[32] A succession of authoritarian governments and brutal suppression of the masses have scarred the Mexican psyche. Mexico has two faces. One has an element of sadness, which is stylized in songs and art forms. The other is the sunny, smiling face that celebrates Mexicans' well-known love of art, singing, dancing, poetry, humor, and lively conversations.[33]

Mexicans consider North Americans to be ignorant of history, and the average Mexican probably knows more about U.S. history than the average North American knows about his or her own history—not to mention the North American's lack of knowledge of Mexican history. In *Limits to Friendship*, in a chapter entitled "The American Mind," Robert Pastor writes that Mexico is mentioned on fewer than 8 of 752 pages of a fifth-grade U.S. history book. The textbook draws a picture of the United States as a country with the manifest destiny to bring democracy to all of North America. In U.S. history texts, Mexico is a way station on the trek of the United States across the continent. The Texas war for independence and the U.S. war against Mexico are not discussed within the context of U.S.–Mexican relations.[34] Given not only that Mexicans have a much more vivid, present appreciation of history than North Americans, but that Mexico was invaded, one can better understand why Mexicans are still touchy about realities such as the Mexican-American war, in which Mexico lost vast areas of its territories to the United States. Imagine a different set of historical events unfolding on the continent, and that 150 years ago Canada had militarily invaded the United States and taken Washington, Oregon, Idaho, Montana, Wyoming, Utah and Colorado—and, furthermore, imposed French as the official language. Such history would probably still be very present in the North American psyche.

Mexicans also remain very wary of the repeated intervention of the United States in Latin American politics.[35] Despite much greater per capita U.S. investment in Canada, Canadian debates about this economic invasion are much less intense than the vitriol with which the subject is approached in Mexico. Recent history may explain the difference in the two countries' fears of U.S. influence and intervention.[36]

Mexicans believe that since they were colonized and Christianized (including the native peoples) by the old and illustrious Spanish civilization, overlaid on and mixed with ancient Amerindian civilizations, they are culturally elite. North Americans believe that they are superior because of their highly industrialized society and the remarkable and rapid advance of their technology and education.[37] There is truth in both perspectives. Mexicans agree that the United States is mechanically and technically advanced at least fifty years ahead of the rest of the world, but they also see the United States as at least a century behind Europe[38] and Mexico in the fine art of living with one's fellow man. Clearly, the cultures of the United States and Mexico have different values.

Historian Schlesinger suggests that North Americans may be described as "an essentially historyless people"—a country of lawyers with respect for legal scripture, while Mexico is the mirror opposite. In Mexico, history and its lessons are revered and laws rhetorically worshipped, "obeyed but not complied with."[39]

Hierarchy

Mexico has inherited a hierarchical social system from both Spain and its highly structured Amerindian civilizations[40] that is steeper than the hierarchical structure of society in the United States. As a result, Mexicans are very class conscious and more formal about interpersonal relations than are North Americans.[41] Whereas some think that the traditional hierarchy and resulting formality of the Japanese and other similar cultures became so stylized and mechanical as to be inhuman, the formality that became a key factor in Mexican society during the long Spanish colonial period (1521–1821) has remained personal and intimate. One desirable aspect of Mexico's hierarchical organization is that it promotes a courteous formality that adds positively to the quality of people's daily lives.[42]

The term "paternalism" is frequently used in connection with the Mexican system of hierarchy. Although this term undoubtedly has negative connotations for the average North American, in Mexico the term connotes an entire system of values, in which the individual is linked to others through hierarchical ties that offer protection in exchange for loyalty.[43]

Because of the formal, hierarchical system of society in Mexico, businesspersons from the United States should always introduce themselves and present a card. Furthermore, they should pay close attention to the information, name, and title on any card they receive.[44] The importance of building a personal relationship as a prelude to business in Mexico can hardly be overstated, and such a relationship cannot be established instantly. Mexicans may resent overfamiliarity. They find North Americans too quick to begin conversations on a first-name basis, and the custom of shortening names and using nicknames is perceived as strange.

San Antonio businessmen Reed and Gray point out that, in Mexican business, there is a caste system in a very real sense. But, unlike the situation in India, in Mexico you can move up or down the social ladder by business success or failure. Businesspeople will judge you by the level at which you approach the company, and an important executive would never start at the bottom and work up.[45] You must, however, have sufficient rank and authority within your own company to warrant reception by high-level executives and officials. Business cards evidencing your title and "credentials" are one essential tool. Always initiate your business dealings at the highest possible level, because where you start negotiations is probably as high a level as you will reach. If you do not understand where in the hierarchy decisions are made, you may not understand why you can never conclude a transaction at mid-level. Face will not allow buyers or mid-level managers to tell you that they do not have authority to commit their company.[46] One of the reasons for the demise of the short-lived Vitro-Corning business venture was that the difference in hierarchical structures of the two companies caused ill-understood communication difficulties.

Respect is an important element in a steep social hierarchy. But *respect* in North America and *respeto* in Mexico have different shades of meaning. In the United States respect is bound up with objective values of equality, fair play, and democratic spirit. There are fewer emotional overtones, and one respects others as one might respect the law. In Mexico, *respeto* involves matters of power, possible threat, and, often, a love-hate relationship. Its meaning arises from powerful human relationships such as those of father and son or *patrón* and *peón:* the parties recognize that they are unequal in power and influence. *Respeto* in Mexico is likely to be more personal and forced by circumstance, whereas respect in the United States is more a matter of principle to which individuals voluntarily commit themselves.[47] *Respeto* in Mexico also strictly requires deference and propriety toward other entities, such as older persons, family members, women, and the church.

Condon writes that North Americans need both to respect the Mexican hierarchy and to understand that when working in management in Mexico, Mexican employees will accord them *respeto* by virtue of their position as managers. A North American business manager assigned to Mexico may, with good intentions, set out to try to earn the respect of subordinates. In his endeavor to demonstrate that he merits respect, the North American will show how hard he works for the company. But instead of trying to earn respect already accorded him, he should rather strive to earn employees' loyalty and trust through his genuine personal concern for them as individuals.[48]

In a business environment, Condon points out, North Americans will find it helpful to understand that "knowing your people" is an art to Mexican workers, and that they are more conscious of working for a particular person than of doing a particular job as mapped out on an organization chart. This is because survival in the Mexican system has always depended more on knowing how to deal with particular people than in fitting into an organizational structure.[49]

Mexicans working with North Americans and in the United States will find it beneficial to adjust to a flatter hierarchy, which North Americans have had instilled in them as representative of fair play and democracy. It is helpful for Mexicans to understand that North Americans are culturally trained to try to treat all people as being equal, and that they therefore may be unaware of the personal interaction rules imposed by Mexico's steep social hierarchy. In turn, North Americans working in Mexico need to realize that it is offensive to address a person in a powerful governmental or business position, for example, in a familiar manner or as an equal unless such equality of position is clearly the case, and that even equals will still use formally courteous forms of address. Likewise, although persons of lower status are addressed courteously in Mexico and the formal *usted* is used, to treat such persons as equals appears ridiculous and is embarrassing both to them and to onlookers.

The formal and rigid hierarchy of social organization in Mexico permeates every segment of daily life and human interaction. As one report on Mexico points out, societal acceptance of hierarchy, by definition, is an acceptance of inequality. People who live in a steep social hierarchy expect and accept that power will be distributed unequally.[50] The vast difference between the United States and Mexico in their hierarchical organization is a significant obstacle to communication with each other, because the difference is a source of misunderstanding and misinterpretation.

Government

Though both Mexico and the United States are described as "democracies," the structure and operation of the institutions that organize these two governments are markedly different. On one hand, society in Mexico is structured primarily on a system of extended interdependent families; the government itself is centralized. In the United States, on the other hand, society is structured around the government, which is decentralized, and small nuclear families tend to exist and operate independently.

Real politics, like everything else in Mexico, takes place behind masks. Presidential elections take place every six years, but Mexicans have seen this as an elaborate ritual because through the 1990s the president traditionally picked his successor, and usually picked Institutional Revolutionary Party (PRI) candidates for all other key posts. The PRI candidate was declared the victor in all elections for president, senator, and state governor from the time of its formation in 1929 up until 1989. The opposition attributed PRI victories in these elections, as well as in elections to choose mayors and members of the Chamber of Deputies, to vote fraud. Like most authoritarian regimes, Mexico's ruling elite is primarily concerned with the perpetuation of its power. To explain its juridical inconsistencies, government officials argue that the purpose of the constitution (which contains an impressive body of individual and social rights) is to establish the sociopolitical "objectives" toward which the system is working.[51] In 1989 the PRI slowly began losing its stranglehold on elections. The opposition has won several state governor seats, and, notably, in 1996 Cuauhtémoc Cárdenas won the influential position of mayor of Mexico City.

The North American revolution gathered theories and actions of various generations and groups to found a nation and create technological advancement, but Mexico's war of independence was the beginning of its instability, with the appearance of many military politicians. Even so, as stated by Mexican writer Octavio Paz, North American democracy emerged stained by the slavery of African Americans and the extermination of American Indians.[52] Basave comments that North America has helped Mexico with medicine and food in times of catastrophe but has taken advantage of local tyranny to dominate and to profit and has not contributed to modernizing Mexico's political structures.[53]

From a Mexican perspective, the greatest contribution of the United States to human history is its peculiar democratic experiment, which is based on Christian ethic and religious pluralism, both of which influence the pluralist democracy that has flourished in the United States more than anywhere else in the world. The historical climate of the United States seems to better prepare its people for democracy than does the history of most other countries. Basave writes that democracy in the United States, despite its deficiencies, is a living reality, thus Mexicans can forgive these disinherited people of Europe their lack of good manners because nowhere else on earth is there more freedom of expression than in the United States. Basave hopes for much to come from the free speech and the right to dissent practiced by the community of free people in the United States.[54]

Given the different governmental environments in which Mexicans and North Americans live, it is not surprising that different things are meant by democracy and freedom of speech, and what is viewed as international assistance by one may well be interpreted as unwonted political intervention by the other. Government officials in Mexico are carefully briefed on what is to be said publicly,[55] if they do not already know it both cognitively and instinctively. Although this is beginning to change, Mexican officials display extraordinary unanimity to the public and to foreigners, whereas in the United States dissension is frequently quite public. It is necessary to have some understanding of the context of the government of any country in order to interpret many local customs, actions, and statements correctly.

Despite these wide differences, however, few Mexicans express hostility toward North Americans as individuals (except toward U.S. immigration enforcers, *la migra*), and many openly admire the North American qualities of honesty, efficiency, and democracy that seem lacking in Mexico.[56]

The Shadow of Power

The "unique fact that a vulnerable developing country shares a 2,000-mile border with the world's richest and strongest power" is the overshadowing factor in the relationship between Mexico and the United States. This asymmetry of power shapes their perspectives of each other.[57] A 1998 article in a U.S. newspaper reported on talks (intercultural by nature) between the United States and Mexico to approve added drug enforcement. The discussions ended "in a failure," and the two countries put off for later talks regarding the right of American narcotics agents to carry weapons for defense in Mexico. The article aptly pointed out that for Mexicans, communication about this issue "raises sovereignty concerns that are particularly acute given the country's long and often painful history with its giant neighbor to the north."[58] Because of Mexico's distrust, if the United States expresses a desire to intervene in Mexican affairs, whatever the declared motive, Mexico's first response is usually to refuse first—or sidestep—and ask questions later, even if the matter might deserve consideration.[59]

Power even affects attempts to obtain accurate news and information. Few Mexicans believe their national press even when it tells the truth—except when it alleges "misdeeds" committed by the United States. But because of the power imbalance, fewer still disbelieve the North American press, even when it does not tell the truth.[60]

Many countries fear what has been the United States' cultural imperialism. Just as the United States cannot keep out immigrants, Mexico cannot keep out North American middle-class influences—the consumption of blue jeans, fast food, television, and music. The border is permeable in both directions at all levels. Pastor and Castañeda comment that the positive aspects of North American culture such as its democratizing, youthful, and irreverent influence can be good for Mexico in some ways, but negative aspects such as blandness, disrespect for "Culture" in the strong European sense, and the lack of a sense of history butt up against Mexico's strong traits. Mexico possesses an extraordinarily rich and diversified cultural personality that is well anchored in its history.[61]

Intercultural communication between Mexico and the United States is negatively affected by the imbalance of power, which exacerbates the problems in communication created by differences of attitude and motivation, and by ethnocentrism and ignorance. The motivation to achieve successful intercultural communication has been asymmetrical between Mexico and the United States because of this imbalance of power. Mexicans have had more reasons to want or need to communicate with North Americans than vice-versa, but since communication is necessarily a two-way process, North Americans will need to adjust their attitudes to make more effort if they desire a more successful outcome in arriving at acceptable shared meaning.

SOCIAL ORGANIZATION

Individualism versus Collectivism

The difference in individualistic versus collective cultures is a significant cause of intercultural communication misunderstanding. Fundamentally, Mexico is a collective culture and the United States is an individualistic culture.

North American families teach their children to be independent, to take initiative, and to compete on a one-to-one basis. They learn to cope actively with the events of life. Mexican parents stress obedience, a respect for elders and superiors, and emotional dependence on the family. This approach leads to a more passive coping style for life events. North Americans value individual opinions and behavior, as long as it does not infringe on the rights of others. Mexicans focus on the relational role that each person should fill in order to contribute the most to the survival, success, and happiness of the family.[62] The common good is generally perceived as more important than the rights of individuals.

Mexico is a collectivist society that is interdependently and affectively organized around the extended family. The group cooperation that holds this organization together is a strong factor in decision-making and in motivation. In comparison, North Americans tend to be self-motivated and distant in personal interaction. Their individual loyalty is often more to institutions or government than to extended family.

Mexicans are taught to behave with humility, and any individual show of arrogance, bragging, or pride is shameful. Since North American culture encourages competition and individual achievement, much normal North American behavior appears to Mexicans to be arrogance or boasting.[63]

Some think that North Americans and other nations that are primarily efficiency-oriented take some of the human element out of living, and that violence in the North American workplace is a symptom of the dehumanization of society. Some of the antidotes—such as nurturing respect and individual dignity, acknowledging employee's lives outside of work—that are prescribed for workplace violence read as if they came from the Mexican rulebook of culture.[64]

A Canadian auto-parts manufacturer in Saltillo, Mexico, has gone a long way toward reconciling cultural differences in communication in the workplace, through understanding and adapting to Mexico's unique work culture, combined with culturally sensitive training. The result is that the director general of the company describes his Mexican employees as diligent, loyal, creative, proud of their work, and extraordinarily cooperative.[65]

Family

The strength and stability of Mexico lie in its ordinary people who preserve family and community traditions and who aspire to more spiritually than they do materially,[66] although consumerism is prevalent in the country's higher socioeconomic levels. Society in Mexico is patriarchal, and Mexicans view society in the United States as more nearly matriarchal. Mexicans feel that children have more respect for their parents in Mexico, and that North American parents dedicate themselves to their own careers and encourage their children to move away early to live independently in separate apartments.[67]

News correspondent Alan Riding explains that society is organized around the family in Mexico rather than around the government, which cannot be relied on to provide much or any assistance to a vast majority of the people. Over 90 percent of Mexicans still live in a nuclear family and are united by adherence to the tribal rules of each extended family. The godparents, the *padrino* and the *madrina,* are key figures in the extended family. Families are enormously self-sufficient, providing the whole gamut of human social interaction, so that outsiders are intruders and distrusted; to be invited into a Mexican home is a special honor. Behind cautious ceremonial behavior, Mexicans are human and warm. The family is the safe haven where unquestioning loyalty is guaranteed.[68]

One practical difference that presents an obstacle to successful intercultural communication is that loyalty in Mexico lies primarily with the extended family, whereas loyalty in the United States for many has shifted from the extended family toward institutions such as an employer.

Riding further points out that the economic role the family plays is central to society in Mexico. Domestic servants arrange to have their relatives hired, so that families have families working for them; in a small factory most employees will be related; in offices cousins and relatives have the best chances of employment; entire families are brought into government bureaucracy by someone with influence. Many of the largest economic groups in the country are family businesses, with numerous relatives employed. The hardship of urban life and the recent economic crises of Mexico have strengthened the family's role even further, because one has the duty to look after a relative. Relatives provide interest-free loans when a job is lost, someone makes room for more in a bedroom, another relative offers some kind of work, and there is always a place at the table. Even the government relies on the family safety net as the principal welfare system of the country.[69]

Viewed in this context, nepotism, rather than seeming corrupt, might be seen as an organized expression of the loyalty, compassion, and generosity that human beings need in order to survive in a difficult economy. Male domination of the family is perceived in Mexico as the price of maintaining traditions, morality, and security of the family structure. Thus through the family much of the good and the bad of old Mexico is perpetuated.[70]

Even so, the recent economic difficulties in Mexico are slowly contributing to change in the traditional family structure. As more women enter or are forced into the workplace, traditional male dominance is being eroded.

Gender Roles

Culture dictates gender roles, which are of great significance in any society, and therefore it is significant when these roles differ between cultures. Gender roles affect the organization of society in the United States and Mexico. It is impossible to interact cross-culturally—even if the interaction is between same sexes—without the effects, positive or negative, caused by the difference of roles of men and women in Mexico and the United States.

Mexico practices its own form of machismo. Riding in *Distant Neighbors* writes that the Spaniard's defense of honor becomes the Mexican's defense of his masculinity. The concept of women involves the Madonna-whore syndrome that is a common theme in literature and cultures that have roots on the Iberian Peninsula. In Mexico men worship the female ideal, exemplified by Mexico's pure Virgin of Guadalupe and personified by the mother. The wife can be associated with the Amerindian historical figure La Malinche— as an object of sex the wife departs from feminine perfection; she is also capable of betrayal, just as La Malinche is characterized by some as having betrayed the Aztecs. If a man demonstrates faithfulness or excessive affection to his wife, it implies vulnerability or weakness. Mistresses provide the man the opportunity to conquer, and to betray in anticipation of any Malinche-like betrayal. The wife translates her resentment into smothering love for her son, who completes the cycle by elevating her to the female ideal, but the son will relate to his wife as his father related to his.[71] The standard for extramarital relationships is double: expected for men, but not acceptable for women.

Acclaimed Mexican novelist Carlos Fuentes, in an opinion piece in the Mexico City newspaper *Reforma,* wondered who would topple a Latin American president for extramarital indiscretions. He wrote that Mexico's macho tradition tends to admire philandering presidents, and he termed the controversy about President Clinton's sexual forays "trivial," pointing out how wife, mistress, and assorted children attended the funeral of France's François Mitterand.[72] There are, of course, differences of opinion. At least one Mexican businessman living in the United States lamented what he perceived in the Clinton scandal a threat to the equal application of the law. He states that this equal application is what he most admires in the United States and is missing the most in Mexico.

Tension and distrust often mark the male-female relationship in Mexico, therefore—like men—women spend most of their time with their same sex. For women, contact with men is too complicated to be casual.[73] Women are assigned the role of mothers and homemakers, and most suffer social and family pressure when they decide to seek careers. Representative of traditional attitudes, in her autobiography about her life in Mexico, Elizabeth Borton Treviño, a North American trained in journalism who married into a Mexican family in the 1950s, recounts that the worst thing that her husband could think of to say to her during a disagreement is that she wanted to be *independiente* (independent)—as if the word itself were an epithet.[74]

In 1998 in Monterrey, Mexico, an economically progressive city, one civic group that promotes good relations between Mexico and the United States still segregated men and women for regular member meetings. The men gathered in the evening at a casino to discuss group projects and socialize, and the women met separately in the afternoons in some acceptable venue. Men and women in the Monterrey chapter meet together for special social events a few times a year. The U.S. counterparts of the Mexican chapters of this organization schedule all meetings jointly for both men and women.[75] As a wife, mother, and career woman in Monterrey confided: "La mujer en México vive siempre bajo la sombra del hombre." (In Mexico a woman lives always under the shadow of a man.) Mexico is, in fact, a man's world.[76]

Women in the United States, by contrast, seem "liberated." Basave summarizes a Mexican viewpoint of U.S. women that has both positives and negatives:

> U.S. women know their intellectual, spiritual, and physical quali-
> ties; they were not willing to accept the paralytic role assigned them.
> They entered universities, factories, business, and politics. And still
> they did not renounce their key role in the home. Mothers guide,
> serve, care for, feed, and give or withhold permission to their chil-
> dren. They almost nullify the function of the father, who abandons
> his authority and behaves like the eldest son—at least that is how
> it appears to Europeans and to Latin Americans. Diet, sports, and
> their combination of European ancestors have given the U.S. woman
> optimal physical attributes. Young women have much more freedom
> than in Mexico, and the Puritan ethic no longer controls the chastity
> of single females. The use of contraceptives, female emancipation,
> hasty marriages, and a high divorce rate are the order of the day.[77]

Young women in Mexico who went to work in the 1950s and 1960s for North American companies were to contribute to a move toward social emancipation for women. They came primarily from affluent families and worked in order to gain a measure of personal freedom. By 1994 there were women on the presidential election committees of Ernesto Zedillo, and a woman became head of the male-dominated PRI. The 1990s saw women in government in Mexico at the state and national levels, which was unheard of not long before.[78] In fact, by 1998, 17 percent of the seats in Mexico's Congress were held by women, compared to 11 percent in the United States Congress.

The biggest change may be taking place because of recent economic conditions in Mexico. In order for families to survive, more women have entered the work place during the past ten to fifteen years than ever before, and at many socioeconomic levels. At the blue-collar level, a quiet revolution is spreading from the border maquiladoras into Mexico. Factory work formerly defamed "decent" women in Mexico, but today women who work in factories, even in unsatisfactory conditions, are fueling a grass-roots shift that grants them an unusual degree of domestic clout and social freedom.[79] Certainly in many families at lower socioeconomic levels, women are becoming more independent because their income allows the family to eat, and they will no longer tolerate an authoritarian, abusive, or drunken husband. Traditional machismo is slowly being diluted.

Because of cultural differences, North Americans should take great care to relate "properly" to the sexes in Mexico. If a male guest for dinner at a Mexican home wishes to send flowers, it is important that he send them not to the hostess (the wife), but rather address them to the family.[80] On one occasion, a Mexican male acquaintance was to send a North American businesswoman some information about business that had come up incidentally in conversation in a social setting. He addressed the letter to both the businesswoman and her husband, and the letter was sent using both his name and his wife's (whom the North American businesswoman had never met). In the context of Mexican culture, his communication properly indicated respect and impeccable manners, with no possible hint of impropriety. In U.S. culture the circumstances would not have dictated the same degree of circumspection.

Despite recent changes in prescribed gender roles in Mexico, deeply ingrained cultural differences cause considerable difficulty for a woman from the United States who attempts to work or relate on her own to Mexicans. Because of these differences, U.S. women seeking to do business in Mexico will benefit from cultural awareness. If a woman wishes to invite a man to a meal, she should invite him to lunch and not go to dinner alone with him. One solution might be to schedule lunch at her hotel and to arrange in advance to have the charges added to her bill, both to avoid embarrassing her guest and to be able to pay. However, Adriana, a bilingual, bicultural attorney who works in the United States and Mexico, states that many Mexican men cannot and will not accept a woman's paying for anything. They consider it an insult to their manhood.

Adriana finds it very difficult to attend social functions at business conferences in Mexico. Even lunchtime entertainment may have sexual overtones. At one 1998 cross-border business conference, the scheduled luncheon included a Las Vegas style female dancer who sat on men's laps and accepted the placement of bills in her scanty attire.

Even so, Adriana finds that Mexican men are much less likely than North Americans to interpret friendliness as a sexual invitation if the woman is not being overtly suggestive. And although many Mexican men stereotype North American women as "loose" and fair game, she states that Mexican men are usually much less likely to try to force themselves on a woman or make overt sexual advances than are North American men.

Latin Americans, including Mexicans, generally believe that men cannot control their sexual drives and that women cannot resist them. In short, they believe that if there is any opportunity for a sexual relationship, it will occur. Appearances are very important. This is partly because of perceived gender roles, but may also be because the United States is a low-context culture and North Americans tend to "protect" themselves in this regard with invisible internal rules rather than through apparent external controls. Mexico's high-context culture imposes more rules externally by context, as evidenced by the chaperone system. The high-context culture of Mexico also requires adherence to more rigid gender roles, and a woman is judged to be either decent or not by how she adheres to certain norms of behavior. If she is considered decent, then strict rules of respect apply. Some of the cross-cultural difficulties lie in the fact that behavior that is acceptable for women in North American culture is not acceptable in Mexico and is therefore misinterpreted. A Mexican woman can dress provocatively and project "hot" sensuality in protected situations and run no risk.

OUTLOOK ON LIFE

Religion

Mexico is a predominantly Catholic country. The Bishop's Conference claims that 92 percent of Mexicans have been baptized into the Catholic Church. Church and State are separated, and in Mexico only civil weddings are legally valid. Most couples (over 70 percent) also marry in church,[81] so two marriage ceremonies usually take place as a consequence. Most often, the civil service is held first, and couples only consider themselves married after the church ceremony.

In many areas Amerindian beliefs and superstitions color the traditions, ceremonies, and tenets of Catholicism. Mexico's patron saint, the Virgin of Guadalupe, is representative of this acculturation.

The United States is primarily Protestant but it is one of the world's countries with the greatest number of different religious sects. Basave writes that Puritanism is a cultural phenomenon of the United States and that although the colonizers left England to find religious tolerance, they became intolerant rulers of a theocracy, dictating what one should eat, wear, believe, and do, and how one was permitted to enjoy life. They were more preoccupied with damnation than salvation.[82]

North Americans believe that religion is a personal and private matter, whereas a Mexican—even one who is not overly devout—typically shows his religion everywhere and in everything. Secularization continues to grow in the United States, and the people argue about such issues as government support for parochial schools and prayer in school. Even so, Basave points out that one should not forget that the preamble to the U.S. Constitution expressly refers to God and even coins of Federal issue are stamped "In God We Trust."[83] Because of the uniformity of religion in their country, Mexicans do not grapple with the same religious versus government issues. Most of the world does not share the United States' preference for separation of church and state.[84]

Fatalism and Free Will

Mexican fatalism, a product of both Hispanic and Amerindian cultures, sees the human condition as a product of destiny. North American culture believes strongly that an individual can control his or her destiny and the destiny of society at large.[85] Writer Basave feels that the North American belief in free will stems from the open frontier where there was always room for hope. The great space of the continent engendered a belief that one could always make one's fortune and that "big" and quantity are important. He writes that North Americans seem driven by the hope of doing better, they are always on the move, and they are always ready to attempt yet another summit; since they therefore always feel transitory, they give the means the value of the end. Their preoccupation with the "technique" leads them to believe that good methods will always produce good results.[86] One viewpoint is that North Americans have an epic sense of life, and the security they typically feel expresses itself in philosophical pragmatism.[87]

Stoic acceptance and Catholic resignation to invasion, territorial mutilation, and poverty as adverse historical destiny are primary characteristics of the Mexican.[88] Disasters are not major disappointments because they are considered unavoidable.[89] "Ni modo" ("no way" or "tough luck") is a traditional response to failure or accident and means that the setback was destined. Mexicans are reluctant to convey bad news, whether it be about production delays in business or other disappointing information.[90] Perhaps bad news is seen as an omen that more adversity is destined to come.

Elizabeth Borton Treviño wrote that study of Mexico's Amerindians, cataloging of handcrafts and music, and research into language and history cannot give a true picture of the soul of the Mexican people. She felt that insight might be gained by understanding the deeply proud and valiant mysticism of one man, Don Eleazar, a cultured lawyer in his sixties who was diagnosed with terminal cancer. He gave strict orders that he not be given opiates. He did not want his senses or his consciousness dulled. A devoted Catholic, he said that God had been lavish with his gifts and that he was being permitted to share in some small measure in Christ's pain. On one occasion Elizabeth had told her Mexican mother-in-law that she would kill herself rather than suffer some incurable disease. She was told "no, you will accept your debts to life when and as God sends them, and you will pay them every one." [91]

Death

Basave's description of how death is handled in the United States illustrates some of its cultural differences with Mexico. He states that in the United States friends and family do not observe a mourning period. Individuals do not die. They "pass away" and are referred to abstractly as "a loved one." The cadavers are cleaned, arranged—and then make-up is applied so that they probably look healthier than when they were living. Well-known Forest Lawn in California has tried to create the happiest and most luxurious cemetery in the world, negating and hiding death. It displays a sculpture group named "the mystery of *life* [author's emphasis]," and endeavors to set aside what is essentially the tragic nature of the death of a human being.[92] What counts in the United States are pep, youth, and present energy; people fear maturity, and they fear old age even more. The subject of death is hardly ever mentioned.[93]

Although Halloween is being imported commercially into Mexico from the United States, the traditional celebration predominates and the Day of the Dead is celebrated on November second. People flock to the cemeteries carrying flowers, and even food and drink, to the graves of their ancestors, in the manner of the ancient Aztecs. Many families even set out a table of refreshments in the home the night before, so that the spirits of the dead can visit (much like children in the United States set out treats for Santa Claus on Christmas Eve). People chat with the dead, and belief in this communion is widespread, not in the sense of psychic contact or because of belief in a Christian afterlife, but rather because the past in Mexico is a part of the living present.[94]

One U.S. newspaper article reported that "Mexico displays its dead in a way that might be considered macabre in other countries." In 1998 the skull of Miguel Hidalgo, a Mexican independence hero, was put on display in a glass case in a crypt in Mexico City. The lower jaw has fallen from the cranium, but the skull has "been through a lot": during Mexico's 1810–1821 war for independence, the Spanish publicly displayed Hidalgo's severed head hanging in a cage. Mexico displays the bodies of its heroes—or what is left of them—perhaps more than any other country. The skulls of three other founding fathers lie next to Hidalgo's on a red velvet cushion. This somber display inspired awe and respect in the schoolchildren who came to its opening. Twelve-year-old Jorge Paz Pérez, a soft-spoken and serious boy, commented, "These are the bodies of our heroes."[95]

Values

Basave remarks that in the United States, a person is said to be worth "so many dollars" ("he must be worth three million"). A person is worth a lot if they are capable of earning a lot of money, but it is the ability to earn that is admired more than the money. Money is the means to acquire things, not the end,[96] but the focus for most people in the United States is more material than spiritual.

The Protestant work ethic, as articulated by German economist Max Weber, sees virtue in people through their actions and their work. Mexicans see North Americans as living to work and as being overly materialistic, but for North Americans this learned, work-oriented behavior is the source of pride and self-respect. North Americans stereotype Mexicans as lazy, untrustworthy, and lacking in that measure which is most important to a culture that emphasizes a work ethic: material development.[97]

An attorney who works in Mexico and the United States points out that a common complaint in business and negotiations is that North Americans perceive Mexicans as theorizers or talkers, whereas North Americans value doing and implementing. They feel that Mexicans will talk an issue "to death" and not move a step toward its resolution.

Basave feels that some people in Mexico confuse their country's spirituality with disdain for material progress, and this confusion generates their myth of U.S. materialism.[98] He explains that Mexicans value the spiritual maturity that comes from striving in the areas of religion, art, and culture, although they do not disdain economic endeavors.[99]

There has been a traditionally graceful element in the lives of many urban Mexicans that is not dependent upon economic affluence. It includes music, singing, dancing, poetry, philosophical discussions, and animated conversation. Many poor Mexicans find emotional, intellectual, and spiritual satisfaction in these activities. Mexicans are interested in such pursuits, a trait that North Americans and other concretely progressive people find economically counterproductive.[100] Today, for example, in the city of Mérida, Yucatan, as in many Mexican cities, events are frequently staged in town squares. Families of men, women, children, teenagers, and courting couples—people from young to old—the well educated and the less educated, all gather to enjoy performances that include singing, folk dances, and the recitation of poetry. It is difficult to imagine the recitation of poetry commanding the same interest and attention from such a general audience in a United States park. There is also the custom of the *tertulia,* which is a gathering to exercise the intellect through the discussion of philosophy, politics, literature, and other topics. In Austin, Texas, a group of expatriate Mexicans and other Latin expatriates gather monthly to perpetuate this tradition.

Basave writes that the average North American equates international progress with the universal diffusion of their material "American way." He finds this conviction naive but not really materialistic, pointing out that no country has less national selfishness in helping other countries. The common person in a state like Iowa or Missouri, for example, will spread the word and generously collect money or goods to send to another country that has suffered a disaster. He asserts that anyone who knows the United States, if they look without prejudice, can observe that the people are generous, of goodwill, and manifest a feeling of human solidarity. Selfishness is shameful for the average North American.[101]

The cultural perceptions of well-being for the comfortable classes in Mexico and the United States differ significantly. In general, Mexican cul-

ture requires fulfillment of more nonmaterial needs for people to feel satisfied with life.

Mexicans recognize that North American industry is the most polished
example of scientific technology in the modern world but feel that it has
greatly developed the *homo faber* at the expense of the *homo sapiens;* that
is, the producer and consumer of goods rather than the creator and enjoyer
of ideas. They feel that U.S. education, as a product of its culture, produces
technically competent but culturally shallow individuals. For these Mexicans, the typical North American has a technical vision of reality and inter-
prets the world in a commercial and economic sense that distorts both the
reality of life and of death. They view efficiency as the despot of the American way of life and see North Americans as philosophical pragmatists. Ideas
function in life as a plan of action and are measured by their success when
the plan is implemented.[102]

Basave writes that Mexico has an excess of *literati* and a lack of specialists; in the United States there is an excess of specialists and a lack of well-
rounded humanists. Mexico's social organization may seem lacking to
North Americans, but the culture of the United States seems uncouth, poor,
and primitive to Mexicans. He states that it is time that the two peoples
learn to know each other well in order to move beyond their mutual disdain
and to achieve cooperation as good neighbors.[103]

Mexicans take care of the emotional and spiritual side of life through
powerful religiosity, ceremonious behavior, and formality of language; the
mechanical efficiency, punctuality, and organization of United States society
seem purposeless to them. The identity of Mexicans is what they are rather
than what they do, the person rather than the job. Mexicans do not live to
work, they work to live.[104]

The North American value system assumes three interrelated premises
about human beings: (1) that people are basically the same, except for social and educational influences, (2) that each person should be judged on individual merits, and (3) that these "merits"—including a person's worth
and character—are revealed through a person's actions. Because a person's
actions are considered to be important, the chief means of judging and
knowing a person is through comparison of accomplishments. In Mexico
the uniqueness of the individual is valued, but this uniqueness is seen to re-
side within each person and not to be necessarily evidenced through actions
or achievements. The worth of an individual is closer to the concept of soul
than it is to character. The inner dignity of the individual must be protected
at all costs, and any communication through words or deed that is inter-

preted as a slight to the person's dignity is a grave provocation. Since most often a Mexican is first part of a family, and secondarily a member of an organization or profession, a slight to any family member will be as provocative as a direct insult. When a Mexican refers to a person's inner quality as the soul or spirit (*alma* or *espíritu*) of the individual, North Americans tend to regard that reference as vague or sentimental and to feel uncomfortable discussing what they consider a private or religious matter. They will avoid or change the subject, which confirms to Mexicans that North Americans are insensitive and not interested in the individual.[105]

Mexico traditionally has not had the same concern for speed and efficiency in mass production as has the United States. This is a product of a culture that *values* a slower-paced, more humanistic approach to life.

Thought Patterns

In arriving at truth (and making decisions), the collectivist, affective Mexican will be more in touch with emotions, feelings, and experience, while the North American will tend to evaluate and decide in a more detached, abstract, and pragmatic manner. The learned organization of rules that is manifested in living patterns differs in the two countries, and this difference affects choice-making and conflict resolution in the two cultures.

Mexico is a high-context culture, where people tend to learn more by rote, demonstration, guidance, and doing; Mexicans are, in general, associative rather than abstract thinkers.[106] The low-context culture of the United States focuses more on abstractions and problem solving when processing new information than does Mexico's high-context culture. This contrast again illustrates cultural relativity, because the French feel that North Americans are too little interested in theory and abstraction and too concerned with application. The attempt to share meaning between Mexicans and North Americans can be frustrated because each communicator tends to present information in his or her own opposing style.

Work, Leisure, and Worldview

The orientation toward God, life, and death differs substantially between the two nations. The sense of fatalism in Mexico contrasts sharply with the North American's pioneering, epic belief that one controls one's future and that there is, figuratively, always a new frontier. Perhaps the most basic difference between Mexicans and North Americans is that North Americans are conditioned to emphasize strength, power, doing, and achieving, while Mexicans focus on being, thought, and human relations.[107]

One writer thinks that television is becoming the most powerful cultural influence in Mexico, and is changing Mexicans' world view—the way they think and behave. It is contributing greatly to the emancipation of women from traditional cultural bonds. It also causes anger and aggressive action among the poor, because it exposes them to the concept of other lifestyles.[108]

In the United States activity and competence are everything. The Spanish word *negocio* translates as "business," and *ocio* translates as "leisure." *Neg-ocio* (the root for the English word negotiate) negates *ocio*: the root meaning is that business negates leisure. Basave writes that in the United States business comes first and leisure comes afterward—if it comes at all. The tautological phrase "business is business" is eloquent in and of itself. From Basave's viewpoint, Mexico's agrarian structure and poorly developed industry make the country economically underdeveloped, but North Americans should guard against doing nothing but work. He argues that to lose the fruits of fertile leisure impoverishes mankind spiritually, even though the United States reaps the material rewards of its work ethic.[109]

Clearly, in many respects Mexicans and North Americans perceive their worlds differently, and this difference in perceptions can impede communication with each other. However, people live their daily lives not only thinking and perceiving, but also engaged in personal interaction. There are additional significant cultural differences that surface through the personal interaction process that contribute to the difficulties of United States–Mexico communication.

SEVEN

Some Mexico—United States Cultural Issues

The causes of friction in communication between two cultures lie not in the shortcomings of either culture but rather in their interaction.[1]

Ana and Blanca Estela drove to a meeting of the Tertulia Literaria held monthly by a group of expatriate Latins in the United States. Participants in the literary discussion group would take turns as hosts, and a Mexican couple was hosting the gathering at the new home into which they had recently moved. It was the first time the group would meet at this address. The location of the house was some distance from the area in which the two women lived, so they allowed enough time to get there and find it. They looked forward to seeing the new house, to lively discussion with friends, and to good food. They wondered who and how many would be able to attend. The group was to meet at 7:00 P.M. Traffic was not bad, and Ana found the address without much difficulty, so they made good time. Ana pulled up and stopped in front of the house. Looking at her watch, Blanca Estela commented to Ana that it was three minutes to seven. The two women looked at each other with dismay; there were no other cars in front of the house. Ana put the car in gear and drove away.

The Tertulia Literaria group has made some concessions to living in a North American city—7:00 P.M. is an early meeting time for Latins, and discussion participants endeavor to be more or less prompt. Even so, Blanca Estela commented to Ana as the pair drove away that the worst *gaffe* that one can make is to arrive early at a Mexican home. Ana drove around the block to the next street, where she parked. She turned on some music on the car radio, and she and Blanca Estela talked for a while about the book that would be discussed that evening. Some fifteen minutes later, Ana drove back to the house where the gathering was scheduled. There was now a car parked in front of the house, and they recognized two other cars just pulling up. With relief Ana turned off the motor and she and Blanca Estela got out, now ready to approach the home.

The Tertulia Literaria is a literary discussion group that was formed in a Texas city and is composed primarily of expatriate Latin participants ("members" implies a greater degree of formality than actually exists). Because of the city's proximity to Mexico, approximately half of the participants are Mexicans. In the same city, there is an anglophone Book Club, where English is spoken. Blanca Estela is bilingual and frequents both groups. The Tertulia group read and discuss books in Spanish. The Book Club members read and discuss books in English. The Tertulia group for years set their next meeting by consensus each time they gathered, meeting approximately once a month on whatever date was selected, except for the months that they decided not to meet. More recently, Tertulia participants agreed that they would meet on the last Wednesday of every month so that participants could reserve and count on that date. However, by consensus, participants change the fixed day of the meeting as often as they keep it. Almost any participant can veto a proposed date if he or she is not available and wants to attend, and the group endeavors to accommodate all. If there is difficulty selecting a date good for everyone, sometimes there is a show of hands to indicate preference, and participants defer to the best date for the greatest number. Friends sometimes invite friends to visit or to participate regularly in the group.

The Book Club meets on the first Tuesday of every month except December. To select books, the Book Club members have an annual planning meeting in August. At that meeting they select all the books that they will read during the coming year. Members agree on the titles by vote. Tertulia participants propose titles of books by authors from different Spanish-speaking countries as they go along, and they choose books by general indication of interest or informal agreement. Participants usually select two or three titles at a time and agree on the order in which they will read them as they go along.

The Tertulia is influenced by its location in the United States, and many Tertulia participants go to work on a North American time schedule the next morning. Participants make an effort to maintain North American punctuality, but although the meeting starts out fairly early with socializing "at 7:00," people straggle in over the next hour. Discussion of the book usually begins around 8:00 P.M., and ends sometime around 9:00. Everyone brings food to share, and they bring whatever inspires them. Participants have dinner around 9:00. There is a group leader who has emerged over time and who takes responsibility for coordinating the meetings and discussions. However, different people lead the discussions of a specific author or work at different meetings. This is sometimes agreed on beforehand and sometimes occurs by circumstance. The members are well educated, articulate, and insightful in their comments. Both men and women participate in the Tertulia, and they usually sit comfortably in a family room or living room, with assorted chairs added in a circular pattern. People enthusiastically jump into the discussion with comments. Aside from the Mexican custom of eating meals later than in the United States, an important reason for eating dinner after the discussion has been explicitly stated: If you allow Latins to start eating and conversing with each other, you cannot stop the activity in which they are involved to get them to organize into the different activity of a "discussion group"—they would never get to the discussion of the book. The group is spontaneous and informal in its structure and activities. Participants are never sure who will attend each gathering.

The Book Club starts at 6:30 P.M., and members arrive promptly. Members are expected to report to the group if they cannot attend. The host home and the person to report on the book for each month are assigned at the yearly meeting. A schedule is mailed for the year, listing in columns the venue, the book, and the person to report. On arrival at a Book Club meeting, people greet each other and chat for a short time. Everyone brings a dish to share, with the food coordinated so that people bring dishes in the different categories of main dishes, salads, and desserts. People start eating dinner by 7:00. Standing at the front of and facing the group, the president initiates the meeting at approximately 7:30. The discussion lasts until 8:30 or 9:00. For decisions there is discussion, a vote, and the majority rules. Members sit comfortably in available living room or family room chairs. Extra chairs are added in straight rows. To speak, members will raise a hand to signal their desire to take a turn. The members are well educated, articulate, and insightful in their comments. The club members are all female, but spouses are included at a special holiday gathering. The group is formally and efficiently organized. Membership is by invitation and limited to twenty-five persons. Any prospective members are discussed at the yearly meeting to determine their compatibility with the group.

Both book discussion groups comprise people who know, enjoy, and respect each other, and are courteous and hospitable. The content of the discussions in both groups is informative and interesting, but the ambience and experience of attending the two groups are very different. A North American might well be frustrated by the lack of formal structure, the informal measure of time, and the spontaneous multiple activities of the Latin Tertulia. A Mexican would not expect the formalized structure of the Book Club. One year, a Latin expatriate who had "joined" the Book Club was very courteously uninvited by letter as a member because she missed meetings without notifying the group and seemed to lack awareness of the importance of the group's schedule and structure. The club members interpreted this as a lack of interest.

Many cultural factors give rise to obstacles in communication between the United States and Mexico. Interaction as affected by the nonverbal processes of chronemics, context, kinesics, and proxemics frequently impede communication, and ethnocentrism and preconceptions filter perceptions differently.

CHRONEMICS

The frequent difficulties that arise in communication between monochronic and polychronic cultures typically provoke emotional reactions that range in intensity from irritation to anger. Therefore time, not surprisingly, is a major factor that causes misunderstanding between Mexicans and North Americans, because Mexico is a polychronic culture and the United States is predominantly monochronic. Although Mexicans react negatively to some North American chronemic cultural traits, Mexico's polychronic culture seems to pose a greater number of problems for North Americans. North Americans view Mexico's informal "*mañana* syndrome" as a symptom of chronic inefficiency or laziness, but Riding points out that it is rather evidence of an entirely different philosophy of time.[2] Because people in the two cultures are conditioned differently, their respective perceptions, measures, and uses of time are quite different. One observer commented that the tyranny of the clock is terrible in the United States, where technology has created a "chronocracy."[3]

Logic does not necessarily apply to time in Mexico, and a maid may leave the day before payday just for *ganas* (she felt like it). Absenteeism after a weekend is so common that it gives rise to a saying that implies a holiday: "St. Monday."[4] So many workers will take off what they call *el puente*—

the day that bridges a holiday and a weekend—that it can close down a plant. Consequently, many companies that have formed United States–Mexico joint ventures create their own new corporate culture with bits and pieces from each side. At Vitro-Whirlpool in Monterrey, when a holiday like Mother's day, for example, falls on a Tuesday, the company will permit workers to take Monday off, but only if they work an extra hour each day for eight days beforehand.[5]

Time Value

Basave states that North Americans are always in a hurry and say that time is money, while Mexicans live at a slower pace and pay attention to the moment. He feels that the saying that "tomorrow is another day" is not so far from "give us this day our daily bread."[6]

Basave explains that in Mexico, temporality exists in human beings and cannot be separated from them without destroying it, so that for Mexicans to live for time is to live for nothing. He states that if one recognizes death, then time in our lives should be seen as opportunity and not as money.[7] Riding explains that cultures that see birth as a beginning and death as an end do not connect with a living past. Future time in Mexico is seen with fatalism as being predestined, so there is no reason to force oneself into a routine, and in business, large, fast, personal profits are preferred to long-term institutional or business expansion plans.[8] North Americans see themselves as long-range planners by comparison.

Simultaneous Activities

Mexico is a polychronic culture where people engage in many activities simultaneously, while by comparison the United States is a more monochronic, linear culture where people tend to focus on a single activity at a time when interacting and communicating. Elizabeth Borton Treviño, in *My Heart Lies South,* wrote that she considered herself a master of Spanish. But on moving to Mexico, she observed that she had not counted on the fact that in a group, everyone talks all at the same time and loudly,[9] which made it very difficult for her to understand and follow conversations. In the United States, people usually prefer to "take turns" when speaking.

In a historical novel published in 1997, Mexico's popular author Ángeles Mastretta writes,

When she was asked how she could carry on two conversations at once, Emily replied that such a practice was genetic to all the women in her family. And that some, like her aunt Milagros, were capable of following up to four. It probably was because of the country in which they lived, because in Mexico so many things happened at the same time that if you did not follow several things at once, you always ended up lagging behind what was really going on.[10]

What appears to be the chaos of simultaneous multiple activities engendered by Mexico's polychronic interpersonal communication style is an obstacle that is primarily monodirectional. It poses more problems to North Americans than the North American monochronic communication style poses to Mexicans.

Measuring Time by Activity and Ritual

Understanding the differences in the cultural measure of time is an important factor in communication between the United States and Mexico. In Mexico, the informal measure of time more often prevails over formal time, and activities, rather than the measurement of time by the abstract symbols on a clock, dictate how time is used. Treviño writes that Mexicans live not by the abstract dates on a calendar, but by the liturgical year. She describes life as progressing by the feasts and rituals (the *activities*) that mark time's progress, the year going from Advent and Nativity to Lent and the Passion and the Pentecosts.[11]

In Mexico, nothing that is being enjoyed now is worth cutting short in order to do something else.[12] If discussions at hand are not finished, Mexicans consider it senseless to terminate a meeting because time as abstractly measured by the clock is up, nor are meetings strictly scheduled as to order and content.

Many North Americans find it difficult to understand or tolerate the unstructured measurement of time by activity rather than by the abstract and more exact measure of the clock.

Establishing Relationships

Another important characteristic of polychronic cultures is that personal relationships are paramount, and such relationships take time to establish. The United States' monochronic approach to time makes North Americans appear to Mexicans to be too blunt (too quick to get to the point) and to be discourteous in the lack of time spent on personal courtesies.

A Mexican woman living in and acculturated to the United States commented on a common experience when telephoning North Americans whom she knows. She will call and identify herself with, "Hello, this is Victoria. . . ." As she opens her mouth to inquire about the well-being of the other person and engage in some amount of personal conversation, the person will often answer with "Oh, hi. It's nice to hear from you. How can I help you?" Victoria says that although she knows the response is meant to be hospitable, she cannot help feeling offended in some small measure. It seems to her as if she is bothering the person she calls, who wants to dispense with any personal conversation to get to the point, in order to quickly move on to something else. She misses the personal interaction that is Mexican protocol, while the North American may genuinely want to indicate his or her availability to be of assistance and may not want or be accustomed to as much personal interaction.

In the Corning-Vitro venture, the Mexicans often thought the North Americans moved too quickly, while the North Americans thought that the Mexicans moved too slowly.[13] The culture of Mexico is more people-oriented than it is task-oriented.[14] Foreign business executives transferred to Mexico should make sure to establish close personal relationships with their top Mexican managers from the beginning. They need to find out about their families and backgrounds, treat them with formal courtesy on the job, and spend time having informal talks away from the office over drinks or meals. Special effort must be made to keep them in the circle of communication. Consideration must also be given to personal events, such as weddings, illness, and deaths in the family.[15]

Hernán García-Corral, an attorney from Monterrey, Mexico, who has lived in the United States, emphasizes the importance of establishing personal relationships before trying to transact business with Mexicans. You have to go to Mexico and call on people in person. To send a brochure and financial statement as an introduction is not just ineffective, it is insulting. "You need to make the personal relationship first."[16] Horace Scherer, director general of Hobart Day Mexicana, the Mexican subsidiary of the Hobart Corporation, points out that his salespeople often must make four trips to complete one transaction. The same single transaction might well be concluded with one visit in the United States. While executives in Mexico can expect the unquestioned loyalty of employees, they tend to view outsiders with distrust,[17] so Hobart's salespeople have to take time to establish a relationship before attempting to do business. Contrary to North American sales training where one is told to keep on asking for the order, in Mexico it is important to bide your time and be patient.[18]

North Americans can also forget what they know about the real estate brokerage business. A broker based in Mexico City says that connections are everything. Who you know is who you are. He sees two entrees into Mexican business, personal contacts or major capital investment ability,[19] although clearly Corning's capital resources did not save the failed Corning-Vitro venture from its cross-cultural communication problems. If, in Mexico, you are who you know in business relations, then it would be wise to take the time necessary to get to know the right people.

At many meetings, a businessperson needs to be able to communicate on issues that are small talk and personal in order to establish relationships before discussing business. Mexican attorney García-Corral also tells U.S. businesspeople to keep lawyers out of negotiations until a verbal agreement is reached. That is the "time" to put the agreement in writing.[20]

Scheduling and Punctuality

Events are scheduled differently in the United States and in Mexico. In Mexico, activities usually take place later in the day than is customary in the United States. Labón's etiquette book states that the usual time for dinner in Mexico is no later than 10:00 P.M., and formal dinners should not start after 11:00 P.M.[21] In the United States the comparable range would be as early as 6:00 P.M. and not later than 8:00 P.M.

Baldrige summarizes U.S. business etiquette by stating that the polite meeting chairman schedules meetings knowing that most people are fresh in the morning, distributes the agenda well in advance, and keeps one eye on the clock and one on the agenda to keep the meeting strictly on schedule.[22] This is diametrically opposed to Mexican protocol. Mexicans schedule meetings later in the day and do not strictly limit them as to time or as to the subjects that can be discussed. It is a wonder that North Americans and Mexicans communicate as well as they do.

Because of a different perspective of time, and because of different cultural habits, simple things like scheduling meetings between Mexicans and North Americans become ballets of clashing customs. Mexicans, with their long lunches, typically have a longer workday, starting at 9:00 A.M. and lasting to 9:00 P.M. Government officials often keep an even later schedule, starting around 10:00 A.M. and finishing up at 11:00 P.M. While North Americans often eat lunch at their desks, in Mexico City bankers go out for hours, for leisurely meals. The solution for Banc One of Columbus, Ohio, hired to assist Mexico's Bancomer in setting up a credit card operation, was to have full lunches in the company dining rooms.[23]

In Mexico, the morning hours before work are family time. There is a great deal of interaction with children before school, which often does not start until 9:00 A.M. Then most parents prefer to take their children to school themselves. There is also family interaction in the late evening, and weekends are "sacred" family time. In the United States, school starts much earlier, as does work for most parents, which makes morning hours more rushed. In winter, many U.S. families leave for school and for work in the dark. A typical U.S. family spends time together in the early evening and, as in Mexico, weekends are typically reserved for family activities.

Mexico's hierarchical system also affects the use of time. In business and government offices, subordinates never leave work before their boss. The person highest in rank will leave first, then the middle ranking persons, and the lower rank of secretaries will be the last to leave. In the United States departure times will usually be the opposite. It seems like the higher one's position in the United States, the longer one stays, and those holding secretarial or clerical positions are usually the first to leave, promptly at five o'clock.

The conventions of "telling time" are also different in the two countries. Arriving late for a dinner party in Mexico is polite by the informal time system—it is arriving on time that is rude. One will most likely catch the hosts in the shower or before they are dressed. If one is invited to a party at 8:00 P.M., the informal measure of time dictates that one should not arrive before 8:30 or 9:00.[24] However, Labón's Mexican etiquette book does recommend that, if the dinner is formal, then one should not be more than thirty minutes late.[25]

A Mexican who speaks in the United States on NAFTA uses the following anecdote to illustrate different time concepts. At a party North Americans leave without saying good-bye, Mexicans say good-bye but never leave, and Canadians say good-bye but then apologize for leaving. He then proceeds to explain that what one needs to understand is that for a Mexican, saying good-bye does not mean that he or she is leaving, but rather signals that the leave-taking ritual is about to begin. This may take forty-five minutes to an hour. North Americans will leave without saying good-bye, which is rude by the standards of Mexican etiquette, but they sometimes intentionally do so in order to be discreet and not break up the momentum of a party or gathering. Interestingly, the French have adopted the expression *filer à l'anglaise* (to slip out English style) for anyone who leaves without saying good-bye.

Appointments are made in Mexico knowing that they may not be kept.[26] One North American trying to speak with a Mexican official was told first that he was available only in the evening, then that he worked from 8:30 A.M. to 3:00 P.M., and then later that he no longer worked there at all. Not only does this illustrate that verbal communication in Mexico is obviously information-nonspecific, which is typical of high-context cultures, but the perception of the importance of schedules and the urgency of conducting business are radically different than in the United States.[27] These differences give rise to major problems. The U.S. perception might be that such responses are inefficient at best and lies or deliberate hostility at worst, when, in fact, they are typical behavior conveying no personal insult nor any meta-message at all about the relationship with the inquirer.

The Grupo Internacional de Austin in Texas is composed of expatriates from Mexico, Central America, South America, and Spain, and includes some North Americans both of Hispanic and other descent. Spanish is spoken at all gatherings. Because this group is so tuned in to cultural differences, they often joke among themselves, and when someone mentions the time for an event another will call out: "¿Hora mexicana o hora norteamericana?" (Mexican time or North American time?). One group newsletter announced that the group was to gather for the traditional Feast of the Magi celebration, and the time was specified as 8:00 P.M.—"puntualidad mexicana" (Mexican punctuality).[28]

Today and *Mañana*

Because of practical implications, it is not surprising that some of the communication obstacles between Mexico and the United States that exist because of a different time sense are primarily monodirectional. But times change. Despite the problems of the Salinas administration, it did set a new result-oriented tone for business. The administration included a clause in foreign investment regulations stipulating that if the Foreign Investment Commission does not officially respond to an application within forty-five days, the request is automatically granted.[29] Today, people working, visiting, and meeting with Mexicans will find many of a new generation who place greater value on efficiency than they do on rhetoric.[30]

In the end, one should maintain a sense of cultural relativity, as well as a sense of humor. As one story goes, an Arab discussing cultural differences with a Mexican friend asked about the meaning of the expression *mañana*. On hearing the explanation, he nodded in understanding and replied, "That is like the Arab *bukara,* but *bukara* does not have the same sense of urgency." [31]

Pastor and Castañeda state that North Americans are exuberant and expansive and feel impatience and frustration in dealing with Mexicans. For a more successful outcome, Pastor and Castañeda recommend that North Americans temper these traits and, instead, stress patience, tolerance, and respect. [32] It is also not helpful to criticize Mexicans for not planning for the future in the same way as North Americans. To put the difference in perspective, North Americans are often criticized for lack of planning and short-range vision by the Japanese. [33]

CONTEXT

High-Context versus Low-Context

The function of context in communication, especially in intercultural communication, is so significant and pervasive that the subject of high- versus low-context appears and reappears, woven like a thread, in and out of multiple areas of discussion and many different categories of potential obstacles to intercultural communication. The use of context to communicate often manifests itself in whether one expresses oneself directly, or whether culture dictates the use of an indirect style of expression.

Low-context communicators usually express themselves directly in words and most often intend the words they use to be taken literally—the contents of the verbal message are information-specific. High-context communicators are less direct in style and often use words in a ritual fashion. The intended message may be communicated by context, with the words of the message being information nonspecific. The greater number of, and more formalized and stylized, interaction rituals of Mexico, in contrast to more informal interaction in the United States, are sources of misunderstanding in intercultural communication.

A traditional Mexican aphorism for dealing with the United States (attributed to Benito Juárez) is "Say yes, but never say when." The United States wished to use in a display a sensitive flag that had been flown at the Alamo and asked to borrow the flag from Mexico. Mexico did not want to lend the flag and therefore responded that it was not then available to lend or to photograph. It was being restored—which would take "considerable time."[34] Any Mexican would have understood this response as a "no."

In the 1991–1994 Corning-Vitro joint venture, the Mexicans often saw North Americans as too direct, while North Americans saw impeccably polite Vitro managers as unwilling to acknowledge problems and faults.[35] Cultural clashes between the two successful companies were fatal to the business alliance, although the independent companies were able to continue to deal with each other at arm's length.

North Americans trust rules and want to trust others to obey the rules so that everyone has the same opportunities and obligations. A Mexican remarked that he was shocked to discover that in the United States a driver would stop at a red light late at night when there was no other traffic. "I used to think you had surrendered to your machines. Now I see that you are actually governed by certain abstract principles." In his opinion, "No Mexican would ever stop like that."[36] In the United States, to stop and wait at a red traffic light before going through an intersection, even late at night with no one around, is the norm. But in Mexico people more often proceed through the intersection. Why stop and wait for the light to change to green if there is no traffic? North Americans respect the abstract *symbol* that the red traffic light represents, whereas for most Mexicans the context of the traffic circumstances will override the low-context symbol. Similarly, in interpersonal communication exchanges, North Americans and Mexicans differ in their reliance on symbolic verbal expression of meaning in contrast to how meaning is conveyed by the context of nonverbal behavior. Further, Mexicans will often ignore an abstract principle in favor of a real person, so a Mexican taxi driver may pick up a friend he sees walking on the street, even while he has a paying passenger in the taxi.[37]

Tact versus Directness

In Mexico, excessive frankness or directness is considered rude; even important discussions must be preceded by small talk.[38] Mexican culture emphasizes hospitality and sympathy. If possible, one should begin to establish a relationship by talking, rather than writing; words should be chosen for their pleasant meaning and connotation. Mexicans are solicitous in their expression of concern for the other person's personal and business needs, refer to him or her by name, and often make mention of the person's city or specific business.[39] The Mexican viewpoint is that North Americans are direct, sincere, and ingenuous, and that Mexicans are refined, courteous, and spiritually elegant, with more agile minds.[40]

In Mexico, society functions through power relationships, and individual rights are determined by level of influence. Mexicans seem like actors who adapt their roles to circumstances and perform against an invisible background of latent violence; confrontation is avoided, since consequences can be dire, and conciliation becomes second nature: you're half right and I'm half right. Even in the mad traffic of Mexico City, insults are rarely exchanged, because many drivers carry weapons.[41] The cultural difference is significant to both business and personal affairs. North Americans tend to be open and frank, to tell all and to trust others to do the same. Mexicans have been conditioned to distrust, to hold back, to be reserved, and to maintain invulnerability by never revealing their true thoughts or feelings.[42]

Information-Specific versus Information-Nonspecific Verbal Content

North Americans expect that the verbal content of a message will be information-specific, but Mexicans regularly use verbal messages that are information-nonspecific. To avoid misunderstanding, the successful businessmen Reed and Gray advise North Americans working with Mexicans to communicate with the four F's: fone, fax, FedEx, and follow-up. Telephone (presuming you have already established a relationship) to personally discuss a matter with a Mexican colleague, then fax a recapitulation of your agreement and request a faxed acknowledgment. FedEx documents or materials necessary (never mail them), and follow up so that action takes place.[43]

Dealing with business contracts intertwines the communication concepts of context, tact and directness, and information specificity.

Mexican attorney García-Corral recommends to North Americans that their written contracts should be specific, because Mexicans are not as literal (information-specific) as North Americans. If, for example, payment on a certain date is important, he suggests that the agreement should explicitly provide for a penalty for payment that is even one day late, which would make the importance of the deadline clear.[44] This is, however, a delicate matter. A bicultural attorney who works in the United States and Mexico points out that North Americans consider a higher level of detail appropriate in the drafting of a contract than do Mexicans. In particular, Mexicans will sometimes take offense because North Americans want to provide in the contract for what happens if things go wrong. She feels that it is important to preface the discussion of certain issues with a statement such as "I know neither party would intentionally do X, but we need to provide for . . ." The concept of penalties in contracts in and of itself can be offensive. A North American businessperson often has to think of ways other than contractual penalties to encourage performance.

KINESICS AND PROXEMICS

Emblems or Gestures

The use of emblems (gestures) in a specific culture is a code and, like language, is a skill that needs to be acquired. The emblem code in Mexico and the United States is different. The use of emblems frequently takes place at a conscious level, and therefore a communicator is aware of not understanding, which is not as great an obstacle to communicating and relating as subconscious misinterpretation and a consequent negative reaction.

Elizabeth Borton Treviño thought she spoke good Spanish, but in Mexico, she stated, half the words are left out and replaced with gestures. She found there to be a whole lexicon of meaning for movement of shoulders, hands, wrists, eyebrows, forehead, and head.[45] And in Mexico, women have developed flirting with the eyes to a fine art.[46]

In the United States, people will hold out their hand flat, with palm down, to indicate the height of a child. To a Mexican, this indicates the height of an animal. The height of a child is demonstrated with two bobs of the hand extended out, palm up, and the index finger curled, like a small hooking motion. Visually, a Mexican understands that this gesture refers to a person. If a North American indicates a child's height using the "animal" palm down gesture, it is—fortunately—more likely to confuse than to offend. A Mexican would probably repeat that the "child is this tall?" with a palm up "person" gesture, to clarify that a child is being discussed, not an animal. The Mexican would most likely go through this clarification process without consciously thinking about it.

Other Body Communication

Kinetic expressions such as posture, stretching, hands behind the head, elbows on the table, use of fork and knife, importance of smell, and use of touch are interpreted differently in the two cultures. The attribution of meaning and its significance is asymmetrical. Kinesics are more important carriers of meaning in the high-context culture of Mexico than they are in the United States, and in intercultural communication the North American unwittingly offends the Mexican more frequently than the reverse is true. Misinterpretation often takes place at a subconscious level, causing a negative reaction. The different meaning of kinesics is a significant obstacle in communication between the two cultures.

Unlike the norm for the majority of cultures in the world, the norm for North Americans for smell as it relates to persons is basically for there to be none that is discernible. Mexicans not only want to be clean, they intentionally communicate clean by a clean smell. Perfumes are used more often and in greater quantities than in the United States (see the later discussion of Artifacts). Mexicans are not only conscious of offending through smell— as are North Americans—but actively enjoy many distinct and pleasant aromas[47] that might be considered too strong or too pungent by North Americans.

Since Mexicans are effusive and expressive, it is wise for a North American to express positive feelings, approval, and thanks in the same nonverbal ways, such as a strong and direct handshake, good eye contact when addressing a person, and a positive tone of voice.[48] In Mexico, it is customary to gesture with one's hands and arms when speaking, which is not the norm in the United States.[49] Mexicans regard people, both men and women, who control their emotions and stay dry-eyed as cold, unfeeling, and without passion—and they believe that passion is the essence of life.[50]

Bodies move to different rhythms in Mexico and the United States. North Americans use neck and head for emphasis; Mexican movement, and Latin American movement in general, involves the trunk. Mexican dance teachers comment on this difference when teaching North Americans. North American seated posture tends to slump more than that of Mexicans, and this difference can be interpreted by Mexicans as a lack of interest or alertness.[51]

Mexicans are sensitive to body language and to movements in public that they consider offensive: stretching in public is too personal and informal; tightening one's belt is not acceptable; to stand with hands on hips is a posture of challenge. Labón in her Mexican etiquette manual "forbids" putting one's hands or arms behind one's head: "Las áxilas, aún tapadas, son una parte íntima del cuerpo" (the armpit, even though covered, is an intimate part of the body).[52]

A North American can easily picture an intense meeting of business people where, upon reaching some decision or agreement, a person will sit back in his or her chair and clasp hands behind the neck, in a gesture of relief or relaxation. It is reported that one such offense ruptured a relationship in Mexico. The gesture was clearly interpreted by Mexicans as more offensive than mere informality. Mexicans may feel that the U.S. visitor is either trying to insult them or that the person is so ill mannered as to not be worth associating or doing business with.[53]

Use of Space and Touch

The different use of informal space in interpersonal encounters is an obstacle in intercultural communication. Mexicans may misinterpret North American preference for maintaining greater physical distance as carrying negatively affective and attitudinal meaning, while North Americans are uncomfortable with the physical closeness typical in Mexican interaction.

Mexicans tend to stand closer to each other when talking than do North Americans and to feel comfortable at eighteen to twenty-one inches apart (a Mexican stands farther from a person of the opposite sex than from a person of the same sex). If a North American stands or moves back to their comfort zone of up to six feet, they run the risk of appearing cold, distant, and disinterested.[54] One can sometimes observe a comical sort of dance, where one person keeps moving away, and the other keeps moving in. Letitia Baldrige, in her manual for North American etiquette, states:

> When you meet someone, don't stand too close. (Remember the angry expression, "Stay out of my face!"). An uncomfortable closeness is very annoying to the other person, so keep your physical distance, or he'll have to keep backing off from you. A minimum of two feet away from the other person will do it.[55]

Mexicans often touch the arm or hand of another person in professional and business interaction. This touch most frequently occurs between persons of the same sex. North Americans tend to be uncomfortable with this physical contact.

ETHNOCENTRISM

Other nations of the Americas react negatively to the statement "I am an American" by a North American, because this statement implies that only citizens of the United States of America really count,[56] and even though these nations may themselves sometimes use *americano/americana* or, more often, *norteamericano/norteamericana* to refer to U.S. citizens. Although it is more acceptable to call oneself a North American, one should realize that this is also a misnomer, because the United States of Mexico is a part of North America. Nonetheless, this study has chosen to refer to citizens of the United States of America as North Americans, which is less awkward than other alternatives, and in English is acceptable to the country's neighbors to the South. In Spanish, the best term for referring to oneself as a North American is "soy estadounidense" (I am from the United States). People from Canada, also located in North America, are, of course, distinguished as Canadians.

Basave writes that North Americans are simple and unpolished and that their ignorance of Mexico's customs hurts Mexican pride.[57] Mexicans themselves are extremely nationalistic and resent any patronizing reference to their country or culture. Over a decade after President Carter's visit, they were still expressing their disapproval of his negative reference to the quality of Mexico's water.[58]

Mexicans think that North Americans naively believe that the United States has a messianic mission to police the world. Mexicans also think that although North Americans take justifiable pride in their technical advances, they are not aware that they are backward in humanism. From the Mexican viewpoint, individually North Americans may be humble, but as a nation the United States is arrogant.[59]

Mexicans do not think the "American Way" is the only way. One must recognize that the political and economic system of Mexico is peculiarly Mexican—a mixture of authoritarianism and paternalism, conciliation and negotiation, cynicism and idealism. If this system loses its national identity, it will lose its way and will not survive. To endure, any changes in the current Mexican political system will have to be firmly based in Mexican culture.[60] A study on the role of culture in the political and administrative transformation of the Mexican state contends that any successful reforms will have to conform to three specific cultural norms: hierarchy, collectivism, and uncertainty avoidance.[61]

All cultures suffer from ethnocentrism when attempting intercultural communication. Basave feels, however, that the United States confuses its economic dominance of the world in the twentieth century with dominance in all aspects of living as a human being in this world.[62] This preoccupation with economic efficiency is an impediment to adaptability, which is a requisite for successful intercultural communication. North Americans, in fact, tend to view most other nations as "underdeveloped Americans" instead of recognizing who and what the "Other" nation is, inevitably, in the context of its culture. According to speakers from both countries at a United States–Mexico business conference, North Americans who want to do business in Mexico should leave their arrogance at home.[63]

PRECONCEPTIONS AND STEREOTYPES

Mexicans are keenly aware of cultural variances in regions of their own country but—like many foreigners—can be unaware of the vast differences within the United States. Stereotyping is a problem for both Mexicans and North Americans. Mexicans often consider North Americans to be cold, insensitive, ill mannered, and provincial,[64] while many North Americans stereotype Mexicans as lazy, ignorant, and unreliable.

Basave writes that Mexican stereotypes of the United States as The Giant of the North and its citizens as Yankee Imperialists oversimplify facts. The United States is neither the chosen of God nor the chosen of the devil.[65] Riding states that Mexico has a disconcerting intellectual disdain for the United States, which it at the same time envies, and, even though Mexico has vainly demanded understanding from the United States, Mexicans have made little attempt to understand their neighbor. Mexicans assume that in the United States the executive branch, Congress, the judiciary, state governments, and even municipalities are all subservient to the president, and therefore, drawing parallels to their own government structure, they conclude that any "anti-Mexican" incident, great or small, is a politically motivated conspiracy.[66]

Negative stereotyping by both nations only serves to create and exacerbate ill will. Like ethnocentrism, all nations and social groups suffer to some degree from this attribute that impedes intercultural communication. Since Mexicans are generally better informed about the United States than vice-versa, North Americans must be better informed about Mexico in order to communicate successfully. It is not realistic to expect that Mexicans can unilaterally compensate for North American lack of knowledge of Mexico's history and culture.

The cultural filters of perception and the interaction of nonverbal behavior all affect communication every day. We need also to look at some specific rituals of daily interaction that involve all people who live their lives in a society, to see how United States–Mexico cultural differences in behavior in these common situations can cause communication difficulty.

EIGHT

Day-to-Day Cultural Interaction

We should compare two cultures to uncover the differences that affect communication between them, not to judge them.

An elegant, perfectly groomed Mexican woman walked into a corporate meeting in the United States. Helena wore a tailored suit, and eyes were drawn to the gold and diamond pin on her lapel. She particularly liked the rich piece of jewelry and often wore it as an accessory. Some months later, a North American friend took her aside and told her that the pin really was "a bit much" for day or business wear.[1] Helena's statement through her accessory was interpreted differently in the United States than it was in Mexico.

CANONS OF CONDUCT

Rules

Culture dictates rules for daily interaction between people, and different cultures regulate day-to-day interaction differently. Many of these rules differ between Mexico and the United States, and the variance in these culturally prescribed norms affects communication between the two countries. As Hall pointed out, there is not much room for digression from the rules that culture imposes.[2]

Artifacts: Extensions of the Physical Self

Voluntary aspects of personal appearance, such as grooming, hairstyle, make-up, fragrances, and dress, symbolize a person's station in life in Mexico much more than in the United States. Generally, you will be taken care of as well as you dress. Women wear more make-up, more and larger jewelry, and longer nails, which are usually polished; both men and women wear fragrances more frequently; grooming is meticulous.[3] Use of noticeable fragrance is requisite for the well-groomed person in Mexico, and its absence is remarked. In the United States, however, the opposite is true. Letitia Baldrige, in her U.S. etiquette manual, states that "the people around you should hardly be aware of your fragrance." Further, she states that "less is more" when it comes to make-up in the United States and that it is considered by some to be perfect if those around one are unaware of it.[4] This look may seem drab and "underdressed" in Mexico.

Helena, who wore a gold and diamond lapel pin as an accessory, was a Mexican government representative in the United States. She herself designed the pin, and she commented that there are obviously different dress codes in Mexico and the United States.[5] Her lapel pin—an artifact—made a different statement in Mexico than it did in the United States. In Mexico City, such an accessory was considered appropriate to her status and did not attract undue attention, but in the United States it was viewed as ostentatious. The Mexican viewpoint is that one's whole persona—carriage, walk, dress, speech, manners, style—declare who one is, and therefore a rich accessory for an educated and successful person not only obviously coordinates with their nonmaterial attributes, but is expected. Baldrige in her U.S. etiquette manual cautions against overstatement with jewelry and specifies that a woman should not wear more than a watch, two rings, and either a bracelet, or a necklace, or a brooch for business.[6] Helena has not worn the pin with business dress in the United States since her North American friend made her observations about it.

Mexicans follow European fashion more closely than United States fashion and are like Parisians in their recognition of style, accessories, and quality; top-quality fabric is important to the middle and upper classes. In Mexico adults do not wear shorts in public except at the beach; men wear little jewelry (men in the U.S. Southwest sometimes wear large or flashy jewelry); men do not wear pink or violet shirts; ponytails and shaved hairstyles for men are considered ridiculous. Casual dress in Mexico is not the same as in the United States. In Mexico casual clothing should be of good quality fabric, shoes should be polished, and jeans worn only by the young. In short, Mexicans tend to dress more formally than do North Americans on all occasions; women wear heels, stockings, and make-up and their hair is done perfectly for trips to the grocery or to walk their children to the bus.[7]

Adriana took her North American fiancé for Christmas dinner to the home of her aunt and uncle, in Monterrey, Mexico. Her uncle's brothers and their families gathered there for the festive occasion, as well. Introductions were made, and good food and company enjoyed. Later, however, her uncle and one of his brothers took her aside with concern to ask her if she was sure her fiancé wasn't gay, because he had worn a peach-colored shirt. She had thought William looked particularly handsome in that color.

The artifacts used in Mexico and in the United States, such as dress, perfume, or gifts, and the interpretation of artifacts used, are different in the two cultures. The use of artifacts is a behavior that communicates, and since the behavioral rules are different, this communication is frequently misunderstood or misinterpreted.

Physical Markers

Biological, physical markers of cultural difference are involuntary and are obviously not governed by rules of conduct. Even so, they can affect intercultural communication. A person's appearance may seem foreign because of height, body type, skin pigmentation, hair texture, or eye color. The physical markers of difference between many of the people of Mexico and the United States are often apparent and accentuate perceptions of difference. These markers are therefore potential obstacles because attraction and desire to communicate are positively correlated to perceptions of similarity between people.

In Mexico, physical markers are perceived differently than in the United States. Classification as an Amerindian is more behaviorally than biologically based. One is *indio,* for example, because of language, clothing, and other habits, not by virtue of physical features. Mexican census takers distinguish *indios* by their behaviors, such as going barefoot or eating certain foods with fingers instead of a fork. But in any case, the people of Mexico consider themselves Mexicanos first and foremost.[8]

Mexicans tend to stereotype North Americans as being blond and blue-eyed. North Americans stereotype Mexicans as all having olive complexions, dark hair, and dark eyes and do not realize that a number of Mexicans are fair, honey-blond, and green-eyed, or some variation thereof.

Table and Meal Etiquette

Mexicans judge their guests by their table manners, and in Mexico good manners are more important than the educational degrees one holds.[9] Therefore, perfect table manners in Mexico, including the proper selection of flatware for each food and how the flatware is used, are extremely important. Baldrige notes that among countries in the world that use a knife and fork to eat, the United States is the only country where one shifts the fork after cutting from the left hand to the right hand.[10] In the Continental style of eating used in Mexico, one keeps the fork in the left hand, which conveys food to the mouth after cutting each piece. In lifting a piece of meat to the mouth, the tines of the fork should always curve down, not up. The right hand uses the knife to cut food and to subtly help food onto the fork, which many describe as more quiet, graceful, and efficient than continually switching flatware from one hand to the other.[11]

In Mexico, one should never put one's hands in one's lap when at the table for a meal.[12] Most Latin Americans, as well as the French, find it curious that this action that is highly unacceptable at the table in many countries is almost a requirement for good table etiquette in the United States.[13] One should also never put his or her elbows on the table in Mexico.[14] In fact, some people consider it impolite to rest any part of the arm above the wrist on the table. North Americans generally learn "no elbows on the table," but Baldrige comments that "it's certainly all right to rest an elbow or two on the table between courses, because that's a gesture that comes naturally to people."[15]

Written Communication

Labón's book of Mexican etiquette states that it is fortunate that the telephone exists, since it is used to communicate most invitations. For very special occasions, one can mail invitations or deliver them personally if one has a chauffeur. Labón classifies as "forbidden" the mailing of wedding invitations to people who are in the same city (the invitations must be delivered).[16] Frequently, wedding invitations will be personally delivered even to people in another city. Conversely, Baldrige's book of U.S. etiquette explains that most social planning involves mailing invitations, well in advance, although occasionally there are last-minute events that occur.[17]

In Mexico, Labón recommends that, as a very courteous gesture, you telephone your hostess to express thanks for a dinner or other social occasion. She further explains that in Anglo-Saxon countries, like the United States or England, one mails a note of thanks.[18]

In regard to holiday cards, Labón qualifies cards with pictures of the family in front of a Christmas tree as in bad taste, and she condemns as absolutely inadequate group letters, where the same letter is reproduced and sent to friends and family as is done in the United States. She states that since one has a different relationship with each friend and relative, with different degrees of intimacy, to give the same news to all makes no sense.[19] With reference to United States custom, Baldrige comments that many people prepare a letter with all the family news in multiple copies and mail it with holiday cards, and that she enjoys these letters thoroughly. With regard to family photos printed on cards, she remarks that recipients usually enjoy getting them.[20]

Written communication functions differently in the cultures of Mexico and the United States and even represents a different reality for people. Greater value is placed on communication or information put in writing for verbal, low-context cultures such as the United States. Consultant Richard Sinkin comments that the Mexican view even of written contracts markedly differs from that held in North America. In Mexico, the terms of contract "are the kinds of ideal things that you strive to achieve . . . while in the United States they are law."[21]

RITUAL AS CONTEXT

Courtesy as Communication

A prevailing characteristic of the Mexican people is their courtesy. Not only do they tend to be polite to strangers, they are polite among themselves; older people are greeted with obvious respect, and often a revered senior's hand is kissed.[22] You have but to compare the general experience of shopping in Mexico with that of shopping in the United States (with, perhaps, the exception of some border shops in Mexico) to be very aware of Mexican courtesy. In contrast with many retail employees in the United States, Mexicans are in general very polite, look at the customer to whom they are speaking, and behave in a warm and attentive manner.

Mexicans are so accommodating and solicitous that it is said that when a traveler in Mexico City asked a pedestrian where to find Calle Santo Domingo, the man addressed said that he regretfully did not know the location of the street. He then queried with solicitude, "but may I offer you another?"

Dr. Basave, the Mexican philosopher and educator from Monterrey, opines that the average North American thinks that good manners and exquisite courtesy are omehow effeminate. North Americans, for example, never take off their hats in elevators and rarely offer seats when appropriate on public transportation; to the European or Latin American this seems rude and offensive.[23] Labón specifically prescribes courtesy when using an elevator that is not the norm in the United States: ". . . es necesario hacer un breve saludo: 'buenos dias'. . . . Los caballeros se descubren la cabeza . . . si hay damas presentes." (One must extend a brief greeting, such as "good morning." Gentlemen should take off their hats . . . if ladies are present.)[24]

North Americans notoriously have visitors stop by their homes without offering them anything to eat or drink. This is anathema in Mexico. Regarding guests at the home, Labón puts in the "Forbidden" category "no ofrecer algun refresco o bebida" (not to offer some refreshment or beverage).[25]

Courtesy, dignity, tact, and diplomacy dominate Mexican culture. Protocol is paramount, and in business social competence is as critical as technical competence.[26] North Americans practice good business manners, but what is customary in the United States often differs from what is considered acceptable in Mexico.[27] Both North Americans and Mexicans feel that they put first things first when conducting business. The North American wants to appear serious and professional, which may seem impatient and cold to Mexicans. The Mexican wants to appear gracious, friendly, and interested in the North American as an individual, which may be taken as lacking in professionalism and seriousness of purpose.[28]

Courtesy is a behavioral ritual that communicates.

Gift Giving Communicates by Context

Gifts express both the wealth of the donor and the importance of the recipient.[29] According to Labón, the most important thing in gift giving is to thoroughly study the personality of the recipient in order to select an appropriate gift.[30] When invited to dinner at a home, one should take a small gift such as flowers or candy, or a toy for the children; if one knows the hosts well one might take wine, a liqueur, or a dessert. For a formal dinner or if one does not know the hosts well, send flowers in advance.[31] Different flowers and colors have different meanings in different cultures. In Mexico, the yellow *zempasúchitl* flower (a species of marigold) is sent when there has been a death. It is wise to check with a florist in selecting or sending flowers to make sure they are appropriate to the culture.

In Mexico, when borrowing anything, courtesy requires that the borrowed object always be returned with a gift—one should not expect something for nothing.[32] If even a small favor is asked of a stranger (including a government official), one must offer something in return for making the request. Mexicans, as part of courtesy, tend to give more gifts than North Americans. Presentation is important, and the gift should always be attractively wrapped. Both cultures usually expect one to open the gift upon receipt.

If you are giving a gift in Mexico in a public ceremony, especially to a public official, you need to be aware of a delicate point of protocol. The gift should be mounted on a presentation board and shrink-wrapped so that everyone can see what it is. An opaque wrapper appears to be an attempt to hide the nature of the gift. Regional handicrafts, books, or pieces of art are appropriate.[33] Because Mexico is renowned for its historical production of silver, it is inappropriate for foreigners to give gifts made of silver to Mexicans.[34]

Food

If one is to spend time and interact with diverse peoples, food is an important factor because it is so central to hospitality and ceremony in most cultures, and because tastes between cultures can vary so vastly.

Most North Americans conceive of Mexican food, which is rich and varied by region, in terms of its perverted re-creation by the U.S. fast food industry: swimming in processed melted cheese and drowned in hot chili-pepper sauce—often not recognizable to Mexicans. Many North Americans think all Mexican food is too hot and overspiced, but few have tasted, for example, a good *pescado a la veracruzana* (fish Vera Cruz style)—deliciously flavorful and not spicy hot. The English language uses the word "hot" for both temperature and spicy-hot, not differentiating between the two. Spanish distinguishes between the two with two different words. *Caliente* refers to temperature, and *picante* to spiciness, which indicates the importance of the difference.

Consider this Mexican perspective of U.S. cuisine, summarized in translation from Basave's *Visión de Estados Unidos* (Vision of the United States):[35]

Hamburgers and apple pie. Watery coffee. Salads that make me physically ill: lettuce, mayonnaise, orange marmalade, sour cream and pineapple (a Hawaiian salad). Children and adolescents deaden their taste buds with spices—mustard, pepper, catsup that they pour liberally over their hamburgers and hot dogs. People smoke between courses. It is not surprising that these palates cannot discriminate. Doctors—the oracles of North American life—advise that all food be kept in the refrigerator to kill bacteria. The refrigerator kills the juicy natural flavor of vegetables and meats. Coffee is served boiling hot; water is served with so much ice that one can hardly drink it. Breakfast is abundant so one can work well, lunch is light so one can continue to work, and dinner is eaten so early in the afternoon that at night one has to forage in the refrigerator. North American food is hygienic and full of vitamins, but insipid (except in the Deep South). The American wants simply to assuage his hunger, not savor food. Food is simple and plentiful. Abundant glasses of good milk are consumed—what we would give in Mexico to have it!

Typically in Mexico lunch is an important and substantial meal over which one lingers, sometimes for hours. Anyone visiting Mexico to work would do well to remember that, in both the public and private sector, many transactions are concluded at lunch. Sandy Sheehy, who contributes articles to *Money* and *Forbes* magazines in the United States, wrote that if you "flunk lunch" in your business dealings in Mexico, you might as well go home.[36]

Entertaining

Appearances are very important in Mexico. Even the poor spend extravagantly and go into debt for such social occasions as weddings, birthdays, and funerals. Men wrestle for the privilege of paying the check in a restaurant, which is expected and considered proper manners. The honor may often go to the oldest or most influential of the group. Inviting someone to lunch in Mexico does not necessarily mean one plans to pay, but "going Dutch" (a split bill) is often considered offensive.[37] Contrast this accepted protocol with the advice given in Baldrige's guide for proper executive manners in the United States. She admonishes that one should make it clear in advance who is going to pay when inviting anyone to lunch, because the entire warm mood of the occasion is ruined when people argue over and grapple for the bill.[38] Clearly the potential for North Americans and Mexicans to unintentionally offend each other is not only great, but almost inevitable—unless they have been cross-culturally sensitized.

Mexicans tend to be very private about inviting a stranger into the home; therefore, hospitality in a home is not to be taken lightly.[39] An invitation to the home becomes an act of great symbolism, with Mexicans showing the real face of how they live and sharing the intimacy of the family.[40] It is an attempt to establish a personal bond. In Mexico, foreigners who wish to establish personal relationships should not turn down such an invitation, even if it is inconvenient.

THE INTERACTION KALEIDOSCOPE

Face, Hierarchy, Contextual Indirectness, and Collectivism

Mexicans have the pride characteristic of the Aztecs and the Spanish—a certain haughtiness and probity. Their national literature suggests a nation consumed by questions of honor.[41] Status and appearances are crucial throughout society,[42] whether it be in entertaining, giving gifts, use of titles, respect for the social hierarchy, and so on.

Basave comments that in the United States there is no shame in a student from a good family working as a waiter, selling newspapers, or baby-sitting to earn money.[43] This does not happen in Mexico. Rather, Mexican students spend their time in political activism or strikes and do not perform menial tasks. Manual labor is looked upon with some disdain in Mexico, while in the United States a lawyer might draft a complex contract at his law firm and then return home to paint his deck. Comfortable Mexican families employ cooks, housekeepers, laundresses, gardeners, and chauffeurs. For an average middle-class family in Monterrey, Mexico City, or Querétaro, for example, to have at least one live-in maid is not uncommon.

In Mexico, "no" is used sparingly in order not to disappoint or offend, and direct confrontation is avoided at all costs. Face must be saved. But "yes" is used sparingly as well, and when expressed as "yes, we might like that" or "yes, we will try," it should not necessarily be taken as unequivocal.[44] Because of the subtleties of diplomatic speech, you may not be able to rely on "yes" for an answer, either.

Truth in Mexico is conceived of as personal reality as opposed to objective reality and may be different to different people and at different times.

The rationale for personal truth is that people are taught to maintain harmony, avoid trouble, and please the other person. The word for lie is *mentira*, and in Mexico the word carries a connotation more like "fib."[45] A Mexican woman, speaking in English at a U.S. social gathering, told her North American husband that he was "such a liar"—*un mentiroso*—to which he reacted negatively. A better equivalent in English of what she intended to express would have been "you tell such stories."

The subtle side of the humility inculcated in people by culture in Mexico manifests itself in the uncritical way they accept outsiders, their natural goodwill and friendliness, their quiet courtesy. They are generally easy to get along with and pleasant to be around.[46] John Gavin, who represented the Reagan administration in Mexico from 1981 to 1986, was seen as a classically arrogant American. He adopted a high profile and outspoken stance, which provoked negative reactions in many sectors of Mexican society. The foreigners who communicate most successfully in Mexico understand that they need to relate to the government (and indeed, to anyone) like a Mexican, not a foreigner, only they should be even more subtle and indirect. They should try to establish a presence, not an influence.[47]

A noted characteristic of Mexican culture is the desire to preserve warm relations with colleagues. This governs a strong unwillingness to confront a co-worker with a mistake, because a comment intended to be objective and constructive is likely to be taken personally and cause offense. Personal conflict needs to be removed from management, business, and quality-control situations. For quality control, it has been recommended that one way to do this is to create teams that rotate through all production stages. Since these teams act much like "families" in the workplace, they seem to be compatible with Mexico's collective versus individual cultural identity. And in this pseudo-family the *patrón* or owner/director has final say, just as the father does in the Mexican family. The crucial distinction between this family-team parallel, is that the *patrón* or any manager must continue to maintain the absolute respect that his workers desire to accord him, even while relinquishing enough authority to get the job done.[48]

Even after the failure of the ill-fated Vitro-Corning venture, the way the two companies responded shows how different the cultures can be. North Americans from Corning wanted to discuss what went wrong, while Mexicans from Vitro were reluctant to criticize a former partner and preferred to focus on the fact that the marketing arrangement between the two companies continued in spite of the joint-venture break-up.[49]

In Mexico it is important, because of face, that negotiations remain friendly and conciliatory.[50] A tourist or businessman who bargains hard, with a take it or leave it attitude, is not welcome. Even so, with a perverse sense of pride, "Entre los partidos políticos brilla por su ausencia el espíritu conciliador." (The spirit of conciliation between [Mexican] political parties is conspicuous by its absence).[51]

Because the United States is powerful, it cannot comprehend Mexico's obsession with respect.[52] The Mexican government more often seeks respect and understanding than specific concessions when it addresses United States officials, but the United States rarely grasps the psychological dimension of the communication and focuses instead on the concrete issues that it believes define the relationship. Despite many substantial disagreements with Mexico during his administration, President Reagan may have understood that Carter's mistakes with Mexico were more of style than of substance. Reagan instructed his cabinet members to treat Mexico with special deference, a courtesy that was perceived positively by some. It is said that "Poor Mexico is so far from God . . . and so close to the United States." Both countries share the feeling that they are condemned to live beside each other.[53]

Even collecting data in Mexico is different. Personal relationships are very important, and telephone interviews are neither common nor very welcome. And since Mexicans are acculturated to be courteous and to avoid conflict, in order to preserve the face of the interviewer, the interviewee may "go along" with the interviewer and, with no bad intent communicate misleading information with poor meaning content.[54] Bicultural attorney Adriana comments that, in her experience, some lawyers preserve the harmony that is so important to Mexican culture by telling clients only what they think they want to hear, sidestepping other issues.

Tact and indirectness are used in Mexico to maintain face. The authors of *Limits to Friendship,* Pastor of the United States and Castañeda of Mexico, were each familiar with the other's culture. They chose to collaborate on a book and wrote a parallel series of chapters giving contrasting perspectives looking north and south. But even in this close, voluntary collaboration, there were limits to the subjects on which they agreed. Castañeda remarked that he had a methodological disagreement with Pastor in writing the book, stating that he tried to confine his comments to his own country but that Pastor felt free to comment on Mexican affairs—that his co-author "strayed over the border."[55] The authors' explicit recognition of this difference in their approach well illustrates their awareness of the different use of direct and indirect style in the two cultures, even when two well-informed political analysts who are friends communicate. This is a good example of how direct North American communication style might smirch Mexican face.

The government representatives of Mexico and the United States—ambassadors, embassy, and consular officials—symbolize the reason for many communication problems. "Essentially, the United States must become more discreet, and Mexico, less." More communication will improve United States–Mexico relations, provided that each country can adapt to the different rules of the other country. "U.S. officials must be more private in Mexico, and Mexican representatives in the U.S. must be more active and public." [56] North Americans must communicate with more consciousness of preserving face, and Mexicans must not allow their concern with preservation of face to keep them from communicating directly enough to be understood by North Americans.

Greetings Embrace Hierarchy, Context, Kinesics, Proxemics, and Immediacy

In Mexico, one can experience a whole series of greetings; men shake hands as a matter of course and often walk arm in arm when engaged in intense conversation. It is insulting for a North American male to pull back from this kind of touch. Handshakes can be simply a handshake, or the greeting may be an *abrazo*—a handshake with a couple of coordinated back slaps and, sometimes, a second handshake and shoulder slap. [57] When they meet, women shake hands with men and with each other, and for social occasions kiss both men and women whom they have met a few times.

Labón points out that Mexican greetings differ from the Anglo-Saxon style, in which it is not always the norm to shake hands, much less to embrace or kiss. Latin temperament is affectionate and demonstrative; to shake hands is a must, and *abrazos* and kisses are used for people with whom one feels friendship. The one kiss on the cheek is normal in Mexican culture and in reality is not a kiss, but rather the contact of skin cheek-to-cheek. It is "forbidden" to kiss someone you hardly know. [58]

On the subject of women kissing as a greeting in the United States, Baldrige comments that to "air kiss" means putting a cheek alongside the other person's cheek while miming a kiss. In her opinion this is the worst kind of artificial behavior. What is commonly enjoyed and expected in Mexico—"two people air-kissing with cries of delight when they had seen one another only a week ago"—Baldrige describes as silly, vacuous behavior for U.S. etiquette. [59] With such diametrically opposed norms for behavior displays, it is not surprising that Mexicans may find North Americans cold and aloof and that North Americans may be overwhelmed by the bodily contact and warm demonstrativeness of Mexicans. Most North Americans have been conditioned to be more restrained in the expression of emotion, and many find it awkward to act in as demonstrative a manner as is expected in Mexican culture.

In Mexico it is quite common that a man kiss a woman's hand in certain social settings. Labón's rules are quite strict. The woman must be married or "of an age that she should be (twenty-five and over)," any head covering must be removed, and the lips should approach the hand in a gesture that does not contact it and is not actually a kiss. A young man of good family practices this custom after the age of eighteen and never kisses the hand of a woman of his own generation, using this courtesy only for a woman older than himself.[60] A poised woman will raise her hand slightly toward the man's lips in a coordinated movement. Baldrige states that "by cultural definition, an American man is not supposed to kiss a woman's hand," and that he usually does not know the correct art of hand-kissing anyway.[61] It would therefore probably be better just to refrain from this unfamiliar formality.

Mexican managers commonly use an effusive style of greeting and elaborate courtesy, making a point of greeting and speaking to everyone in their employ, treating them with the same respect they extend to people on their own level.[62] The ritual of greeting is very visible and highly important in Mexico—much more so than in the United States.

High-context Mexican culture displays greater immediacy behaviors signaling availability for approach and communication, and expression of emotion is both permissible and expected. Mexicans seem to react more to North American "coldness" and "distance," which may be interpreted as negatively judgmental avoidance, than North Americans react negatively to Mexican immediacy displays. The difference in immediacy displays is apparent in many areas of behavior such as conversation, greeting, and courtesy.

LANGUAGE AND COMMUNICATION

Hierarchy Affects Formality of Address

Professional titles are paramount, and the commonly used *Licenciado* (referring to any person with a university degree) does not have an English equivalent.[63] Business cards commonly carry this title, often abbreviated as *Lic.*, or the professional degree a person might have, such as *Ingeniero* (Engineer) Marcos Ayala. In referring to a person in an office in Mexico, one commonly uses the appropriate title and would say "El Licenciado" or "El Ingeniero," rather than "Sr. Ayala" or "Marcos" or "he"; for example, "El Licenciado needs the documents," or "El Ingeniero is not in."

Mexicans find it hard to understand the apparent informality that can exist between an American manager and his or her employees; for example, employees commonly calling their superiors by their first names, a reflection of the flatter social hierarchy in the United States. North Americans in Mexico should not dress casually in the office, nor behave in an excessively casual manner (like putting your feet on your desk during an informal meeting). Mexican behavior in general, including attire, tends toward the formal.[64]

Mexicans are quick to point out that the supposed equality in the United States is an illusion, since the manager clearly has more power. They prefer to keep the lines of authority more clear and will address a manager on a last name basis or by a professional title.[65] Labón in her manual of Mexican etiquette admonishes one to respect the authority of one's superiors and the hierarchy of the workplace to maintain good relationships.[66] When addressing Mexicans, North Americans should use last names and titles, as is the custom, unless one is specifically invited to do otherwise.

Rank is so important in Mexico that Labón gives telephone-protocol instructions for the secretaries of important persons. When a secretary needs to use the telephone to contact another person of the same level as her superior, he or she should arrange in advance with the contact's secretary to have both personages come on the telephone at the same time. Some persons will hang up if the caller is not on the line when they answer.[67]

The Spanish language indicates familiarity or formality through the use of two pronouns for "you": the familiar *tu,* and the formal *usted.* According to Labón, in Mexico *tu* is used between persons of the same social status, age, or trade union, for example. "Usted" is used when addressing persons who are older than oneself or more prestigious, and also for those who are at a lower level, such as employees and servants. Children, "of course," are addressed as "tu" because of their age. In an office or social encounter when addressed as "tu," one can politely say that one prefers to "speak with the usted," indicating that one desires to maintain more formality or personal distance in the relationship, or else one can simply continue to speak to the other person using "usted"—the latter alternative being more subtle and perhaps, therefore, preferable. To use "tu" to service persons, unless you have known them for many years, is forbidden. It is absolutely forbidden to use "tu" to the personnel in a public place or to the servants at someone else's home. To do so is an act of disrespect, and everyone deserves to be treated with respect as a person, including domestic servants.[68] A professional from Mexico City comments that the poor or those who perform menial labor have so little in Mexico that the use of "usted" at least adds some dignity to their lives. The poorer or more desperate the situation of Mexicans, the more important their dignity is to them.[69]

The North American Elizabeth Borton Treviño always addressed her mother- and father-in-law, to whom she was very close, with the formal "usted" (which originally meant "your Mercy"). All the Treviño children also used "usted" to address their parents; however, the parents used the familiar "tu" to address their children and the children's respective spouses. Because Elizabeth had not learned to conjugate the familiar *tu* verb forms well, she also used the formal "usted" to address her husband, which created rumors that Luís was very "strict" with his wife.[70] The use of "tu" and "usted" among family members will differ from family to family, and in current generations "tu" is more commonly used.

For good Mexican etiquette, Labón recommends that one address a person by his or her name or title, such as "*Don* Luís," "Mario," "Doctor," "Señor Secretario," "Señor Hernández," to establish a positive and friendly relationship. If one does not know the name or title, an adequate form of address would be "señora" or "señor."[71]

Since the social hierarchy in the United States is much less strict than that in Mexico—it is "flatter"—much less ceremony and ritual is required in personal interaction, and North Americans thus potentially face many pitfalls in interacting with Mexicans. Many North American actions can be interpreted as deliberately insulting or, at best, uneducated and rude. The essence of Mexican *formalidad* (formality) is respect—to parents, elders, friends, people in general, and to oneself. Mexicans believe that respect for oneself includes dress as well as behavior and that respect for others manifests itself in manner and speech.[72]

A North American engineer with forty years of experience in his country's industries points out that during the course of his career he has seen United States business etiquette evolve from formal address, communication, and attire to the more casual end of the spectrum. He wonders if this is not a natural evolution in today's technological world, and whether Mexico's communication style may not also change in this direction. A bicultural professional who has worked both in Mexico City and in the United States comments that he does not think that Mexico's steep social hierarchy will ever permit the same degree of informality in communication that is found in the United States. With the many changes taking place in Mexico today, it will be interesting to observe the degree of change that takes place in the formality of both verbal and nonverbal communication styles.

The Language Process

The languages of the United States and Mexico create a different reality because they are essentially different codes that evolved in different cultural contexts. A North American may find it difficult to understand the concept of *malinchismo* based on the Amerindian La Malinche or to understand the symbolism of the Virgin of Guadalupe, while the Mexican may find the expression "a self-made man" meaningless.

Although both cultures are certainly literate, and without entering into discussions of literacy rates, the primary difference between the two cultures when considering verbal processes is that in Mexico the language code is amplified much more by context than in the United States, where one focuses on the information content of the language code itself. This presents a significant impediment to communication between the two cultures.

There is certainly a difference in cultural rules as to when and how written communication is appropriate and when personal oral communication is preferred, as exemplified by how invitations are transmitted in the two cultures. A number of factors probably contribute to the opposing viewpoints between Mexican and United States culture. Mail may be less reliable in Mexico, personal and oral communication are higher context and therefore better typify Mexican culture, while written communication better represents the low-context communication style of the United States. In addition, Labón's comment regarding the importance of observing the differences in relationships and intimacy when writing letters[73] is quintessentially Mexican in its personal attention and caring style and better adapts to the Mexican respect for hierarchy and the importance of degrees of formality.

Formality, when it comes to language, is also significant. English does not provide the nuance of a formal "you" form of address, although one should note that a person sensitized to the formality requirements of another culture can increase formality in English by the use of titles, surnames, and choice of words.

Learning the language code, i.e., Spanish or English in the case of Mexico and the United States, is a technical skill that must be refined by familiarity with the language's culture in order to achieve competency in application of the skill and raise it to the level of the art of successful communication.

Language Style

The ability to speak well is of great importance in Mexico, and since the style is more ornate,[74] North Americans may take as literal words intended for effect, and then later—when the "literal" result does not occur—they may interpret those words as empty promises. *Momentito* can mean "just a moment" or "never"; "my home is your home" is a Hispanic expression of hospitality that goes back centuries and is not meant literally. A refined Mexican woman told participants in Austin's Tertulia Literaria that the next gathering would be held in "su casa." This translates as "your home" in this context, but means "my home"—because "my home is your home"—which may be confusing for a non-native speaker of Spanish. Style is important to convey even a simple request. To ask for something one should courteously use the conditional, and say "I would like to speak to Mr. Ortega, please" (the Spanish form *quisiera*), rather than the blunt statement "Mr. Ortega, please," or "Let me speak with Mr. Ortega."

In the United States, with its cultural focus on efficiency, parsimony is prized in most writing and speaking, in contrast with Mexican language style. The United States is information-specific in language, whereas in Mexico language is often information-nonspecific as a matter of courtesy. This can be frustrating for the North American, as when trying to find out when someone will be available by telephone, or when trying to arrange appointments. Formality (form) tends to be valued over the accuracy of specific statements (content) in Mexico.[75]

In the United States great value is placed on using the verbal code to convey precise meaning abstractly with as little reliance on context as possible. The high-context culture of Mexico uses such effects as volume, repetition, tone, vocal segregates, and rate of speech to add to meaning when speaking. North American spoken use of the verbal code can be misinterpreted as insincere or lacking in enthusiasm and conviction because of less use of vocalics as a conveyor of meaning.

In the autobiography *My Heart Lies South,* Aunt Rosa was so lavish in her endearments that Elizabeth, with her North American inhibitions, thought her affected. But Elizabeth soon found the aunt's devotion to the family sincere. Expressions like "precious," "my life," or sing me a song "in your glorious voice, little George of my life" expressed Aunt Rosa's genuine, demonstrative affection. And although Elizabeth spoke good Spanish, she also had difficulty because Mexicans use many words of Indian origin—

which she observed that the Spanish Academy had not included in her Spanish dictionary.[76]

Differences in language style also surface in business negotiations. Negotiating techniques in Mexico generally differ from those in the North American style. In real estate, for example, the owner of a property may well start with a price triple its value and talk as if he really expects to obtain it. In North America, it is generally accepted that selling is more effective if the offering price is near real market value. A North American buyer might walk away from the property if the initial asking price is greatly inflated.[77]

But, lest one think that placing importance on language style results only in elaborate but empty discourse, consider the following excerpts from the speeches made in 1977 when President Carter met with President López Portillo in Mexico City.

President López Portillo: It has been two years now since we met for the first time. Since then a great deal of water has flowed beneath the bridges of the Rio Grande. A great deal also has happened within our countries and between our countries, as it has in the world and to the world. . . . Among permanent, not casual neighbors, surprise moves and sudden deceit or abuse are poisonous fruits that sooner or later have a reverse effect. Mexico has thus suddenly found itself the center of American attention—attention that is a surprising mixture of interest, disdain, and fear, much like the recurring vague fears you yourselves inspire in certain areas of our national subconscious. Let us seek only lasting solutions—good faith and fair play—nothing that would make us lose the respect of our children.

Response by President Carter: President López Portillo and I have, in the short time together on this visit, found that we have many things in common. We both represent great nations; we both have found an interest in archeology; we both must deal with difficult questions like energy and the control of inflation. . . . we both have beautiful and interesting wives; and we both run several kilometers every day. As a matter of fact, I told President López Portillo that I first acquired my habit of running here in Mexico City. My first running course was from the Palace of Fine Arts to the Majestic Hotel, where my family and I were staying. In the midst of the Folklórico performance, I discovered that I was afflicted with Montezuma's revenge.

President Portillo's speech was eloquent and candid; President Carter appeared to respond with triviality and not to understand what Portillo said.[78] In addition, President Carter's public reference to an attack of diarrhea was seen as indelicate and a criticism of Mexico. Although one can debate how much of the difference in style in these two speeches is attributable to the individual and how much to culture, each speech contains many elements that are typical of the speaker's culture.

Although English has become an "international" language, the United States is challenged today by other nations in competing for business. It is important for North Americans to make an effort to speak the language of the country they are visiting, even though they learn to use just a few courteous phrases. Because of the value that the United States places on efficiency and pragmatism, North Americans sometimes feel that if they cannot speak the language perfectly, they should not speak it at all. But Mexicans are very pleased when U.S. visitors, even those who cannot speak Spanish fluently or well, attempt to speak the language as a courtesy for social interaction.[79] The effort communicates respect for and interest in the Mexican people. It is, of course, to be understood that competent interpreters and translators should handle technical, sensitive, or important communication in the absence of total language fluency.

Names

Personal interaction is difficult to sustain without knowing and using people's names. It seems this would be a simple matter and that the only difficulty would be in finding out and remembering the name of a person. But for a North American in Mexico, it is not self-evident what name one should use and remember. Mexicans are more formal, and one most often would use a last name when not using a title. In the case of author Dr. Agustín Basave Fernández del Valle, how would one address him? Basave is his father's surname and, therefore, his surname. Fernández del Valle is his mother's name (more commonly the mother's surname would be only one name). One would correctly call this gentleman "Dr. Basave."

Georgina García Domínguez de Ramírez is a married woman. García was her maiden surname, after her father, while Domínguez is her mother's surname. Georgina's married surname is de Ramírez, so one would address her as Sra. de Ramírez (or more informally as Sra. Ramírez), unless one knew her well enough to be on a first name basis. Her husband's name is Juan Carlos Ramírez Gutiérrez. Ramírez is his father's surname, and Gutiérrez his mother's. One would call him Sr. Ramírez.

Mexicans sometimes hyphenate their surnames when working in the United States. By using Manuel García-Hernández, Mr. García can avoid being called by his mother's surname, his last name will be alphabetized correctly, and he can retain the use of what he considers his full and correct name on his business cards, for correspondence, and for general use.

Although family or friends may use shortened names or nicknames in Mexico, their general use is not as widespread in practice as it is in the United States. A Mexican finds it hard to understand how one can be so familiar with their president as to call him by a nickname,[80] such as Bill Clinton instead of William Clinton. It would be wise, in Mexico, to assume that a nickname is not an acceptable form of address. In contrast, in the U.S., Baldrige recommends that one include a nickname, if that is how one is known, on one's business card: "Marianne ('Buffy') Endicott, Vice-President."[81]

Richard Sinkin, a bilingual corporate consultant, comments that in general, corporate style is more formal in Mexico than in the United States. Titles are common, and nearly everyone is *licenciado*, which sometimes loosely refers to having any professional training. To forget the honorific can be a serious insult. The president of a successful food distribution service in San Antonio uses a special business card in Mexico to conform to local custom. It includes the title "Dr.," courtesy of his Princeton doctorate in English literature.[82]

Although in many countries it is common to name a child after a parent, in Mexico the custom is very prevalent. One can easily have "Jorge's" of three generations at one family gathering. However, Labón's Mexican etiquette manual does concede that it is not "obligatory" to name the firstborn after the child's father if it is a boy or after the mother if it is a girl.[83]

It is not unusual for a Mexican to have both an Indian and a Hispanic given name, even for persons of primarily Hispanic families in urban settings. Pronunciation of Indian names (of both people and places) is particularly difficult for non-Mexicans, so ask for help with pronunciation if you need to use the name. The given name Yoloxóchitl (which means "the heart of a flower"), for example, is pronounced "yo-lo-SO-chee."

TABLE 4.   Major United States–Mexico Cultural Differences

United States	Mexico
Product oriented.	People oriented.
Hard working, with emphasis on the value of time.	Hard working, with emphasis on enjoying time.
Decision-making by middle management together with top management.	Decision-making by top management.
Confrontation acceptable.	Confrontation not acceptable.
Pride in competitiveness.	Pride in cooperation.
Emphasis on getting down to business. "Time is money."	Emphasis on getting to know clients before doing business.
Direct communication style, even on painful subjects.	Indirect communication style for dignity of both parties.
Willing to accept close supervision from superiors.	Feel that close supervision shows a lack of trust.
Try to be informal as soon as possible.	Prefer formality until a real relationship exists.
Patriotic and convinced that North Americans "are the best."	Proud of culture. Fear others who are convinced they are the best.

HIGH HURDLES

In examining the perspectives and practices affecting communication in the United States and in Mexico, respectively, we see that the difference in required and preferred behavior is often striking. It is easy to see how friction, misunderstanding, and serious incidents can unwittingly be generated even in simple, daily interaction between the two cultures.

For business people, Table 4 provides a list of major cultural differences between the United States and Mexico, taken almost exactly from a summary by Langtex International.[84]

From a communication perspective, the most frequent clashes in Mexico–United States communication occur because of cultural differences in the following categories:

Perception
  1. Collectivism versus Individualism
  2. Ethnocentrism

3. Hierarchy
4. Master Symbols
5. Preconceptions
6. Values

Nonverbal Processes
1. High- versus Low-Context Communication Behavior
2. Chronemics (Time Sense)
3. Kinesics (Body Motion Communication)
4. Physical Characteristics: Artifacts or Extensions of Self

DIFFERENT — NOT DEFECTIVE

Mexicans perceive their relationship with the United States as shaped by military, economic, and cultural aggression. Most future-oriented North Americans are unaware that the "War of North American Invasion" ever occurred (with reference to this piece of history, Mexican writer Carlos Fuentes speaks of the United States of "Amnesia"[85]), while Mexicans cannot forget it. North Americans communicating with Mexicans should be sensitive to the importance of such a historical event. It will also help communication if Mexicans do not blame current generations of Americans for the invasion.[86]

Each and every one of us is thoroughly conditioned by our own culture from birth to respond to any deviation from the norms to which we are acculturated as being unacceptable. In this and the two preceding chapters that contrast the cultural norms for the United States and Mexico, persons from either culture may react negatively to reading comments about attributes of their own culture. This examination of the two cultures does not attempt to make value judgments about which is "better," but rather to highlight the differences that most frequently impede communication. Certainly, we may not agree with an interpretation that we read. But when we react negatively, we should pause and consider whether we are construing as a negatively judgmental comment what may be simply an informative statement or a demonstration of difference. Whether or not one agrees or empathizes with the cultural perspectives in the data gathered as pertinent to United States–Mexico communication, and whether or not one approves of the behavior described, these opinions and behavior do exist as products of the respective cultures of the two countries. The differences set forth do present real obstacles to communication. Cultural difference is the primary obstacle to intercultural communication. Simple cognizance of the contrasting cultural information about the United States and Mexico irrevocably alters one's perception of the other culture.

In addition to cultural differences, political analysts Robert Pastor and Jorge Castañeda point out, the United States and Mexico have different interests that are real. The two countries' perspectives often diverge and contradict each other. Pastor and Castañeda feel that the two nations could better improve their relationship by recognizing why they differ than by pretending that their differences result only from transient errors and misperceptions. They also think that the establishment of major centers in Mexico for study of the United States would be an important long-term contribution to improving relations between the two countries. Such centers for the study of Mexico already exist in the United States. And journalists, especially, should be trained and informed about any country to which they are assigned.[87]

There are positives and negatives to living in the United States, as there are positives and negatives to living in Mexico. On the one hand, the standard of living in the United States is high, and there is great freedom of expression. On the other, the close interaction with family and friends, and the appreciation of life, death, and history as it is lived daily in Mexican culture are missed by many who are caught up in the fast pace and the focus on achievement of the North American world. Perhaps, in fact, cross-cultural communication can benefit both nations for other than the pragmatic reasons which, of themselves, warrant the effort required to communicate successfully.

Basave states that the peoples of Mexico and the United States should learn to know each other well in order to move beyond their mutual disdain and to achieve cooperation as good neighbors.[88] To quote Basave:

> Lo cierto es que los obstinados extremismos interpretativos no contribuyen a la compatabilidad en las relaciones mexicano-norteamericanas. Solo el respeto mútuo a las peculiaridades y a las diversidades pueden conducirnos a la conciliación y al reforzamiento de las buenas relaciones entre vecinos. [What is certain is that obstinate and extremist interpretations (of words and behavior) do not contribute to compatibility in Mexico–United States relations. Only mutual respect for peculiarities and diversities can reconcile and reinforce good relations between neighbors.][89]

The experience of trying to understand culture can be like looking in a mirror. Most often we see ourselves as comfortably familiar, but sometimes we are surprised when we catch a momentary glimpse of ourselves as a stranger, the Other—and sometimes we are privileged to see clearly through the looking glass into another world.

PART THREE

CONCLUSION

NINE

Transcending Culture

The real challenge for all of us in intercultural communication is to accept the idea that another culture can be different without being defective.[1]

Self-altering, creative adaptation capacity is the metacompetence for intercultural communication.[2]

FEAR OF THE OTHER

As the reach of our daily activities explodes outward, Richard Pells points out that many people find themselves asking the question, How do we enjoy the benefits of a global world and economy but still maintain the local, regional, and national culture that we value and find comfortably familiar? In the last two decades of the twentieth century, in the face of rapid technological change and the impact of mass communications, people of all nations began to fear the decline of their national languages and identities and the emergence of a global culture, particularly in the Western Hemisphere. Cable, satellites, telecopiers, computers, the Internet, e-mail, VCRs, travel, and immigration can override any attempt by a government to protect its heritage.[3] And today, many people of the dominant culture of a country feel they have the right to ask why they should make an effort to understand visiting or resident foreigners, and why foreigners do not adapt or leave.[4] Even more ethnocentrically, many people of a culture that dominates a region or the globe in any area of human activity may expect foreigners to adapt to them, even when they interact with those foreigners in their own countries.

Critics of globalism want a revival of cultural pluralism, and many have joined movements with a renewed appreciation of traditional religion, local language, and ethnic origin. Interest has grown in preserving dialects such as Gaelic, Welsh, Provençal, and Catalan. In French Polynesia there is heightened pride in the Tahitian language that people still commonly speak, but now it is taught formally in local schools, which was not true a generation ago. But Pells further observes that bigotry is not what critics of global culture have wanted to preserve in the movements to preserve cultural pluralism. Because Europeans have preserved in great part their national and ethnic identities while participating fully in the new global economy, they may be in a position to teach others a valuable lesson. Despite the flood of North American products and mass culture into Europe after World War II, the people of Western Europe have dealt with U.S. "cultural imperialism" by adapting it to their own needs, tastes, and traditions. They have Europeanized what they have received from the United States, each country preserving its cultural distinctiveness.[5]

Day-to-day interaction with people from other cultures has become a reality for most of us living in developed nations, whether we or the Others we encounter are travelers or residents. Those fearful of cultural domination misjudge the ability of national culture, both democratic and authoritarian, to survive and flourish under the assault of globalism.[6] Just as when we learn another language, so learning another culture does not necessarily make us lose our own. To communicate, we can make surface adaptations to another culture without changing the fundamental premises that we have learned and value in our own cultures. In fact, our acculturation from birth is so thorough that we cannot rid ourselves of our culture even when we will to do so.[7] People should not fear the intercultural exchanges that have historically contributed to robust societies. We can benefit from what we learn from other cultures.

Just as we have to learn from birth how to adapt to our own societies in order to survive, the frequency with which we now face crossing cultural boundaries may make it necessary for us to learn to adapt to other cultures to survive in today's multicultural, global society.

CULTURE CROSSING

A successful Japanese executive once said that to be effective in two cultures is like handling two swords at the same time. In one culture you must be assertive, quick, and to the point. The other culture may require you to be unassertive, patient, and indirect. You have to learn to shift style, like handling two swords.[8]

Nations can have different interests, and their perspectives often diverge and contradict each other. To improve relations, nations should recognize why they differ instead of pretending that the differences are a product of misperception.[9] Differences between Europe and the United States, or the United States and Mexico, are not shaped simply by misinformation and misunderstanding, but involve real conflicts concerning basic conceptions of national interest. Diplomatic communiqués or cultural exchanges do not easily erase these profound differences.[10]

A people should be sensitive to the importance of undesirable events in their history with another culture; it is important to acknowledge collective history.[11] But in acknowledging this history, it will help communication if one culture does not blame current generations of the other for past transgressions.[12] There are times when we need to forgive and forget. To overcome cultural differences, we should strive to conduct our relationships in the present. We need to evaluate one another as individuals based on personal and direct experience, regardless of culture or nationality, and independent of the impersonal and stereotypical expectations instilled in us by history. Ethnocentrism and empathy are opposites.[13]

Research in the field of intercultural communication clearly shows that we are not attracted to people who seem different—the Other—which makes it difficult to evaluate a person from another culture as an individual. Most people try to avoid the unfamiliar.[14] The key challenge that we encounter in intercultural communication is cultural difference between persons who interact and the stress that results from such encounters. This stress can be managed in several ways.

A GUIDE

From two-thirds to three-fourths of our communication takes place through nonverbal behavior. Our culture inculcates our behavior in us from birth, and we learn it so well that we internalize it at a subconscious level. Since culture is learned, culture can in great part be taught. To communicate across cultures, we need first to raise our own internal rules to the level of a conscious, externalized map. This will allow us to interact more through conscious choice, so that we examine differences in behavior rather than automatically reacting negatively. We then need to study the culture we are targeting in order to cross cultural barriers to achieve successful communication. We need either to find or create a set of rules as our guide.

Clearly, a dual etic-emic approach is necessary to overcome intercultural communication obstacles. The obstacles that we can identify from an external perspective of a target culture may, in many cases, only be understood or overcome by internal study of the culture, thereby gaining understanding of the perspectives and behaviors the culture engenders. A manageable approach is to use the artifice of comparing units of perception and behavioral categories in the two cultures between which communication is being attempted. This can give us the key to avoid or overcome many of the obstacles that commonly arise.

A broad-based etic approach should be used to first sensitize people to their own concept of culture and to foster appreciation and awareness of cultural diversity, so that emic or target cultural training will then be much more meaningful.[15] Part I of this book, in fact, uses such an approach by examining the concept of culture and the common categories of cultural differences that a person can expect to encounter in setting out to communicate across cultural boundaries. We need to know ourselves. We need to become conscious of what is in our heads and how we behave around others, and we also need to be aware that how we see ourselves may not be how others see us.[16] Looking into the face of the Other may show you your own. Viewing a target culture through this large, external frame sensitizes one to anticipate pitfalls and deal with many unforeseen circumstances of interaction as they arise—unfamiliar situations—thereby greatly increasing one's adaptability.

Internal cultural information about the target culture should then be examined; for example, the look we have taken in Part II at the differences between Mexico and the United States. This type of culture-specific information is useful for persons from either of these two cultures in attempting to communicate with persons from the other. One needs to look internally at factors such as the historical background of a culture and its major institutions (such as religion, government, and family) as part of the cultural frame in which the situational units of personal interaction take place. One must learn the rules of behavior for specific situations in a culture. A practical approach for obtaining target cultural information is to consult travel guides, to read current publications, and to watch videos on the country. When in the country it is valuable to attend local cultural events, and businesspersons should also endeavor to join some kind of business group.[17] People of different countries need to learn to know each other well in order to move beyond mutual disdain and achieve cooperation.[18]

Fortunately, cultural norms do not exist for every situation that individuals face in life, even for persons who may spend their whole lives in their own hometowns.[19] We can consciously evaluate new situations and make decisions about how to handle them. Thus, we can and do act to transcend the binding fetters of our cultural norms and rules.[20] People who communicate effectively between their own and a target culture seem to create a "third culture perspective"[21]—a neutral third zone into which they step to communicate. There they retain their basic native acculturation while partially adapting to traits of the target culture. If they are fortunate, they will communicate with others who can do the same and will meet them in this third zone. In communication, however, it is often necessary and useful for one person to consciously assume the responsibility to adapt in order to communicate with another as successfully as possible, because sometimes the other person cannot or will not do the same. Etic adaptive capacity coupled with emic culture-specific knowledge and skills allow us to approach each intercultural communication encounter as an interested learner and talented negotiator for the most successful outcome possible.[22]

Hall wrote that there is error "in two assumptions: first, that an outsider can, within a matter of months or even years, adequately understand, explain, and describe a foreign culture; and secondly, that he or she can transcend their own culture."[23] However, transcendence is not a positive or negative state, but rather a matter of degree; one can certainly adequately transcend cultural differences for many types of desirable human interaction. There will always be those situations where one cannot interpret culture well enough to communicate successfully, or where the other person impedes communication by withholding cooperation, but this is true even between the microcultures of two persons who grew up in the same city.

This model for improving intercultural communication competency has been illustrated by first considering intercultural communication from an external, etic perspective, and then emically targeting communication between two specific countries, the United States and Mexico.

AN INTERCULTURAL PRESCRIPTION

We all have a strong need to understand both the self and the Other when we communicate interpersonally, and we strive to increase predictability, which is often difficult with people of other cultures. To increase our intercultural communication competence, we can apply the following steps to communicate between any two cultures:

1. To communicate with another culture, start by knowing your own. Write down what you know about each category of Potential Obstacles to Intercultural Communication (Table 2, Chapter 2) as it applies to your native culture.

2. Have a positive attitude. To go beyond simplistic understanding of communicative meaning, such as attacking with a stick or greeting with flowers, goodwill in intercultural communication is essential. Obstinate or extremist interpretations of words and behavior do not contribute positively to cross-cultural communication. Only mutual respect for peculiarities and diversities can reconcile difficulties and reinforce good communication.[24]

3. You must be motivated to communicate—whether for survival, for pleasure, for business purposes, or to satisfy the curiosity of incurable xenophiles. To avoid or overcome intercultural communication obstacles usually requires enough effort that one must engage one's will to succeed. We need to overcome our subconscious tendency to automatically interpret anything or anyone "different" in a negative manner.

4. Overcome ethnocentrism. Replace ignorance with knowledge through education. Through knowledge, you will become more objective and will not automatically make negative judgments about that which is different. Furthermore, examination of foreign cultural characteristics can make them seem familiar rather than alien, and we tend to be positively attracted to that which is familiar. Knowledge will also help increase the predictability of interacting with an individual from a foreign culture.

5. Learn the target culture's rules. To do so the rules must be identified. Start by identifying the cultural information for each category of Potential Obstacles to Intercultural Communication listed in Table 2 for the culture with which you wish to communicate. Remain alert for difference issues that do not seem to fit the

framework of this table of obstacles so that you can discover any new categories, because every culture is different, and because cultures are dynamic and change over time. Do not neglect the obvious: seek out the areas of communication difficulty between the two cultures which members of the respective cultures themselves have already expressed. These difficulties are often written about in published sources. You may need to create your own map of cultural perceptions and processes to successfully travel through this foreign cultural territory. Explicitly put cultural differences into words for yourself.

6. The category of context stands out as common and greatly significant in intercultural communication. We should constantly seek to determine if communication is high-context or low-context. Should we consider the words as information-specific? What nonverbal behavior do we need to interpret? We need to be mindful of cultural differences in communication styles.

7. Be flexible—adaptability is the metacompetence for intercultural communication. Some have said that the United States has advanced technologically fifty years beyond the rest of the world. If so, just by reason of the pragmatic, information-specific, low-context communication style thereby generated, it is imperative that North Americans acquire the capacity to culturally adjust and adapt if they wish to communicate, interact, or do business with the majority of other world cultures.

8. Take responsibility for successful communication if you want to achieve it. You may have to do most of the work.

9. The mind-sets that may be the most universal for successful intercultural communication are a positive attitude, adaptability, effort, and assuming responsibility.

IN CONCLUSION

Rather than live in a world where cultural identities go to war, Pells suggests that it would be preferable to live in one with some common, global cultural traits. Mass communications may ultimately offer people more choice, and people may end up retaining much of their particular culture while acknowledging that they live in a pluralistic and interdependent world. They can give up the old battle for cultural supremacy and thrive on cultural differences.

At its best, nationalism coupled with diversity might create societies that are both diverse and tolerant.[25]

Cultural differences are impossible to avoid and, for many of us, daily intercultural encounters are here to stay. Understanding and adapting to others do not have to change the aspects of ourselves that we consider essential, but rather can enrich us. We will no longer fear that which is foreign just because it is different. We will read our own great literary masterpieces and find new meaning. We will learn to read cultural differences in persuasion styles, in logic, in behavior. Exploring another culture is an adventure.[26]

The data presented here were intended to sensitize and to inform. If the reader was left with some feeling of self-consciousness and was afforded even a small glimpse of her- or himself as the Other, then a major objective was attained. For without self-consciousness, some feeling of nonrecognition when looking in a mirror, one cannot transcend one's culture into that neutral "third" culture zone that lies between the communicator and the target culture, where meaning can be acceptably shared.

The raising of one's culture consciousness through education, like the biblical knowledge of good and evil, gives the intercultural communicator the freedom to consciously choose behavior and attitude in personal interaction, rather than submitting to the control of subconscious cultural norms and just reacting, usually negatively, to any deviation from these norms. Such consciousness also then gives the communicator personal responsibility in the interaction between cultures.

APPENDIX   **Author's Note**

Because of my interest in *how* members of one culture successfully communicate with those of another, I researched communication theory to identify and find explanations for many common obstacles that one encounters when interacting with any culture foreign to one's own. To illustrate how the resulting categories of obstacles that I constructed from communication literature affect intercultural communication, I then chose to relate these categories to current communication between two specific cultures: Mexico and the United States.

To do so, I felt I needed a Mexican perspective of communicating with North Americans that was not contaminated by North American culture. I therefore looked in Mexico to Mexicans addressing other Mexicans in Spanish, drawing on both published sources and personal interviews. No attempt was made to exclude information about communication problems for either North Americans or Mexicans because the problems did not neatly pigeonhole into predetermined categories of obstacles. It is also important to state explicitly that in the context of this book the objective is not to judge a cultural trait right or wrong, but to consider how the trait affects the attempt to communicate across cultures. I have striven to present information and perspectives with a minimum of monocultural bias, although, according to anthropologist E. T. Hall, it is impossible to "purely" overcome the culture or cultures of one's youth.

In collecting information, I selected business and social situations that are significant, common, and repetitive in occurrence. Because of the nature of the sources both in the United States and in Mexico, the cultural data represent fairly well educated people who live at a comfortable socioeconomic level. Every culture has its microcultures, and this analysis, to be meaningful, therefore endeavored to compare mangos to mangos.

Glossary

ADAPTABILITY: Adaptability is the capability to alter the structure and attributes of the psychic system to meet the demands of the environment, and to suspend or modify cultural ways to creatively manage the dynamics of cultural difference. *Self-altering, creative adaptation capacity is the meta-competence for intercultural communication.*[1]

ANXIETY: A high degree of unfamiliarity and uncertainty produces high anxiety or stress on the part of communicators, and anxiety compounds the problems[2] presented by other intercultural communication obstacles.

ARTIFACTS (extensions of physical self):   People communicate consciously and unconsciously by physical extensions of themselves,[3] such as dress, gifts, or cars. These extensions are interpreted differently in different cultures.

ATTITUDE: Attitudes are psychological states that influence overt behavior and distort perception. They cause interpretation of events in predisposed ways (*see* Preconceptions).[4]

CHRONEMICS: Formal time is measured abstractly by units such as hours, days, months, and years, and by different calendars. Informal time is measured by systems such as moons, weather seasons, or customs. People easily understand the differences in formal time between cultures but find it more difficult to understand a foreign culture's informal time system. Informal time elements are loosely defined by a culture, not explicitly taught, and typically operate outside consciousness. Chronemic cues can be intentional or unintentional and are often ambiguous. Time cues in communication have an ability to evoke strong emotional reactions.[5]

CODE: A cultural code is a system of words or nonverbal behavior that has acquired certain arbitrary meaning within a culture. A code is a systematic collection of regulations and rules of behavior.

COGNITION: Different cognitive styles result in different perceptions of reality.[6]

COLLECTIVISM: One of the most fundamental ways in which cultures differ is in the dimensions of individualism versus collectivism. Collectivists interact closely and are interdependent.[7] They are best encouraged by appealing to their group spirit and by requesting cooperation. Persons in individualistic cultures are motivated by stressing individual competition.[8]

COMMUNICATION: Communication takes place when communicators arrive at acceptable shared meaning of an intended message, or when an unintended message has been correctly interpreted.

CONTEXT: Nonverbal behavioral context, in addition to communicating on its own, affects, amplifies, explains, and supplements verbal language behavior. It is estimated that two-thirds to three-fourths of communication is through context. Different cultures use context differently to communicate, and this difference greatly affects intercultural communication.

High-context cultures emphasize formalized and stylized interaction rituals, which are a type of nonverbal behavior; the context communicates in place of,[9] or in addition to, verbal language. Nonverbal expression seldom occurs in isolation from verbal and other nonverbal cues, and we use nonverbal cues to interpret verbal expression.[10] Verbal communication in high-context cultures often uses words to represent cultural rituals which often results in the verbal content being information nonspecific.[11]

Low-Context cultures focus relatively more on words to convey meaning. The verbal content of messages in low-context cultures is information-specific.

COURTESY: Courtesy is culturally dictated communicative ritual. *See* Context.

CROSS-CULTURAL: This term is used synonymously with *intercultural.*

CULTURAL UNIT: *See* Situational unit.

CULTURE: Culture refers to "knowledge, experience, meanings, beliefs, values, attitudes, religions, concepts of self, the universe and self-universe, relationships, hierarchies of status, role expectations, spatial relations, and time concepts" accumulated by a large group of people over generations through individual and group effort. "Culture manifests itself both in patterns of language and thought, and in forms of activity and behavior."[12]

CUSTOMS: *See* Rules.

DIRECTNESS: Low-context communicators usually express themselves directly

in words and most often intend the words they use to be taken literally—
the contents of the verbal message are direct and information-specific.
High-context communicators are less direct in style and often use words
in a ritual fashion: the intended message may be communicated by context, with the words of the message being information-nonspecific.

EMBLEMS (gestures): A gesture assigned a specific meaning in a culture is called
an emblem. Gestures that are foreign to us create non-understanding,
and we know that we do not understand. Homomorphic gestures are the
same or similar in form, but since they carry different meanings, these
gestures frequently generate misunderstanding.[13]

EMIC: Emic means viewed from an internal, *intra*cultural perspective, that is,
culture-specific. It refers to cultural characteristics that pertain to or are
significant units that function with other units in a language or other system of behavior. "The emic view is monocultural with its units derived
from the internal functional relations of only one . . . culture at a time."[14]
Pronunciation rhymes with "anemic."

ETHNOCENTRISM: When perceptions learned through acculturation are narrow
and cause rigid behavior they are ethnocentric.[15]

ETIC: Etic means viewed from an external, *inter*cultural perspective, that is,
culture-general. It refers to cultural characteristics that pertain to, or are
raw data of, a language or other area of behavior, without considering
the data as significant units functioning within a system. "The etic view
is an alien view—the structuring of an outsider" looking in.[16] Pronunciation rhymes with "phonetic."

EYE CONTACT: Cultures have explicit rules regarding eye behavior such as staring, frequency of contact, and lowering the eyes. The same behavior can
have different meanings in different cultures, giving rise to misinterpretation. Direct eye contact can signify honesty and attentiveness or disrespect and boldness, depending on the culture.

FACE: Face is a person's value, standing, or prestige in the eyes of others. In
many cultures maintaining face is of great importance, and one must take
great care in disagreeing, criticizing, or competing.[17]

FACIAL EXPRESSIONS: There may be some universal patterns of facial expression,[18] such as an expression indicating happiness. However, since cultural rules may dictate the use of a facial expression for other purposes,
an expression of "happiness" may express anger or mask sadness.[19]

GENDER: Cultures regard some behaviors as masculine or feminine; behavior associated with one sex is usually considered inappropriate for the
other.[20]

GESTURES: *See* Emblems.

HAPTICS (touch): Although human beings are born with a need for touch, cultures train humans as to what and how much touch is acceptable as they mature. People in collective cultures touch each other more than those in cultures that stress the individual.[21] Collective cultures are called high-contact, and individualistic cultures are called low-contact.

HIERARCHY: All living things have a ranking order,[22] and the use of hierarchy differs from culture to culture. The concept of hierarchical distance affects the degree of formality in communication.[23] Steep hierarchy in a society encourages respect of classification, rank, order, and harmony. A flat hierarchy has a decentralized and democratic perspective that encourages participation based on declassification, equality, exploration, and adventure. There is, of course, some overlap. The use of language and ritual courtesies can change or reinforce the steepness or flatness of hierarchy.

HIGH-CONTEXT: Relative to low-context cultures, high-context cultures rely more on nonverbal context or behaviors than on abstract, verbal symbols of meaning to communicate. *See* Context.

HISTORY: The history of a country molds individuals' perceptions. Some cultures maintain history as a part of the living present, and it colors people's perceptions of their lives on a daily basis.

IDIOMS: The use of idioms, jargon, figurative expressions, exaggeration, and understatement in intercultural communication frequently causes misunderstanding.[24]

IGNORANCE: *See* Ethnocentrism.

IMMEDIACY: Actions that simultaneously communicate warmth, closeness, and availability for communication are immediacy behaviors which signal approach rather than avoidance. Such actions are typical of cultures that have high physical contact (high-contact), as contrasted with low-contact cultures.[25] It is assumed that persons approach things they like and avoid things they dislike, so people interpret immediacy behaviors as communicating positive or negative evaluations of the interaction partner.

INDIVIDUALISM: One of the most fundamental ways in which cultures differ is in the dimensions of individualism versus collectivism. Individualists tend to be distant in their personal interactions with others and must acquire affective relationships.[26] They tend to be self-motivated and can be stimulated to achieve by individual competition.[27]

INFORMATION-SPECIFIC: *See* Directness.

INTERCULTURAL: A macrodefinition of "intercultural" is used, indicating one or several differences between communicators relating to language, national origin, race, or ethnicity. (In contrast, a microdefinition might, for example, indicate the difference in "culture" between the Women's Bar Association and a local electricians' union in the United States.) This book addresses the obstacles in communicating across cultures that are *inter*national, rather than targeting diverse, *intra*national subcultures (sometimes called co-cultures) that share the experience of living in the same polity, such as the United States of America.

INTERCULTURAL COMMUNICATION: Intercultural communication is "a transactional, symbolic process involving the attribution of meaning between people from different cultures."[28]

INTRACULTURAL COMMUNICATION: Communication between people who share a common culture is intracultural.

JUDGMENT: *See* Preconceptions.

KINESICS: Body-motion language, like vocalic language, culture by culture is composed of distinctive elements that can be combined in a virtually infinite number of ordered combinations which rule the communicative aspects of human behavior. We can term verbal language digital and body motion language analogic.[29]

LANGUAGE COMPETENCY: Language competency is positively correlated to "attractiveness" in intercultural communication.[30] The majority of people prefer to communicate with a foreign person who speaks their language well. The language barrier makes intercultural interaction more difficult than intracultural interaction.[31]

LANGUAGE CONNOTATION: The connotative meanings of symbols arise from one's experience in the context of culture. Connotative and multiple meanings of a word are difficult to learn.[32] "Lie," "fib," and "equivocate" do not have the same shades of meaning.

LANGUAGE, VERBAL: Language should be considered a mirror of its culture.[33] Not only is language a product of culture, culture is a product of language, as well.[34] The Sapir-Whorf hypothesis states that language is a guide to social reality and builds up the real world through the language habits of a group. No two languages are sufficiently alike to consider that they represent the same social reality.[35] One must learn to "speak" the culture to learn its verbal language well.[36]

LEARNING DIFFERENCES: Different cultures learn to learn differently, as by rote, by demonstration, by guiding, or by doing.[37]

LITERACY / ORALITY: Literacy gives cultures the key to symbolic, abstract thinking. Written language fixes thought and uses subordination and analysis. This kind of logic may escape a person from an oral language tradition. Sound is evanescent, and oral language strings thoughts together like beads on a string.[38]

Writing stabilizes a language and develops a special kind of dialect. Some languages (more correctly called dialects) have invested centuries in writing. An established written language is called a grapholect. To deal with the unfamiliar expressively and precisely, an elaborated text-based code is imperative.[39] Compared to an oral-based language code, a grapholect has resources of a totally different order of magnitude.[40]

LOW-CONTEXT: Communication styles that focus relatively more (by comparison with high-context styles) on words to communicate, and relatively less on behavior—the context in which the words are used—are said to be "low-context." *See* Context.

MANNERS: *See* Rules.

MASTER SYMBOLS: A culture often has highly abstract master symbols that are agreed upon and respected by groups, such as "Allah" or "Christ" or a rising sun.[41] If a culture is tightly organized around a master symbol, it is difficult and sometimes impossible for communication to take place with another culture that has a very different, or no, master symbol.

MATERIALISM: *See* Values.

METAMESSAGE: Communication carries messages at least at two important levels: one level carries the content of the message, and another carries a metamessage about the relational aspect of the communicators.[42] Non-verbal communication often carries the metamessage, and verbal communication more often contains the content. The simple question "What do you want?" can be asked in a variety of ways that carry a metamessage beyond the verbal content of the question.

MEXICAN: A citizen of the United States of Mexico. This book focuses on communication with Spanish-speaking Mexicans, and not on Mexican citizens who speak an Amerindian language as their first language.

MEXICAN-AMERICAN: A citizen of the United States of America who is of Mexican heritage.

MISCOMMUNICATION: Miscommunication occurs when a receiver attributes erroneous meaning to a verbal or nonverbal message, whether the message was intended or unintended, and whether or not the message was adequately or properly encoded and transmitted.

MONOCHRONIC: This is a linear and sequential approach toward time that is rational, suppresses spontaneity, and tends to focus on one activity at a time when communicating interpersonally. People of monochronic cultures are punctual, efficient, and "get to the point" quickly.

MOTIVATION: Willingness or desire to make the effort required to reduce uncertainty in intercultural interaction.

NONVERBAL COMMUNICATION: The nonverbal behavior through which a person communicates; behavior in this sense includes gestures, facial expressions, tone of voice, dress, body language, and the rituals (such as courtesies) one observes.

NORMS: *See* Rules.

NORTH AMERICAN: This term refers to an English-speaking citizen of the United States of America (not a Canadian or Mexican citizen) sometimes called an anglophone. An anglophone can be of any ethnic origin or ancestry; however, in common United States usage, the shortened term "anglo" usually refers to a North American of northern European origin and has a different connotative meaning than the word "anglophone."

OBSTACLES OF PERCEPTION: Perception is the internal process by which we select, evaluate, and organize the stimuli of the outside world. From the time we are born, we learn our perceptions and the resulting behaviors from our cultural experiences.[43] Behaviors "natural" to different cultures do not necessarily conflict,[44] but when they do, the conflict frequently causes communication obstacles.

OBSTACLES OF PROCESS: Differences in the situational units of cultures create communication obstacles in the *process* of verbal and nonverbal interaction between persons. A situational unit is the smallest viable unit of a culture that can be analyzed, taught, and transmitted as a complete entity.[45] Examples of such units might be greeting, gift-giving, introductions, eye contact, and table manners.

ORALITY: *See* Literacy / orality.

OTHER, THE: The Other is someone who is perceived as foreign, alien, diverse, not one of "us."

PERCEPTION: Perception filters behavior and interaction.

PHYSICAL APPEARANCE: A person's physical features such as hair or skin color can be "markers" that accentuate perceptions of cultural difference.[46] Markers of difference can discourage interaction, because the higher the perceived similarity between two individuals, the greater their attraction to each other[47] to communicate.

PHYSICAL CHARACTERISTICS: These are physically observable "markers" of cultural difference, such as dress or physical features. *See* Artifacts; Physical appearance.

POLITE LANGUAGE USAGE: The actual language forms required in a target language may have no analogues in one's own and may therefore be difficult to learn or to use correctly.[48] Polite usage closely relates to two perceptual categories of communication behavior: hierarchy and rules.

POLYCHRONIC: This is a multiple-activity, "matrix" concept of time. Polychronic cultures only loosely measure time with the symbols of a formalized system. Business relationships are personalized, based on trust, and take "time" to establish. It is "time" to move on to the next activity when the current set of activities is over, because activity is more important than the abstract measure of time by a clock. Persons in polychronic cultures frequently carry on many activities at the same time when communicating interpersonally.

POSTURE: The meaning and use of body posture or stance can vary culturally. Standing with hands on hips can signify relaxation, bad manners, or a challenge, depending on the culture. Sitting with legs crossed may be unacceptable, depending on one's gender and the culture with which one is interacting. Cultures orient themselves differently to communicate, such as directly face-to-face or indirectly with persons standing at an angle to each other.[49]

POWER: A significant discrepancy in power or status between groups causes acute intergroup posturing tendencies, which can present obstacles to intercultural communication.[50]

PRECONCEPTIONS: People tend to see what they expect to see and, furthermore, to discount that which conflicts with these preconceptions, stereotypes, or prejudices toward persons.[51]

PREJUDICE: *See* Preconceptions.

PROXEMICS (space sense): People communicate with space far more than is consciously apparent, and people of different cultures communicate differently through use of space.[52]

RIGIDITY: *See* Adaptability.

RITUALS: *See* Context; Rules.

ROLE: Prescribed roles for persons can vary culturally, such as by gender or social class.[53]

RULES: Cultural rules are based on ideas.[54] They govern formality and ritual, and what types of interaction take place when and where.[55] There is not much flexibility in cultural rules,[56] and one must learn the rules of a target culture in order to communicate effectively.

SILENCE: Silence is viewed by some cultures as an important form of speech and rhetoric, and a silence gap in speaking is used differently by different cultures.[57] Silence can also be considered nonverbal behavior.

SIMILARITY ASSUMPTIONS: To assume that surface similarity in communication or behavior means the same thing in different cultures can result in misinterpretation. Likewise, surface differences may represent underlying similarity. Unless assumptions are overtly reported, there is no chance of correcting misinterpretations.[58] It is easy to underestimate the effect of an unfamiliar cultural environment.

SITUATIONAL UNIT: A situational unit is the smallest viable unit of a culture that can be "analyzed, taught, transmitted, and handed down" as a complete entity.[59] We learn our culture in units such as greeting, gift-giving, table manners, and so on.

SMELL: Smell is one of our most basic modes of communication and can sustain a message when the person is gone. Some cultures perceive smell as an extension of the person and actively smell others, while other cultures prefer an absence of any personal smell.[60]

SOCIAL ORGANIZATION: The institutions of a culture, such as family or government, can be formal or informal, and they affect how the culture organizes itself.[61]

SPACE, FIXED-FEATURE: Fixed-feature space tells us what we do where and how: we know what behavior is appropriate in a dining room or in a church.[62] People wrest and defend space (territoriality) and use space to indicate status or rank by the amount or location of their territory.[63]

SPACE, INFORMAL: Informal space includes the distance maintained in interpersonal encounters, which varies culturally.[64] In some cultures people stand and sit very close when interacting, and they judge those who interact at a greater distance to be cold, condescending, or disinterested. Other cultures perceive close interaction as pushy, disrespectful, or sexually aggressive.[65] Culture usually determines orientation (whether persons interact face-to-face or side-by-side), as well as whether people wait in line or jockey for the best position to be served.[66]

SPACE, SEMIFIXED-FEATURE: Semifixed-feature space communicates through movable objects. Some cultures easily move furniture, and others do not.[67] Some cultures keep the doors in their offices and homes closed to protect privacy and property.[68] Rank or status can be communicated by such space arrangements as the placement of tables and seating.[69]

STEREOTYPING: *See* Preconceptions.

TACT: In some cultures, directness is considered rude; even important discussions must be preceded by small talk. *See* Directness.

THOUGHT PATTERNS: Different cultures arrive at their concepts of reality in different ways. A culture's perception of reality may come through faith or belief, independent of fact. It may come from fact based on evidence,

which is the most predictable concept of reality. Or, a culture may perceive reality primarily through feelings or instinct, which is the most
common basis for reality perception in the world.[70]

TOUCH: *See* Haptics.

UNCERTAINTY: People have a strong need to understand both the self and the
Other in interpersonal interaction. In order to reduce uncertainty, they
strive to increase predictability—which is often difficult with people of
"Other" cultures.[71] Culture teaches individuals to behave in prescribed
ways that permit the other group members to recognize and anticipate
the individual's behavior.[72] Most people prefer to interact in predictable
social environments.

VALUES: Values are the learned (through acculturation) organization of rules
for making choices and resolving conflicts,[73] and differences in values can
be an obstacle to intercultural communication.[74] Religious values are
manifested not only in dogma, but also in living patterns and outlook.[75]
Materialism places value on money, work, and material success. To respect another culture's values can conflict with one's own values as a basis for judgment. There is much debate over relative and absolute values.[76] *See also* Master symbols.

VERBAL COMMUNICATION: Communication by word symbols of meaning, both
written and oral.

VOCAL CHARACTERIZERS: Vocalizations such as laughing, crying, yelling, moaning,
whining, belching, and yawning are vocal characterizers.[77] These characterizers communicate by themselves, or they can amplify or modify
other communication.

VOCAL QUALIFIERS: Volume, pitch, rhythm, tempo, resonance, and tone are vocal qualifiers.[78] For example, loudness of voice connotes sincerity and
strength to some but seems aggressive to others.[79]

VOCAL RATE: This is the vocalizing speed at which people speak.[80] A fast talker
may be viewed as glib and untrustworthy in one culture but as intelligent
and involved in another.[81]

VOCAL SEGREGATES: "Un-huh," "shhh," "ooh," "uh," and "mmh" are vocal segregates.[82] The Japanese use an essential gap or silence interval, which is
called *ma*.[83]

VOCALICS: The term "vocalics" encompasses any vocal-auditory behavior except the spoken word.[84] Vocalics is "how something is said," rather than
the actual meaning of the words.[85] The voice is a rich channel in the system of nonverbal communication. Vocalic cues are among the most powerful cues in the nonverbal repertoire and, next to kinesics, are the largest

in number. Some vocalic cues are so brief as to be missed in intercultural communication. Vocalics can be divided into four categories: vocal characterizers, qualifiers, segregates, and rate.[86]

WORLDVIEW: This may well be the most important cultural perception and the most difficult to describe. It is a culture's orientation toward God, nature, life, death, the universe—the meaning of life and "being."[87]

Notes

CHAPTER 1: WHY COMMUNICATE ACROSS CULTURES?

1. P. Watzlawick, J. B. Bavelas, and D. D. Jackson (1967), *Pragmatics of human communication: A study of interactional patterns, pathologies, and paradoxes* (New York: W. W. Norton).

2. Watzlawick et al., 1967.

3. K. S. Sitaram (1972), What is intercultural communication? in *Intercultural communication: A reader,* edited by L. A. Samovar and R. E. Porter (Belmont, Calif.: Wadsworth), pp. 18–23.

4. R. L. Birdwhistell (1970), *Kinesics and context: Essays on body motion communication* (Philadelphia: University of Pennsylvania Press).

5. E. T. Hall (1976), *Beyond culture* (Garden City, N.Y.: Doubleday).

6. Ibid.

7. J. K. Burgoon, D. B. Butler, and W. G. Woodall (1996), *Nonverbal communication: The unspoken dialogue* (New York: McGraw-Hill).

8. Ibid.

9. Interview, January 1997, with women who had lived in Colombia and Venezuela.

10. R. H. Pells (1997), *Not like us: How Europeans have loved, hated, and transformed American culture since World War II* (New York: Basic Books).

11. See, for example: J. W. Carey (1993), Everything that rises must diverge: Notes on communication, technology and the symbolic construction of the social, in *Beyond agendas: New directions in communication research,* edited by P. Gaunt (Westport: Greenwood Press), pp. 172–184; P. Gaunt (1993), The future of communication research, in *Beyond agendas: New directions in communication research,* edited by P. Gaunt (Westport: Greenwood Press), pp. 1–16; W. B. Pearce (1993), Achieving dialogue with "the Other" in the postmodern world, in *Beyond agendas:*

New directions in communication research, edited by P. Gaunt (Westport: Greenwood Press), pp. 101–116; B. D. Ruben (1989), The study of cross-cultural competence: Traditions and contemporary issues, *International Journal of Intercultural Relations* 13: 229–240.

12. R. E. Porter (1972), An overview of intercultural communication, in *Intercultural communication: A reader,* edited by L. A. Samovar and R. E. Porter (Belmont, Calif.: Wadsworth), pp. 3–18.

13. T. H. Inman, A. C. Ownby, H. R. Perreault, and J. N. Rhea (1991), Internationalizing the business communication curriculum, *Business Education Forum* 46(2): 19–22.

14. A. Toffler, cited in R. T. Moran and J. D. Abbott (1994), *NAFTA: Managing the cultural differences* (Houston: Gulf Publishing), p. 128.

15. Carey, 1993.

16. Ruben, 1989.

17. W. B. Gudykunst and Y. Y. Kim (1984), *Communicating with strangers: An approach to intercultural communication* (Reading, Mass.: Addison Wesley).

18. K. L. Pike (1956), *Language and life* (Glendale, Calif.: Summer Institute of Linguistics), p. 145.

19. Ibid.

20. T. Sowell (1994), *Race and culture: A world view* (New York: Basic Books).

21. M. A. Glendon (1994), *A nation under lawyers: How the crisis in the legal profession is transforming society* (Cambridge, Mass.: Harvard University Press), p. 168.

22. Sowell, 1994.

23. Glendon, 1994.

24. Sowell, 1994.

25. R. A. Pastor and J. G. Castañeda (1988), *Limits to friendship: The United States and Mexico* (New York: Knopf).

CHAPTER 2: WHAT CONSTITUTES A CULTURE?

1. E. T. Hall (1959), *The silent language,* 1st ed. (Garden City, N.Y.: Doubleday).

2. H. W. Ellingsworth (1977), Conceptualizing intercultural communication, in *Communication yearbook I,* edited by B. D. Ruben (New Brunswick, N.J.: Transaction Books), pp. 99–106; Ruben, 1989.

3. Sitaram, 1972.

4. J. Altman (1989), Overcoming babel: The role of the conference interpreter in the communication process, in *Babel: The cultural and linguistic barriers between nations,* edited by R. Kolmel and J. Payne (Aberdeen: Aberdeen University Press), pp. 73–83.

5. Conversation in 1998 with Chinese graduate students attending the University of Texas at Austin. The name has been changed.

6. Porter, 1972.

7. Pearce, 1993.

8. Gaunt, 1993.

9. A. Gonzalez (1990), Mexican "otherness" in the rhetoric of Mexican Americans, *Southern Communication Journal* 55: 276–291.

10. M. Tixier (1993), Obstacles to internal communication among subsidiary and headquarters executives in Western Europe, in *Beyond agendas: New directions in communication research,* edited by P. Gaunt (Westport: Greenwood Press), p. 101.

11. I. Torbiorn (1987), Culture barriers as a social psychological construct, in Cross-cultural adaptation: Current approaches, edited by Y. Y. Kim and W. B. Gudykunst, *International and intercultural communication annual XI,* pp. 168–190.

12. R. Carroll (1987), *Evidences invisibles: Américains et français au quotidien* (Paris: Editions du Seuil). [Available in translation: R. Carroll (1988), *Cultural misunderstandings: The French-American experience,* translated by C. Volk (Chicago: University of Chicago Press).

13. Porter, 1972, p. 3.

14. Hall, 1959.

15. Birdwhistell, 1970.

16. Ibid.

17. Watzlawick et al., 1967.

18. Hall, 1976, p. 3.

19. Hall, 1976.

20. F. Boas (1940), *Race, language and culture* (New York: Free Press).

21. Hall, 1976.

22. Ibid.

23. Hall, 1959.

24. J. Streeck (1994), Culture, meaning, and interpersonal communication, in *Handbook of interpersonal communication,* edited by M. L. Knapp (Thousand Oaks, Calif.: Sage), pp. 286–319.

25. Hall, 1976.

26. Hall, 1959.

27. Ibid.

28. Hall, 1976.

29. Birdwhistell, 1970.

30. E. Goffman (1963), *Behavior in public places: Notes on the social organization of gatherings* (New York: Free Press).

31. Streeck, 1994.

32. E. Goffman (1969), *Interaction ritual: Essays in face-to-face behavior* (Chicago: Aldine).

33. Birdwhistell, 1970.

34. R. Benedict (1934), *Patterns of culture* (Boston: Houghton Mifflin).

35. Hall, 1959.

36. E. Goffman (1971), *Relations in public: Microstudies of the public order* (New York: Basic Books).

37. J. J. Gumperz (1972), Introduction, in *Directions in sociolinguistics: The ethnography of communication,* edited by J. J. Gumperz and D. Hymes (New York: Holt, Rinehart and Winston), pp. 1–25.

38. Goffman, 1963.

39. Hall, 1976.

40. Pells, 1997.

41. J. K. Conway (1995), *True north: A memoir* (New York: Vintage Books), p. 93.

42. Ibid., p.179.

43. Ibid., p.166.

44. Hall, 1976.

45. Pells, 1997.

46. Ibid.

47. Hall, 1959.

48. Hall, 1976.

49. N. Dresser (1996), *Multicultural manners: New rules of etiquette for a changing society* (New York: John Wiley and Sons).

50. Ibid.

51. Hall, 1976.

52. Hall, 1959.

53. Hall, 1976.

54. Pells, 1997.

55. Hall, 1959.

56. Pells, 1997.

57. L. A. Samovar and R. E. Porter (1991), *Communication between cultures* (Belmont, Calif.: Wadsworth).

58. R. Shuter (1990), The centrality of culture, *Southern Communication Journal* 55: 237–249.

59. Inman et al., 1991.

60. Y. Y. Kim (1991), Intercultural communication competence: A systems-theoretic view, in *Cross-cultural interpersonal communication,* edited by S. Ting-Toomey and F. Korzenny (Newbury Park, Calif.: Sage), pp. 259–275.

61. Torbiorn, 1987.

62. Samovar and Porter, 1991.

63. T. Novinger (1996), *Intercultural communication: The cultural factors that create obstacles between Mexico and the United States* (unpublished master's thesis, Wichita State University, Wichita, Kans.).

CHAPTER 3: OBSTACLES OF PERCEPTION

1. Pells, 1997.

2. Samovar and Porter, 1991.

3. Carroll, 1987.

4. Ibid.

5. Ibid.

6. Torbiorn, 1987.

7. Moran and Abbott, 1994.

8. L. M. Barna (1988), Stumbling blocks in intercultural communication, in *Intercultural communication: A reader,* edited by L. A. Samovar and R. E. Porter, 5th ed. (Belmont, Calif.: Wadsworth), pp. 322–329; Wedge, B. (1972), Barriers to un-

derstanding, in *Intercultural communication: A reader,* edited by L. A. Samovar and R. E. Porter (Belmont, Calif.: Wadsworth), pp. 3–18.

9. Y. Kim, 1991,

10. Samovar and Porter, 1991.

11. A. Kardiner and R. Linton, cited in Moran and Abbott, 1994.

12. Ibid.

13. Moran and Abbott, 1994.

14. P. Andersen (1988), Explaining intercultural differences in nonverbal communication, in *Intercultural communication: A reader,* edited by L. A. Samovar and R. E. Porter, 5th ed. (Belmont, Calif.: Wadsworth), pp. 272–287.

15. Samovar and Porter, 1991.

16. Carroll, 1987.

17. Ibid.

18. C. Thompson (1998), Lost tongues, lost spirits: Native Americans struggle to preserve fading tribal languages, *Austin American-Statesman,* July 12, p. C-1.

19. Burgoon et al., 1996.

20. Ibid.

21. M. Argyle (1988), Intercultural communication, in *Intercultural communication: A reader,* edited by L. A. Samovar and R. E. Porter, 5th ed. (Belmont, Calif.: Wadsworth), pp. 31–44; J. Johnston (1988), Japanese firms in the U.S.: Adapting the persuasive message, *Bulletin of the Association for Business Communication* 51(3): 33–34.

22. Pells, 1997.

23. Hall, 1959.

24. Pells, 1997.

25. A. R. Brown-Gort (1998), *The role of culture in the political and administrative transformation of the Mexican state* (unpublished master's thesis, The University of Texas at Austin).

26. A. Swardson (1998), Many of France's best minds bid it adieu: High-tech talent joins in fleeing for opportunity, *Austin American-Statesman,* April 6, pp. G1, G8.

27. Hall, 1959.

28. Tixier, 1993.

29. J. P. Bowman and T. Okuda (1985), Japanese-American communication: Mysteries, enigmas, and possibilities, *Bulletin of the Association for Business Communication* 48(4): 18–21.

30. Inman et al., 1991.

31. Pells, 1997.

32. Burgoon et al., 1996.

33. Ibid.

34. Ibid.

35. Pells, 1997.

36. J. W. Fesler and D. F. Kent, cited in: Brown-Gort, 1998.

37. H. Wilensky, cited in: Brown-Gort, 1998.

38. Pells, 1997.

39. S. I. Hayakawa (1958), Communication and the human community. *Etc.* 60: 5–11.

40. Y. Kim, 1991.

41. Pastor and Castañeda, 1988.

42. Pells, 1997.

43. Pastor and Castañeda, 1988.

44. Inman et al., 1991; Porter, 1972.

45. Andersen, 1988; Hall, 1959.

46. Conway, 1995.

47. E. T. Hall and W. F. Whyte (1960), Intercultural communication: A guide to men of action, *Human Organization* 19: 5–20.

48. Mujeres, por importantes, el futuro les pertenece [The future belongs to women because of their importance] (1997), *Atractivos de la Huasteca* 3 (July–August): 52–53 (Xilitla, San Luís Potosí, México).

49. W. B. Gudykunst (1994), *Bridging differences: Effective intergroup communication* (Thousand Oaks, Calif.: Sage).

50. Argyle, 1988; Inman et al., 1991.

51. Bowman and Okuda, 1985.

52. Hall, 1959.

53. P. Platt (1996), *French or foe?* (Cincinnati, Ohio: C. J. Krehbiel Co.).

54. Pells, 1997.

55. E. T. Hall (1954), The anthropology of manners, *Scientific American* 192: 85–89.

56. Samovar and Porter, 1991.

57. T. Morrison, W. Conway, and G. A. Borden (1994), *Kiss, bow, or shake hands: How to do business in sixty countries* (Holbrook, Mass.: Bob Adams).

58. Wedge, 1972.

59. Platt, 1996.

60. Pells, 1997.

61. Hall, 1959.

62. Wedge, 1972.

63. Morrison et al., 1994.

64. Ibid.

65. Ibid.

66. Samovar and Porter, 1991.

67. Barna, 1988; Hall and Whyte, 1960.

68. W. Feinberg (1989), A role for philosophy of education in intercultural research: A reexamination of the relativism-absolutism debate, *Teachers College Record* 91: 161–176.

69. Tixier, 1993.

70. Torbiorn, 1987.

71. Samovar and Porter, 1991.

72. Pells, 1997.

73. Platt, 1996.

74. Carroll, 1987.

75. Samovar and Porter, 1991.

76. C. R. Berger and R. Calabrese (1975). Some explorations in initial interaction and beyond, *Human Communication Research* 1: 99–112; Birdwhistell, 1970.

77. Barna, 1988; Y. Kim, 1991; T. Pettigrew, 1986, The intergroup contact hypothesis reconsidered, in *Contact and conflict in intergroup encounters,* edited by Hewstone and R. Brown (Oxford: Basil Blackwell).

78. Berger and Calabrese, 1975; Lee and Boster, 1991.

79. Berger and Calabrese, 1975.

80. Birdwhistell, 1970.

81. W. Gudykunst and S. Ting-Toomey (1988), *Culture and interpersonal communication* (Beverly Hills, Calif.: Sage).

82. Porter, 1972.

83. H. O. Lee and F. J. Boster (1991), Social information for uncertainty reduction during initial interactions, in *Cross-cultural interpersonal communication,* edited by S. Ting-Toomey and F. Korzenny (Newbury Park, Calif.: Sage), pp. 189–212; Y. Kim, 1991.

84. Porter, 1972.

85. Wedge, 1972.

86. H. J. Kim (1991), Influence of language and similarity on initial intercultural attraction in *Cross-cultural interpersonal communication,* edited by S. Ting-Toomey and F. Korzenny (Newbury Park, Calif.: Sage), pp. 213–229.

87. Samovar and Porter, 1991.

88. Hall, 1959.

89. Pells, 1997.

90. Ibid.

91. Moran and Abbott, 1994.

92. Barna, 1988; R. Schneller (1989), Intercultural and intrapersonal processes and factors of misunderstanding: Implications for multicultural training, *International Journal of Intercultural Relations* 5: 175–191.

93. Platt, 1996.

94. Carroll, 1987.

95. Moran and Abbott, 1994.

96. Y. Kim, 1991.

CHAPTER 4: OBSTACLES IN VERBAL PROCESSES

1. Porter, 1972; Samovar and Porter, 1991; V. Terpstra (1978), *The cultural environment of international business* (Cincinnati: South Western Publishing).

2. Porter, 1972.

3. E. Sapir (1949), Time perspective in aboriginal American culture: A study in method, in *Selected writings of Edward Sapir in language, culture, and personality,* edited by D. G. Mandelbaum (Berkeley and Los Angeles: University of California Press).

4. Terpstra, 1978.

5. Streeck, 1994.

6. Hall, 1976.

7. B. Bryson (1990), *The mother tongue: English and how it got that way* (New York: William Morrow).

8. Thompson, 1998.

9. Bryson, 1990.

10. Hall, 1959.

11. Burgoon et al., 1996.

12. Birdwhistell, 1970.

13. Torbiorn, 1987.

14. Samovar and Porter, 1991.

15. Birdwhistell, 1970.

16. Andersen, 1988.

17. H. Kim, 1991; M. J. Schneider and W. Jordan (1981), Perceptions of the communicative performance of Americans and Chinese in intercultural dyads, *International Journal of Intercultural Relations* 5: 175–191.

18. H. Giles and P. F. Powesland (1975), *Speech style and social evaluation* (London: Academic Press); W. B. Gudykunst (1983), Similarities and differences in perceptions of initial intracultural and intercultural encounters, *Southern Speech Communication Journal* 49: 40–65; T. T. Imahori (1987), Intercultural interpersonal epistemology: Behavioral comparisons of intimacy and interrogative strategies between initial intracultural and intercultural interactions, paper presented at the Speech Communication Association Annual Convention, Boston; Lee and Boster, 1991; Samovar and Porter, 1991; L. M. Simard (1981), Cross cultural interaction: Potential invisible barriers, *Journal of Social Psychology* 113: 171–192.

19. Barna, 1988.

20. Bowman and Okuda, 1985; R. H. Kilpatrick (1984), International business communication practices, *Journal of Business Communication* 21 (4): 33–44.

21. Argyle, 1988.

22. Bryson, B., 1990.

23. Bowman and Okuda, 1985; Gudykunst and Kim, 1984.

24. W. J. Ong (1982), *Orality and literacy: The technologizing of the word* (New York: Methuen).

25. Ibid.

26. B. Bernstein, cited in Ong, 1982.

27. D. R. Olson, cited in Ong, 1982.

28. B. Bernstein, cited in Ong, 1982.

29. Ong, 1982.

30. Ibid.

31. Inman et al., 1991; Tixier, 1993.

32. E. D. Hirsch, Jr. (1973), *The philosophy of composition* (Chicago: University of Chicago Press).

CHAPTER 5: OBSTACLES IN NONVERBAL PROCESSES

1. Hall, 1976.

2. Birdwhistell, 1970.

3. Burgoon et al., 1996.

4. Ibid.

5. Watzlawick et al., 1967.

6. Burgoon et al., 1996.

7. Hall, 1959, p. 15.

8. Andersen, 1988; Barna, 1988.

9. Burgoon et al., 1996.

10. Carroll, 1987.

11. Hall, 1976.

12. Andersen, 1988; Y. Kim, 1991.

13. P. Collett (1971), Training Englishmen in the non-verbal behavior of Arabs: An experiment in intercultural communication, *International Journal of Psychology* 6: 209–215.

14. Nonverbal communication has been categorized by drawing on Knapp, 1972; Samovar and Porter, 1991; communication literature; and the author's years of living in diverse cultures.

15. Andersen, 1988; Hall, 1959; Y. Kim, 1991.

16. Gudykunst and Kim, 1984.

17. Porter, 1972; Samovar and Porter, 1991.

18. Moran and Abbott, 1994.

19. The discussion of chronemics draws on: Burgoon et al., 1996; Hall, 1959; Hall and Whyte, 1960; Porter, 1972; Samovar and Porter, 1991; Tixier, 1993.

20. Burgoon et al., 1996.

21. Ibid.

22. R. Gesteland (1998), Do's and taboos: Proper etiquette in the global marketplace, *The Rotarian,* April, pp. 26–29, 59.

23. Pells, 1997.

24. Sapir, 1949.

25. Birdwhistell, 1970.

26. Ibid.

27. Hall, 1976.

28. Birdwhistell, 1970, p. 187.

29. Birdwhistell, 1970.

30. Ibid.

31. Ibid.

32. Ibid.

33. Argyle, 1988; Bowman and Okuda, 1985; Inman et al., 1991. R. Jakobsen (1972), Motor signs for 'yes' and 'no,' *Language in Society* 1: 19–96; W. La Barre (1947), The cultural basis of emotions and gestures, *Journal of Personality* 16: 49–68; D. Morris, P. Collett, P. Marsh, and M. O'Shaughnessy (1979), *Gestures, their origin and distribution* (New York: Stein and Day); Schneller, 1989.

34. Dresser, 1996.

35. Birdwhistell, 1970.

36. G. J. Brault (1962), Kinesics and the classroom: some typical French gestures, *French Review* 36: 374–382.

37. M. Argyle and M. Cook (1976), *Gaze and mutual gaze* (New York: Cambridge University Press); Bowman and Okuda, 1985; Inman et al., 1991; Samovar and Porter, 1991.

38. Carroll, 1987, p. 30.

39. D. M. Cuceloglu (1970), Perception of facial expressions in three different

cultures, *Ergonomics* 13: 93–100; P. Ekman (1973), Crosscultural studies of facial expressions, in *Darwin and facial expression: A century of research in review,* edited by P. Edman (New York: Academic Press); C. E. Izard (1971), *The face of emotion* (New York: Appleton-Century-Croft); J. E. Kilbridge and M. Yarczower (1976), Recognition of happy and sad facial expressions among Baganda and U.S. children, *Journal of Crosscultural Psychology* 7 (2): 181–183; Samovar and Porter, 1991; K. Shimoda, M. Argyle, and P. R. Bitti (1978), The intercultural recognition of emotion expression by three national-racial groups: English, Italian and Japanese, *European Journal of Social Psychology* 8 (2): 169–179.

40. Argyle, 1988; O. Klineberg (1938), Emotional expression in Chinese literature, *Journal of Abnormal and Social Psychology* 33: 517–520.

41. Birdwhistell, 1970.

42. Ibid.

43. Samovar and Porter, 1991.

44. Argyle, 1988; Hall and Whyte, 1960.

45. Inman et al., 1991.

46. Samovar and Porter, 1991.

47. Ibid.

48. Ibid.

49. Burgoon et al., 1996.

50. Gudykunst and Kim, 1984; Hall, 1959; Hall, 1969; Hall and Whyte, 1960; Porter, 1972.

51. Pells, 1997.

52. Ibid.

53. Hall, 1969.

54. Hall, 1959.

55. M. Kirch (1979), Nonverbal communication across cultures, *Modern Language Journal* 63: 416–423.

56. Hall, 1969.

57. Kirch, 1979.

58. Hall, 1959.

59. Platt, 1996.

60. Hall, 1969.

61. Argyle, 1988; Hall and Whyte, 1960; Inman et al., 1991; Kirch, 1979; Porter, 1972.

62. Samovar and Porter, 1991.

63. Platt, 1996.

64. Dresser, 1996.

65. Andersen, 1988.

66. Burgoon et al., 1996.

67. Gudykunst and Kim, 1984; Samovar and Porter, 1991.

68. Burgoon et al., 1996.

69. Hall, 1959; K. H. Kim (1977), Misunderstanding in nonverbal communication: America and Korea, *Papers in Linguistics* 10: 1–22; Samovar and Porter, 1991.

70. Y. Kim, 1991.

71. D. Byrne (1971), *The attraction paradigm* (New York: Academic Press).

72. Burgoon et al., 1996.
73. Hall, 1959.
74. Burgoon et al., 1996.
75. Samovar and Porter, 1991.
76. Ibid.
77. Hall and Whyte, 1960.
78. Porter, 1972; Tixier, 1993.
79. L. Di Mare (1990), Ma and Japan, *Southern Communication Journal* 55: 319–328.

CHAPTER 6: THE MEXICO–UNITED STATES CULTURAL ENVIRONMENT

1. Pastor and Castañeda, 1988, p.375. Paraphrased from "Cooperation between the United States and Mexico will always be difficult but never impossible."
2. A. DePalma (1994), Cultural clashes fatally wound a cross-border alliance, *Austin American-Statesman,* July 5, p. C5.
3. G. Reed and R. Gray (1997), *How to do business in Mexico: Your essential and up-to-date guide for success* (Austin: University of Texas Press).
4. A. Oppenheimer (1996), *Bordering on chaos: Guerrillas, stockbrokers, politicians, and Mexico's road to prosperity* (New York: Little, Brown).
5. C. Lemire (1998), Ambassador lauds Texas, Mexico ties, *Austin American-Statesman,* March 24, p. B5.
6. DePalma, 1994.
7. Reed and Gray, 1997.
8. H. A. Kissinger, cited in Moran and Abbott, 1994, p. 70.
9. J. Fallows, cited in Pastor and Castañeda, 1988.
10. Carroll, 1987.
11. Pastor and Castañeda, 1988.
12. A. Riding (1986), *Distant neighbors: A portrait of the Mexicans* (New York: Random House).
13. Oppenheimer, 1996.
14. Riding, 1986.
15. A. Kardiner and R. Linton, cited in Moran and Abbott (1994).
16. Morrison et al., 1994.
17. A. Basave Fernández del Valle (1974), *Visión de Estados Unidos* [A view of the United States] (Mexico, D.F.: Editorial Diana).
18. Riding, 1986.
19. Ibid.
20. R. Labón Collado (1992), *Modos, modas y modales: Manual de buenas maneras y etiqueta* [Manners, style, and customs: A manual of good manners and etiquette] (Mexico, D.F.: Trillas).
21. O. Paz, cited in A. Basave Fernández del Valle (1990), *Vocación y estilo de México: Fundamentos de la mexicanidad* [The vocation and style of Mexico: The foundations of Mexicanness] (Mexico, D.F.: Editorial Limusa).
22. Basave, 1990.
23. O. Paz, cited in Basave, 1990, p. 768.

24. Basave, 1990.
25. Basave, 1974.
26. Anonymous interview, 1997, with the cultural attaché of a Mexican consulate in the United States.
27. B. L. De Mente (1996), *NTC's dictionary of Mexican cultural code words* (Lincolnwood, Ill.: NTC Publishing Group).
28. J. C. Condon (1985), *Good neighbors: Communicating with the Mexicans* (Yarmouth, Maine: Intercultural Press).
29. Basave, 1990.
30. Ibid.
31. S. R. Ross and R. Erb, cited in Moran and Abbott, 1994, p. 30.
32. Condon, 1985.
33. De Mente, 1996.
34. Pastor and Castañeda, 1988.
35. C. B. McKinniss and A. A. Natella, Jr. (1994), *Business in Mexico: Managerial behavior, protocol and etiquette* (Binghamton, N.Y.: Haworth).
36. Pastor and Castañeda, 1988.
37. Basave, 1990.
38. Basave, 1974.
39. A. M. Schlesinger, Jr., cited in Pastor and Castañeda, 1988.
40. Riding, 1986.
41. McKinniss and Natella, 1994.
42. De Mente, 1996.
43. Brown-Gort, 1998.
44. McKinniss and Natella, 1994.
45. Reed and Gray, 1997.
46. Ibid.; A. Serralde (1987), El estilo mexicano de dirigir [The Mexican style of management], *Management Today en Español*, January, pp. 5–20.
47. Condon, 1985.
48. Ibid.
49. Ibid.
50. Brown-Gort, 1998.
51. Riding, 1986.
52. O. Paz, cited in Basave, 1990.
53. Basave, 1990.
54. Basave, 1974.
55. Riding, 1986.
56. Ibid.
57. Ibid., p. 459.
58. U.S. and Mexico approve added drug enforcement (1998), *Austin American-Statesman*, February 6, p. A2.
59. Pastor and Castañeda, 1988.
60. Ibid.
61. Ibid.
62. De Mente, 1996.
63. Ibid.

64. Ibid.

65. Moran and Abbott, 1994.

66. Riding, 1986.

67. Basave, 1990.

68. Riding, 1986.

69. Ibid.

70. Ibid.

71. Ibid.

72. C. Fuentes, cited in *Mexico Watch* (1998) 4 (2), February.

73. Riding, 1986.

74. E. B. Treviño (1972), *My heart lies south: The story of my Mexican marriage* (New York: Thomas Y. Crowell).

75. Anonymous interview, 1998, at an annual convention of the *Consejo Internacional de Buén Vecindad* in Guanajuato, Mexico.

76. Anonymous interview, 1997, with the cultural attaché of a Mexican Consulate in the United States.

77. Basave, 1974, p. 243 (author's translation).

78. De Mente, 1996.

79. A. M. O'Connor (1998), The new women of Mexico: Border plant workers breaking down gender barriers, *Austin American-Statesman*, February 22, pp. H1, H5.

80. Riding, 1986.

81. Ibid.

82. Basave, 1990.

83. Ibid.

84. Morrison et al., 1994.

85. McKinniss and Natella, 1994.

86. Basave, 1974.

87. P. Romanell, Prologue, in Basave, 1974.

88. Basave, 1990.

89. Riding, 1986.

90. McKinniss and Natella, 1994.

91. Treviño, 1972, p. 233.

92. Basave, 1974.

93. Basave, 1990.

94. Riding, 1986.

95. M. Stevenson (1998), Mexican crypt opens to show heroes' skulls, *Austin American-Statesman*, March 29, p. A7.

96. Basave, 1974.

97. Moran and Abbott, 1994.

98. Basave, 1974.

99. Basave, 1990.

100. De Mente, 1996.

101. Basave, 1974.

102. Ibid.

103. Basave, 1990.

104. Riding, 1986.

105. Condon, 1985.

106. Morrison et al., 1994.

107. De Mente, 1996.

108. Ibid.

109. Basave, 1974.

CHAPTER 7: SOME MEXICO–UNITED STATES CULTURAL ISSUES

1. Condon, 1985.

2. Riding, 1986.

3. Romanell, 1974.

4. Riding, 1986.

5. DePalma, 1994.

6. Basave, 1974.

7. Ibid.

8. Riding, 1986.

9. Treviño, 1972.

10. A. Mastretta (1997), *Mal de amores* [Lovesick] (Mexico, D.F.: Alfaguara), p. 272 [author's translation].

11. Treviño, 1972.

12. Riding, 1986.

13. DePalma, 1994.

14. Moran and Abbott, 1994.

15. De Mente, 1996.

16. B. Hight (1994), Americans advised on Mexico trade: Cuatro Caminos speaker suggests leaving 'arrogance at the airport,' *Austin American-Statesman,* May 20, p. D1.

17. DePalma, 1994.

18. C. A. Simpson (1998), Real estate south of the border: Opportunities abound in Argentina, Brazil, Chile, and Mexico, *Commercial Real Estate Investment Journal,* March–April, pp. 20–24.

19. Ibid.

20. Hight, 1994.

21. Labón, 1992.

22. L. Baldrige (1993), *Letitia Baldrige's new complete guide to executive manners* (New York: Macmillan).

23. DePalma, 1994.

24. McKinniss and Natella, 1994.

25. Labón, 1992.

26. Riding, 1986.

27. McKinniss and Natella, 1994.

28. Grupo Internacional de Austin, Texas (1996), *Newsletter,* January.

29. Reed and Gray, 1997.

30. Oppenheimer, 1996.

31. Platt, 1996.

32. Pastor and Castañeda, 1988.
33. Condon, 1985.
34. Pastor and Castañeda, 1988.
35. DePalma, 1994.
36. Condon, 1985, p. 20.
37. Condon, 1985.
38. Riding, 1986.
39. McKinniss and Natella, 1994.
40. Basave, 1974.
41. Riding, 1986.
42. De Mente, 1996.
43. Reed and Gray, 1997.
44. Hight, 1994.
45. Treviño, 1972.
46. De Mente, 1996.
47. McKinniss and Natella, 1994.
48. Ibid.
49. Labón, 1992.
50. De Mente, 1996.
51. Condon, 1985.
52. Labón, 1992, p. 18.
53. McKinniss and Natella, 1994.
54. Ibid.
55. Baldrige, 1993, p. 121.
56. McKinniss and Natella, 1994.
57. Basave, 1990.
58. McKinniss and Natella, 1994.
59. Basave, 1990.
60. Riding, 1986.
61. Brown-Gort, 1998.
62. Basave, 1974.
63. Hight, B., 1994.
64. McKinniss and Natella, 1994.
65. Basave, 1974.
66. Riding, 1986.

CHAPTER 8: DAY-TO-DAY CULTURAL INTERACTION

1. Anonymous interview, 1997, with the cultural attaché of a Mexican Consulate in the United States.
2. Hall, 1959.
3. McKinniss and Natella, 1994
4. Baldrige 1993, p. 222.
5. Anonymous interview, 1997, with the cultural attaché of a Mexican Consulate in the United States.
6. Baldrige, 1993.

7. McKinniss and Natella, 1994.

8. Condon, 1985.

9. McKinniss and Natella, 1994.

10. L. Baldrige (1990), *Letitia Baldrige's complete guide to the new manners for the '90s* (New York: Macmillan).

11. O. Geler (1974), *Urbanidad y buenas maneras* [Courtesy and good manners] (Mexico, D.F.: Editorial Pax).

12. Ibid.

13. Baldrige, 1990; Geler, 1974.

14. McKinniss and Natella, 1994.

15. Baldrige, 1990, p. 133.

16. Labón, 1992.

17. Baldrige, 1990.

18. Labón, 1992.

19. Ibid.

20. Baldrige, 1990.

21. R. Sinkin, cited in DePalma, 1994, p. 5.

22. McKinniss and Natella, 1994.

23. Basave, 1974.

24. Labón, 1992, p. 184.

25. Labón, 1992.

26. Moran and Abbott, 1994.

27. Reed and Gray, 1997.

28. Condon, 1985.

29. McKinniss and Natella, 1994.

30. Labón, 1992.

31. Baldrige, 1993.

32. McKinniss and Natella, 1994.

33. Reed and Gray, 1997.

34. Moran and Abbott, 1994.

35. Basave, 1974, pp. 236–237 (author's translation).

36. S. Sheehy, cited in De Mente, 1996, p. 59.

37. McKinniss and Natella, 1994.

38. Baldrige, 1993.

39. McKinniss and Natella, 1994.

40. Riding, 1986.

41. Basave, 1990.

42. Riding, 1986.

43. Basave, 1990.

44. Reed and Gray, 1997

45. De Mente, 1996.

46. De Mente, 1996.

47. Pastor and Castañeda, 1988.

48. Moran and Abbott, 1994.

49. DePalma, 1994.

50. McKinniss and Natella, 1994.

51. Basave, 1990, p. 779.
52. Riding, 1986.
53. Ibid., p. 458.
54. Moran and Abbott, 1994.
55. Pastor and Castañeda, 1988, p. 17.
56. Ibid., p. 372.
57. McKinniss and Natella, 1994.
58. Labón, 1992.
59. Baldrige, 1993, p. 16.
60. Labón, 1992, p. 30.
61. Baldrige, 1993, p. 16.
62. De Mente, 1996.
63. McKinniss and Natella, 1994.
64. De Mente, 1996.
65. McKinniss and Natella, 1994.
66. Labón, 1992.
67. Ibid.
68. Ibid.
69. De Mente, 1996.
70. Treviño, 1972.
71. Labón, 1992.
72. De Mente, 1996.
73. Labón, 1992.
74. McKinniss and Natella, 1994.
75. Ibid.
76. Treviño, 1972.
77. Simpson, 1998.
78. Moran and Abbott, 1994, pp. 1–2.
79. McKinniss and Natella, 1994.
80. Ibid.
81. Baldrige, 1993, p. 199.
82. DePalma, 1994.
83. Labón, 1992.
84. Report on Langtex International of Austin, Texas, *Austin American-Statesman,* 1994.
85. C. Fuentes (1997), *The crystal frontier* (New York: Farrar, Straus and Giroux).
86. Ross and Erb, cited in Moran and Abbott, 1994, p. 30.
87. Pastor and Castañeda, 1988.
88. Basave, 1990.
89. Ibid., p. 786 [author's translation].

CHAPTER 9: TRANSCENDING CULTURE

1. Pells, 1997.
2. Y. Kim, 1991.
3. Pells, 1997.

4. Carroll, 1987.
5. Pells, 1997.
6. Ibid.
7. Carroll, 1987; Hall, 1959.
8. Moran and Abbott, 1994.
9. Pastor and Castañeda, 1988.
10. Pells, 1997.
11. Hayes, 1998.
12. Ross and Erb, cited in Moran and Abbott, 1994.
13. Moran and Abbott, 1994.
14. Samovar and Porter, 1991.
15. Armstrong et al., 1988.
16. Samovar and Porter, 1991.
17. Simpson, 1998.
18. Basave, 1990.
19. Torbiorn, 1987.
20. S. Sudweek et al. (1990), Developmental themes in Japanese–North American interpersonal relationships, *International Journal of Intercultural Relations* 14: 207–233.
21. Gudykunst et al., 1977.
22. Y. Kim, 1991.
23. Hall, 1976, p. 194.
24. Basave, 1990, p. 786.
25. Pells, 1997.
26. Carroll, 1987.

GLOSSARY

1. Y. Kim, 1991.
2. Barna, 1988; Y. Kim, 1991; Pettigrew, 1986.
3. Hall, 1959; K. Kim, 1977; Samovar and Porter, 1991.
4. Porter, 1972.
5. Burgoon et al., 1996; Hall, 1959; Hall and Whyte, 1960; Porter, 1972; Samovar and Porter, 1991; Tixier, 1993.
6. Morrison et al., 1994.
7. Andersen, P., 1988.
8. Samovar and Porter, 1991.
9. Andersen, 1988; Hall, 1959; Y. Kim, 1991.
10. Porter, 1972; Samovar and Porter, 1991.
11. Moran and Abbott, 1994.
12. Porter, 1972, p. 3.
13. Argyle, 1988; Bowman and Okuda, 1985; Inman et al., 1991; Jakobsen, 1972; La Barre, 1947; Morris et al., 1979; Schneller, 1989.
14. Pike, 1956, p. 145.
15. Samovar and Porter, 1991.
16. Pike, 1956.

17. Argyle, 1988; Johnston, 1988.

18. Cuceloglu, 1970; Ekman, 1973; Izard, 1971; Kilbridge and Yarczower, 1976; Samovar and Porter, 1991; Shimoda et al., 1978.

19. Argyle, 1988; Klineberg, 1938.

20. Andersen, 1988; Hall, 1959.

21. Samovar and Porter, 1991.

22. Hall, 1959.

23. Tixier, 1993.

24. Bowman and Okuda, 1985; Kilpatrick, 1984.

25. Andersen, 1988.

26. Ibid.

27. Samovar and Porter, 1991.

28. Gudykunst, 1984.

29. Birdwhistell, 1970.

30. H. Kim, 1991; Schneider and Jordan, 1981.

31. Giles and Powesland, 1975; Gudykunst, 1983; Imahori, 1987; Lee and Boster, 1991; Samovar and Porter, 1991; Simard, 1981.

32. Barna, 1988.

33. Porter, 1972; Samovar and Porter, 1991; Terpstra, 1978.

34. Porter, 1972.

35. Sapir, 1949.

36. Terpstra, 1978.

37. Hall, 1959.

38. Ong, 1982.

39. Bernstein, 1982.

40. Ong, 1982.

41. Hayakawa, 1958.

42. Watzlawick et al., 1967.

43. Samovar and Porter, 1991.

44. Carroll, 1987.

45. Hall, 1976.

46. Y. Kim, 1991.

47. Byrne, 1971.

48. Argyle, 1988.

49. Samovar and Porter, 1991.

50. Y. Kim, 1991.

51. Barna, 1988; Wedge, 1972.

52. Gudykunst and Kim, 1984; Hall, 1959; Hall, 1969; Hall and Whyte, 1960; Porter, 1972.

53. Inman et al., 1991; Porter, 1972.

54. Argyle, 1988; Inman et al., 1991.

55. Bowman and Okuda, 1985.

56. Hall, 1959.

57. Bowman and Okuda, 1985; Gudykunst and Kim, 1984.

58. Barna, 1988; Schneller, 1989.

59. Hall, 1976.

60. Samovar and Porter, 1991.
61. Ibid.
62. Hall, 1969.
63. Hall, 1959.
64. Hall, 1969.
65. Argyle, 1988; Hall and Whyte, 1960; Inman et al., 1991; Kirch, 1979; Porter, 1972.
66. Samovar and Porter, 1991.
67. Hall, 1969.
68. Kirch, 1979.
69. Hall, 1959.
70. Morrison et al., 1994.
71. Berger and Calabrese, 1975; Lee and Boster, 1991; Samovar and Porter, 1991.
72. Birdwhistell, 1970.
73. Samovar and Porter, 1991.
74. Barna, 1988; Hall and Whyte, 1960.
75. Torbiorn, 1987.
76. Feinberg, 1989.
77. Samovar and Porter, 1991.
78. Ibid.
79. Hall and Whyte, 1960.
80. Samovar and Porter, 1991.
81. Porter, 1972; Tixier, 1993.
82. Samovar and Porter, 1991.
83. Di Mare, 1990.
84. Burgoon et al., 1996.
85. Samovar and Porter, 1991.
86. Hall, 1959.
87. Samovar and Porter, 1991.

Bibliography

Altman, J. (1989). Overcoming babel: The role of the conference interpreter in the communication process. In *Babel: The cultural and linguistic barriers between nations*, edited by R. Kolmel and J. Payne, pp. 73–83. Aberdeen: Aberdeen University Press.

Andersen, P. (1988). Explaining intercultural differences in nonverbal communication. In *Intercultural communication: A reader*, edited by L. A. Samovar and R. E. Porter, pp. 272–287. 5th ed. Belmont, Calif.: Wadsworth.

Argyle, M. (1988). Intercultural communication. In *Intercultural communication: A reader*, edited by L. A. Samovar and R. E. Porter, pp. 31–44. 5th ed. Belmont, Calif.: Wadsworth.

Argyle, M., and M. Cook (1976). *Gaze and mutual gaze.* New York: Cambridge University Press.

Armstrong, R. N., R. Sisson, and J. H. Page (1988) *Cross-cultural communication training in business: A sensitizing module.* Paper presented at the seventh annual conference of languages and communication for world business and the professions; sponsored by Eastern Michigan University, April, Ann Arbor, Mich.

Baldrige, L. (1990). *Letitia Baldrige's complete guide to the new manners for the '90s.* New York: Macmillan.

———. (1993). *Letitia Baldrige's new complete guide to executive manners.* Rev. ed. New York: Macmillan.

Barna, L. M. (1988). Stumbling blocks in intercultural communication. In *Intercultural communication: A reader*, edited by L. A. Samovar and R. E. Porter, pp. 322–329. 5th ed. Belmont, Calif.: Wadsworth.

Basave Fernández del Valle, A. (1974). *Visión de Estados Unidos* [A view of the United States]. México, D.F.: Editorial Diana.

———. (1990). *Vocación y estilo de México: Fundamentos de la mexicanidad* [The vocation and style of Mexico: The foundations of Mexicanness]. México, D.F.: Editorial Limusa.

Benedict, R. (1934). *Patterns of culture*. Boston: Houghton Mifflin.

Berger, C. R., and R. Calabrese (1975). Some explorations in initial interaction and beyond. *Human Communication Research* 1: 99–112.

Birdwhistell, R. L. (1970). *Kinesics and context: Essays on body motion communication*. Philadelphia: University of Pennsylvania Press.

Boas, F. (1940). *Race, language and culture*. New York: Free Press.

Bowman, J. P., and T. Okuda (1985). Japanese-American communication: Mysteries, enigmas, and possibilities. *Bulletin of the Association for Business Communication* 48 (4): 18–21.

Brault, G. J. (1962). Kinesics and the classroom: some typical French gestures. *French Review* 36: 374–382.

Brown-Gort, A. R. (1998). *The role of culture in the political and administrative transformation of the Mexican state*. Unpublished master's thesis. The University of Texas at Austin.

Bryson, B. (1990). *The mother tongue: English and how it got that way*. New York: William Morrow.

Burgoon, J. K., D. B. Butler, and W. G. Woodall (1996). *Nonverbal communication: The unspoken dialogue*. New York: McGraw-Hill.

Byrne, D. (1971). *The attraction paradigm*. New York: Academic Press.

Carey, J. W. (1993). Everything that rises must diverge: Notes on communication, technology and the symbolic construction of the social. In *Beyond agendas: New directions in communication research*, edited by P. Gaunt, pp. 172–184. Westport: Greenwood Press.

Carroll, R. (1987). *Evidences invisibles: Américains et français au quotidien*. Paris: Editions du Seuil. [Available in translation: Carroll, R. (1988). *Cultural misunderstandings: The French-American experience*. Translated by C. Volk. Chicago: University of Chicago Press.]

Collett, P. (1971). Training Englishmen in the non-verbal behavior of Arabs: An experiment in intercultural communication. *International Journal of Psychology* 6: 209–215.

Condon, J.C. (1985). *Good neighbors: Communicating with the Mexicans*. Yarmouth, Maine: Intercultural Press.

Conway, J. K. *True north: A memoir*. New York: Vintage Books.

Cuceloglu, D. M. (1970). Perception of facial expressions in three different cultures. *Ergonomics* 13: 93–100.

De Mente, B. L. (1996). *NTC's dictionary of Mexican cultural code words*. Lincolnwood, Ill.: NTC Publishing Group.

DePalma, A. (1994). Cultural clashes fatally wound a cross-border alliance. *Austin American-Statesman*, July 5, p. C5.

Di Mare, L. (1990). Ma and Japan. *Southern Communication Journal* 55: 319–328.

Dresser, N. (1996). *Multicultural manners: New rules of etiquette for a changing society*. New York: John Wiley and Sons.

Ekman, P. (1973). Cross-cultural studies of facial expressions. In *Darwin and facial expression: A century of research in review,* edited by P. Edman. New York: Academic Press.

Ellingsworth, H. W. (1977). Conceptualizing intercultural communication. In *Communication yearbook I,* edited by B. D. Ruben, pp. 99–106. New Brunswick, N.J.: Transaction Books.

Feinberg, W. (1989). A role for philosophy of education in intercultural research: A reexamination of the relativism-absolutism debate. *Teachers College Record* 91: 161–176.

Fuentes, C. (1997). *The crystal frontier.* New York: Farrar, Straus and Giroux.

Gaunt, P. (1993). The future of communication research. In *Beyond agendas: New directions in communication research,* edited by P. Gaunt, pp. 1–16. Westport: Greenwood Press.

Geler, O. (1974). *Urbanidad y buenas maneras* [Courtesy and good manners]. México, D.F.: Editorial Pax.

Gesteland, R. (1998). Do's and taboos: Proper etiquette in the global marketplace. *The Rotarian,* April, pp. 26–29, 59.

Giles, H., and P. F. Powesland (1975). *Speech style and social evaluation.* London: Academic Press.

Glendon, M. A. (1994). *A nation under lawyers: How the crisis in the legal profession is transforming society.* Cambridge, Mass.: Harvard University Press.

Goffman, E. (1963). *Behavior in public places: Notes on the social organization of gatherings.* New York: Free Press.

Goffman, E. (1969). *Interaction ritual: Essays in face-to-face behavior.* Chicago: Aldine.

Goffman, E. (1971). *Relations in public: Microstudies of the public order.* New York: Basic Books.

Gonzalez, A. (1990). Mexican "otherness" in the rhetoric of Mexican Americans. *Southern Communication Journal* 55: 276–291.

Grupo Internacional de Austin, Texas (1996). *Grupo Internacional de Austin Newsletter,* January.

Gudykunst, W. B. (1983). Similarities and differences in perceptions of initial intracultural and intercultural encounters. *Southern Speech Communication Journal* 49: 40–65.

———. (1994). *Bridging differences: Effective intergroup communication.* Thousand Oaks, Calif.: Sage.

Gudykunst, W. B., and Y. Y. Kim (1984). *Communicating with strangers: An approach to intercultural communication.* Reading, Mass.: Addison Wesley.

Gudykunst, W., and S. Ting-Toomey (1988). *Culture and interpersonal communication.* Beverly Hills, Calif.: Sage.

Gudykunst, W. B., R. Wiseman, and M. Hammer (1977). Determinants of a sojourner's attitudinal satisfaction. In *Communication yearbook I,* edited by B. Ruben. New Brunswick, N.J.: Transaction.

Gumperz, J. J. (1972). Introduction. In *Directions in sociolinguistics: The ethnography of communication,* edited by J. Gumperz and D. Hymes, pp. 1–25. New York: Holt, Rinehart and Winston.

Hall, E. T. (1954). The anthropology of manners. *Scientific American* 192: 85–89.
———. (1959). *The silent language.* 1st ed. Garden City, N.Y.: Doubleday.
———. (1969). *The hidden dimension.* New York: Doubleday.
———. (1976). *Beyond culture.* Garden City, N.Y.: Doubleday.
Hall, E. T., and W. F. Whyte (1960). Intercultural communication: A guide to men of action. *Human Organization* 19: 5–20.
Hayakawa, S. I. (1958). Communication and the human community. *Etc.* 60: 5–11.
Hayes, R. (1998). Juneteenth's lessons form this year's message. *Austin American-Statesman,* June 14, p. B6.
Hight, B. (1994). Americans advised on Mexico trade: Cuatro Caminos speaker suggests leaving 'arrogance at the airport.' *Austin American-Statesman,* May 20, p. D1.
Hirsch, E. D. Jr. (1973). *The philosophy of composition.* Chicago: University of Chicago Press.
Imahori, T. T. (1987). *Intercultural interpersonal epistemology: Behavioral comparisons of intimacy and interrogative strategies between initial intracultural and intercultural interactions.* Paper presented at the Speech Communication Association Annual Convention, Boston.
Inman, T. H., A. C. Ownby, H. R. Perreault, and J. N. Rhea (1991). Internationalizing the business communication curriculum. *Business Education Forum* 46 (2): 19–22.
Izard, C. E. (1971). *The face of emotion.* New York: Appleton-Century-Croft.
Jakobsen, R. (1972). Motor signs for 'yes' and 'no.' *Language in Society* 1: 19–96.
Johnston, J. (1988). Japanese firms in the U.S.: Adapting the persuasive message. *Bulletin of the Association for Business Communication* 51 (3): 33–34.
Kilbridge, J. E., and M. Yarczower (1976). Recognition of happy and sad facial expressions among Baganda and U.S. children. *Journal of Crosscultural Psychology* 7 (2): 181–183.
Kilpatrick, R. H. (1984). International business communication practices. *Journal of Business Communication* 21 (4): 33–44.
Kim, H. J. (1991). Influence of language and similarity on initial intercultural attraction. In *Cross-cultural interpersonal communication,* edited by S. Ting-Toomey and F. Korzenny, pp. 213–229. Newbury Park, Calif.: Sage.
Kim, K. H. (1977). Misunderstanding in nonverbal communication: America and Korea. *Papers in Linguistics* 10: 1–22.
Kim, Y. Y. (1991). Intercultural communication competence: A systems-theoretic view. In *Cross-cultural interpersonal communication,* edited by S. Ting-Toomey and F. Korzenny, pp. 259–275. Newbury Park, Calif.: Sage.
Kirch, M. (1979). Nonverbal communication across cultures. *Modern Language Journal* 63: 416–423.
Klineberg, O. (1938). Emotional expression in Chinese literature. *Journal of Abnormal and Social Psychology* 33: 517–520.
Knapp, M. L. (1972). *Nonverbal communication in human interaction.* New York: Holt, Rinehart and Winston.
La Barre, W. (1947). The cultural basis of emotions and gestures. *Journal of Personality* 16: 49–68.

Labón Collado, R. (1992). *Modos, modas y modales: Manual de buenas maneras y etiqueta* [Manners, style, and customs: A manual of good manners and etiquette]. México, D.F.: Trillas.

Lee, H. O., and F. J. Boster (1991). Social information for uncertainty reduction during initial interactions. In *Cross-cultural interpersonal communication,* edited by S. Ting-Toomey and F. Korzenny, pp. 189–212. Newbury Park, Calif.: Sage.

Lemire, C. (1998). Ambassador lauds Texas, Mexico ties. *Austin American-Statesman,* March 24, p. B5.

McKinniss, C. B., and A. A. Natella, Jr. (1994). *Business in Mexico: Managerial behavior, protocol and etiquette.* Binghamton, N.Y.: Haworth.

Mastretta, Á. (1997). *Mal de amores* [Lovesick]. México, D.F.: Alfaguara.

Moran, R. T., and J. D. Abbott (1994). *NAFTA: Managing the cultural differences.* Houston: Gulf Publishing.

Morris, D., P. Collett, P. Marsh, and M. O'Shaughnessy (1979). *Gestures, their origin and distribution.* New York: Stein and Day.

Morrison, T., W. Conway, and G. A. Borden (1994). *Kiss, bow, or shake hands: How to do business in sixty countries.* Holbrook, Mass.: Bob Adams.

Mujeres, por importantes, el futuro les pertenece [The future belongs to women because of their importance] (1997). *Atractivos de la Huasteca* 3 (July–August): 52–53. Xilitla, San Luís Potosí, México.

Novinger, T. (1996). *Intercultural communication: The cultural factors that create obstacles between Mexico and the United States.* Unpublished master's thesis. Wichita State University, Wichita, Kans.

O'Connor, A.M. (1998). The new women of Mexico: Border plant workers breaking down gender barriers. *Austin American-Statesman,* February 22, pp. H1, H5.

Ong, W. J. (1982). *Orality and literacy: The technologizing of the word.* New York: Methuen.

Oppenheimer, A. (1996). *Bordering on chaos: Guerillas, stockbrokers, politicians, and Mexico's road to prosperity.* Boston: Little, Brown.

Pastor, R. A., and J. G. Castañeda (1988). *Limits to friendship: The United States and Mexico.* New York: Knopf.

Pearce, W. B. (1993). Achieving dialogue with "the Other" in the postmodern world. In *Beyond agendas: New directions in communication research,* edited by P. Gaunt, pp. 101–116. Westport: Greenwood Press.

Pells, R. H. (1997). *Not like us: How Europeans have loved, hated, and transformed American culture since World War II.* New York: Basic Books.

Pettigrew, T. (1986). The intergroup contact hypothesis reconsidered. In *Contact and conflict in intergroup encounters,* edited by M. Hewstone and R. Brown. Oxford: Basil Blackwell.

Pike, K. L. (1956). *Language and life.* Glendale, Calif.: Summer Institute of Linguistics.

Platt, P. (1996). *French or foe?* Cincinnati, Ohio: C. J. Krehbiel Co.

Porter, R. E. (1972). An overview of intercultural communication. In *Intercultural communication: A reader,* edited by L. A. Samovar and R. E. Porter, pp. 3–18. 1st ed. Belmont, Calif.: Wadsworth.

Reed, G., and R. Gray (1997). *How to do business in Mexico: Your essential and up-to-date guide for success.* Austin: University of Texas Press.

Riding, A. (1986). *Distant neighbors: A portrait of the Mexicans.* New York: Random House.

Romanell, P. (1974). Prologue. In *Visión de Estados Unidos,* by A. Basave Fernández del Valle. México, D.F.: Editorial Diana.

Ruben, B. D. (1989). The study of cross-cultural competence: Traditions and contemporary issues. *International Journal of Intercultural Relations* 13: 229–240.

Samovar, L. A., and R. E. Porter (1991). *Communication between cultures.* Belmont, Calif.: Wadsworth.

Samovar, L. A., and R. E. Porter, eds. (1972). *Intercultural communication: A reader.* 1st ed. Belmont, Calif.: Wadsworth.

———(1988). *Intercultural communication: A reader.* 5th ed. Belmont, Calif.: Wadsworth.

Sapir, E. (1949). Time perspective in aboriginal American culture: A study in method. In *Selected writings of Edward Sapir in language, culture, and personality,* edited by D. G. Mandelbaum. Berkeley: University of California Press.

Schneider, M. J., and W. Jordan (1981). Perceptions of the communicative performance of Americans and Chinese in intercultural dyads. *International Journal of Intercultural Relations* 5: 175–191.

Schneller, R. (1989). Intercultural and intrapersonal processes and factors of misunderstanding: Implications for multicultural training. *International Journal of Intercultural Relations* 5: 175–191.

Serralde, A. (1987). El estilo mexicano de dirigir [The Mexican style of management]. *Management Today en Español,* January, pp. 5–20.

Shimoda, K., M. Argyle, and P. R. Bitti (1978). The intercultural recognition of emotion expression by three national-racial groups: English, Italian and Japanese. *European Journal of Social Psychology* 8 (2): 169–179.

Shuter, R. (1990). The centrality of culture. *Southern Communication Journal* 55: 237–249.

Simard, L. M. (1981). Cross cultural interaction: potential invisible barriers, *Journal of Social Psychology* 113: 171–192.

Simpson, C. A. (1998). Real estate south of the border: Opportunities abound in Argentina, Brazil, Chile, and Mexico. *Commercial Real Estate Investment Journal,* March–April, pp. 20–24.

Sitaram, K. S. (1972). What is intercultural communication? In *Intercultural communication: A reader,* edited by L. A. Samovar and R. E. Porter, pp. 18–23. Belmont, Calif.: Wadsworth.

Sowell, T. (1994). *Race and culture: A world view.* New York: Basic Books.

Stevenson, M. (1998). Mexican crypt opens to show heroes' skulls. *Austin American-Statesman,* March 29, p. A7.

Streeck, J. (1994). Culture, meaning, and interpersonal communication. In *Handbook of interpersonal communication,* edited by M. L. Knapp, pp. 286–319. Thousand Oaks, Calif.: Sage.

Sudweek, S., W. B. Gudykunst, S. Ting-Toomey, and T. Nishida (1990). Developmental themes in Japanese-North American interpersonal relationships. *International Journal of Intercultural Relations* 14: 207–233.

Swardson, A. (1998). Many of France's best minds bid it adieu: High-tech talent joins in fleeing for opportunity. *Austin American-Statesman,* April 6, pp. G1, G8.

Terpstra, V. (1978). *The cultural environment of international business.* Cincinnati: South Western Publishing.

Thompson, C.(1998). Lost tongues, lost spirits: Native Americans struggle to preserve fading tribal languages. *Austin American-Statesman,* July 12, p. C-1.

Tixier, M. (1993). Obstacles to internal communication among subsidiary and headquarters executives in Western Europe. In *Beyond agendas: New directions in communication research,* edited by P. Gaunt, pp. 101–116. Westport: Greenwood Press.

Torbiorn, I. (1987). Culture barriers as a social psychological construct. In Cross-cultural adaptation: Current approaches, edited by Y. Y. Kim and W. B. Gudykunst. *International and Intercultural Communication Annual, XI,* pp. 168–190.

Treviño, E. B. (1972). *My heart lies south: The story of my Mexican marriage.* New York: Thomas Y. Crowell.

Watzlawick, P., J. B. Bavelas, and D. D. Jackson (1967). *Pragmatics of human communication: A study of interactional patterns, pathologies, and paradoxes.* New York: W. W. Norton.

Wedge, B. (1972). Barriers to understanding. In *Intercultural communication: A reader,* edited by L. A. Samovar and R. E. Porter, pp. 3–18. Belmont, Calif.: Wadsworth.

Index

learning styles, 39
leisure, 104–105
licenciado: defined, 143
line, 68–69
literacy/orality, 51–52
López Portillo, José, 141–142
low-context culture, 48, 58–59, 116;
    defined, 6–7
lunch, 113–114

machismo, 95
madrina, 93
mail, 118, 139
makeup, 125
malinchismo: defined, 84
mañana, 109, 116
manners, 4, 5, 127, 129. *See also*
    Baldrige, Letitia; Labón Collado, R.
Maoris (New Zealand), 46
master symbols: defined, 34
Mastretta, Angeles, 110
materialism, 103
Mediterranean cultures, 61. *See also*
    Greek culture
men. *See* gender
Mérida (Yucatán), 102
mestizo culture, 83–84
Mexican-American war, the, 86
Mexican culture, 5, 80, 82, 122; abstract
    symbols and, 117; Arab culture and,
    81; artifacts in, 125–126; body lan-
    guage in, 120; and Canadian culture,
    93; chronemics in, 109–116; as collec-
    tive culture, 92; communication ob-
    stacles of, 109–123, 144–145; context
    in, 7, 116–119; courtesy in, 128–129;
    death views of, 100–101; directness
    in, 117–118; dress and, 72; elitism
    of, 86–87; entertaining in, 131–132;
    ethnocentrism and, 121–123; face and
    pride in, 132, 134, 135; family in, 38,
    93–94; fashion in, 125–126; fatalism
    and, 99, 100; food and, 130–131;
    gender in, 36, 94–98; gift-giving in,
    129–130; government in, 89–91;
    greetings and parting in, 114, 135–
    136; and Guatemalan culture, 56; hier-
    archy in, 33, 78, 87–89; history and,
    84–87; kinesics in, 119–121; lan-
    guage in, 140–142, leisure in, 104–

105; life in, 146; and *machismo,* 95;
and *mañana,* 116; master symbols of,
84; and North American culture, 72,
77–123, 145, 153; proxemics in, 119–
121; racism in, 83–84; religion in,
98–99; and respect, 134; sexuality
and, 98; social class and, 37; stereotyping in, 123; table manners in, 127;
thank-you notes in, 128; thought patterns in, 104; touch in, 121; and the
United States, 72, 77–123, 145, 153;
values of, 101–104; work in, 104–
105; worldview in, 104–105; written
communications and telephone in,
127–128
Mexican Revolution, the, 85
Mexico: colonization of, 81; comparison
    of, 72, 77–146; indigenous peoples of,
    82; and the United States, 77–78. *See
    also* Mexican culture
Middle Eastern culture, 36, 64, 66. *See
    also* Arab culture; Muslim culture
Mitterand, François, 95
monochronic culture, 110–111; concept
    of, 61
Montaigne, Michel de, 3
Monterrey (Mexico), 85, 96
Moors, the, 81. *See also* Arab culture
Morning Owl, Thomas, 31, 46
Muslim culture, 66. *See also* Arab culture;
    Middle Eastern culture
My Heart Lies South, 110, 140. *See also*
    Treviño, Elizabeth Borton

NAFTA (North American Free-Trade
    Agreement), 77–78
Náhuatl (language), 82
names, 142–143
Native American culture. *See* Indian
    culture (Native American)
Navajo culture, 46
negocio: defined, 105
negotiations, 134, 141
nepotism, 94
New England culture, 85
New Guinea, 46
New Mexico culture, 21
New Spain: culture of, 85
New Zealand, 46
Nigerian culture, 64

About the Author

Tracy Novinger has lived intercultural communication. She was born on the island of Aruba, Netherland Antilles, where three generations of her family resided. When she was ten years old, her father accepted a contract with Petrobrás of Brazil, and her free-spirited mother enrolled her in a Brazilian school in Santos, São Paulo. She learned Portuguese through sink-or-swim total immersion and studied other required languages. When she picks an outstanding event in her life, her acculturation to Brazil through immersion qualifies as the most significant—and as the best.

When Ms. Novinger was to begin university studies, her father opted for the United States—the family spoke English at home, and he said hers was getting strange. She found the United States to be culturally strange. On finishing college, she moved to live and work for nine years in Tahiti, French Polynesia. In Tahiti she had occasion to interpret and translate from French to English for the courts of French Polynesia. She also learned "island" French—complete with the requisite changes in intonation, forms of address, and other nonverbal behavior that go with language. This allows her to contrast non-Western island dialect with continental French, which adds to her understanding of what takes place in intercultural communication.

Since Ms. Novinger speaks English, French, Portuguese, and Spanish, and has some knowledge of other languages, she does not minimize the importance of language in communication. But even though one speaks a language well, or has a good interpreter, she is personally aware of the gaffes one can make due to differences in cultures.

Cultural differences present more than obstacles, however. Because the author has internalized more than one language and culture, she states that her life is infinitely richer. She steps, like Alice, into and out of several worlds, each with its own flavor, smells, cadences, physical shape and feel of phonology in the mouth and throat, body language, ambience, emotions . . . and even attitude.